FOUR FAVOURITES

FOUR FAVOURITES

BY

D. B. Wyndham Lewis

EVANS BROTHERS LIMITED
LONDON
1948

First Published 1948

PRINTED AND BOUND IN ENGLAND BY
HAZELL WATSON & VINEY LTD
AYLESBURY AND LONDON

To
PAULINE AND JAMES GUNN,
amantissime

ON THE FAVOURITE AS HERO

AMONG the Yahoos of Houyhnhnm Land, we learn from the amiable pages of Dean Swift, each tribal leader has his favourite, who is hated intensely by the whole herd. "He usually continues in Office till a Worse can be found; but the very Moment he is discarded, his Successor, at the Head of all the *Yahoos* in that District, young and old, male and female, come in a Body . . ." after which the Dean ceases, as so often, to be quotable in any decent modern page.

Of the four historic favourites with whom these pages are concerned—a Frenchwoman, an Englishman, a Spaniard, and a Russian, all products of the eighteenth century—only one finds a destiny in any way comparable to that of his Yahoo exemplar. They have in common (apart from Lord Melbourne, born to the purple and in a class apart) a swift upward trajectory from more or less obscure origins, due to personal magnetism and a considerable skill in manipulating the policy of the Crown they serve, in the teeth of rivals and enemies. And in all four cases the sovereign they rule, whether Louis XV, Victoria, Carlos IV, or Catherine the Great, may be infatuated but is certainly not weak-minded.

It may be plausibly argued that such specialists in careerism cannot be dismissed with the contempt (again excepting Lord Melbourne) they often inspire in high-minded historians. They had qualities far above the average. However they began their careers, something more than charm and insolence enabled them to establish themselves so firmly against such odds. The aim of these pages, therefore, is to survey the entertaining trajectory of this international quartet, to contemplate the influence they exercised and, if they fell, to discern the reason. Entertainment

apart, the value of such a survey as a textbook for the ambitious
need hardly be insisted on.

The profession of Favourite is not as spectacular as it was,
perhaps, but it is none the less attractive and profitable, and must
incidentally be distinguished from the equally flourishing profession of Parasite, with which it should never be confused.
That it has temporarily declined to some extent in scope and
splendour under modern democracy is undoubted. At the present
moment the most active patrons of the Favourite are not so much
kings and statesmen as noblemen of the Press and Finance, many
of whom require merely a lackey or yes-man on the model of
Ben Jonson's Mosca. Nevertheless one of the headiest delights
of the Favourite's career, that first dizzy upward swoop to
fortune, may be enjoyed even by these. A celebrated Fleet Street
journalist was once observed, on issuing from one of the lifts in
his wayward overlord's marble halls, to raise his hat with
Castilian grace and gravity to the lift-boy. Asked why, he replied
simply : "To-morrow he may be Editor." It is plain that a study
of the technique involved in a Favourite's ascent and deportment
may still be of use to many, and can harm none.

By the earnest-minded it may be objected that in the Egalit-
arian Utopia of the future there will be little room for professional
favourites. The student of affairs is nevertheless sadly aware that
whoever rules a given country there will invariably (as the
financial wizard Joseph Pasquier points out in M. Duhamel's
delightful pages) be a top-crust of privileged consumers of vin-
tage champagne and caviar. To exploit these mighty ones, possessing all the weaknesses of their kind, should be a simpler task than
that achieved by La Pompadour, Melbourne, Godoy, or Potemkin; simpler, chiefly and above all, because the steady decline
in culture and civilisation and manners since the eighteenth—
not to speak of the thirteenth—century will make the masters of
our future world less exacting, less complicated in their requirements, more swiftly amused, more easily soothed. Moreover, no
future Favourite will have to cope with that curious illusion of

automatic progress which afflicted Europe in the late-eighteenth century, and is no longer the axiom and bugbear it was. Those worshippers of Progress who still remain will observe that in these pages their idol is treated with no great respect. To assuage just resentment I would amiably direct their attention to the preface to *Cæsar and Cleopatra* (1900), in which Mr. Shaw blows up the whole chimera with admirable verve and thoroughness. "The notion that there has been any such progress since Cæsar's time (less than twenty centuries) is too absurd for discussion," observes Mr. Shaw before proceeding to discuss it, and a world containing some twenty million unfortunates rotting in slave-camps supplies an adequate footnote nearly fifty years later. So much for the Voltairean and Revolutionary gospel which permeates the second half of the eighteenth century and so strongly influences at least two of the characters in these pages. Their successors will be free at least of the Dogma of the Rosy Dawn.

The principal authorities on which these sketches are based, apart from those cited in the text, will be found in an appendix. A few explanatory notes on treatment seem desirable.

Melbourne has been already written about by a cloud of authorities, all principally concerned with his career as a statesman. I have largely confined myself to his no less interesting feats as a Favourite, at the same time endeavouring to throw into more adequate relief that Puckish streak in Melbourne's character which, I think, most of his biographers (all good and serious men) have tended either to ignore or to dismiss too sharply, possibly being as much bewildered by it as were Melbourne's contemporaries. If I have exhibited the Essential Clubman rather than the British Prime Minister, I trust I have not done so to the exclusion of his other qualities. Melbourne seems to me an eighteenth-century rather than a Victorian type, lacking Victorian earnestness and Victorian naïveté about equally. For this judgment I have no authority to cite but my own, and the reader may applaud or hiss accordingly.

In the case of the Marquise de Pompadour, a point involving

her correspondence seems to call for a note. That particular collection of her letters published in London by Barbé-Marbois ten years after her death has been dismissed by many French historians on what seem to me not totally conclusive grounds. Barbé-Marbois himself claimed to have acquired the originals from the Marquise's private secretary, lately deceased in Holland. Considering this, together with the matter of style, I conclude that if the suspect letters are not the Pompadour's they are the work of an extremely skilful imitator of her manner, with an intimate knowledge of her affairs and her correspondents' equally. I have therefore quoted from one or two without prejudice, as lawyers say, and with due warning. The reader is invited to recall that the eighteenth century was an age of literary forgery, and the charge was flung about fairly indiscriminately. It is not a Star Chamber matter in any case.

Don Manuel Godoy's memoirs I have utilised with becoming discretion. They were published three years after the death of his principal enemy, Ferdinand VII of Spain. Other notable adversaries like Napoleon were also in the grave or, like the aged Talleyrand, preparing for death, or otherwise unable to challenge Don Manuel's pages, had they cared to do so. As he is answering the charges of a lifetime and is concerned to place himself in the best light possible, Godoy tactfully omits from the memoirs one or two curious incidents which might have marred his claim to a white toga; moreover, he is sometimes the sole witness of scenes which may have become blurred or distorted, a long time later, in the memory of a man in his seventieth year. Modern Spanish historians of distinction like Don M. Fernández Almagro, of the Royal Academy of History, and Don Ángel Salcedo Ruíz, of the Royal Academy of Moral and Political Sciences, have practically no use for Godoy at all. I have striven to hold a just balance between the Almagro-Ruíz school, the neutral Lord Holland, and what might be called (without offence) the Rogue-Whig school of d'Esmenard and d'Auvergne, which canonises Godoy as a martyr to reactionary injustice.

Reasonably close acquaintance with contemporaries of his like Goya, Jovellanos, and Quintana, and with the modern Spanish scene, has enabled me, I trust, to fill in Godoy's background not too unhandily.

In the case of Potemkin, I have preserved the usual British spelling of his name (correctly, I am assured, "Patiomkine-Tavrichesky"). Ignorance of the Russian language is no great handicap in surveying him, since apart from French translations of his leading Russian biographers there are the fascinating impressions of the Prince de Ligne and the Comte de Ségur, two admirable Western connoisseurs of the baroque, to draw upon, with the despatches of two British Ambassadors. What are called Potemkin's memoirs, which are not of his own composition and which were published in an English translation "from the German" in 1813, I have used sparingly. If a personal note may be added, some contact with the Russian temperament acquired in Paris in the 1930's has been of immense value. Bizarre as some aspects of Potemkin must appear to Western eyes, such things are a commonplace to his countrymen past and present, and none of the great Russian novelists seems to be a caricaturist to any extent. My concluding chapter is dedicated to the gallant memory of a personage of Potemkinesque attraction and addiction who may here be called (since he has relatives in Russia, possibly still unliquidated) Colonel Boris Nitchevov; in whom diabolic verve as a hired long-distance chauffeur mingled with a wide culture, the gayest of courage in poverty and exile, a fantastic, unpredictable topsy-turveydom of outlook, an inexhaustible gift of conversation, and that fundamental brooding melancholy and *Weltschmerz* which is the classic Russian heritage, it seems. It is possible that one evening with such a character could throw more light on the veritable Russia than a dozen treatises; as G. K. Chesterton also discovered on a memorable night, described in his Autobiography, when, amid the crash of bombs all round, a wild-eyed Russian friend of Maurice Baring's offered him the Crown of England.

From the maze of politics in which my four personages are constantly involved I have selected only those items which seem necessary to explain or corroborate their influence. The serious student, as I have hinted already, will find Melbourne's considerable political achievements reviewed in other places. Similarly with the others. My intention has been to discard, where possible, details interesting only to the specialist. The specialist's loss is so easily reparable that this intention seems to me to call for no apologies, so long as one is able to show one's figures capable of statecraft yet not stuffed. Long ago, ploughing through a densely packed study of Robespierre by a conscientious French historian of the 1860's, I came on the solitary fact that Robespierre's only parlour-trick, in which he took excessive pride, was peeling an orange neatly with one hand. At once (though the historian mentioned it with an embarrassed smirk, as of one caught by the Rector of the Sorbonne in the act of throwing a somersault) did a lay-figure come alive. The essential spinsterish quality of Robespierre, that frigid decorum and Messianic complacency were suddenly illuminated, and his attitude to bloodier problems than an unpeeled orange made manifest in those arid pages for the first time. So, too, when in his jogtrot life of Charlemagne Eginhard mentions incidentally that the Emperor had a high voice (*clara vox*), the great legendary figure moves and breathes, quite unexpectedly. History is full of such opportunities, too rarely taken.

In this connection it may be permitted to observe generally that, like Mme de Pompadour, the figures of Melbourne, Godoy, and Potemkin demand little resuscitative labour in any sensitive biographer, being already alive, both in their letters and memoirs and in the vivid impression they made on their contemporaries. It needs no imagination worth speaking of to see and hear these people moving against their natural background. The crushing dullness of many books written about and around the eminent dead is in the writers, of whom their victims might well complain, as Dr. Johnson said of Dr. Birch, that as soon as they pick up a pen it turns to a torpedo. At the other extreme are the Macaulays and the Michelets, who concentrate on effect rather than veracity—apart from having a case, and a Whig case especially, to prove at all costs—and are hardly more to be endured. The remarkable feat of Carlyle, whose portraits of the men of the French Revolution are so free, amid all that thunderous rhetoric and lavish, vigorous word-painting, from serious blunder, shows that to combine truth with vividness in an historical study is not impossible, as Mr. Belloc—himself a master in this art—has pointed out. The entrancing Revolutionary studies of Lenotre reveal this even more. Here is a living historian who can tell you, as André Bellessort has admiringly remarked, the colour of Robespierre's quilt; the exact mechanism of Couthon's invalid-chair on wheels; the Christian names of Gabrielle Danton's housemaid; the items of Marat's last meal on earth; and the material, with its design, covering the armchair occupied by the President of the Tribunal during the Terror. Pedants who since La Bruyère have sneered at such reconstructive passion do so principally, I think, in envy. Without having gone to such lengths, involving long and now impossible research, I have done what I can to supply such details of contemporary *décor* as help to make the actors, I hope, come more vividly alive. Does one not see the Pompadour a little more clearly when one discovers, in the yellowed pages of some obscure satire on eighteenth-century Parisian high life, the names of the half-dozen principal styles of face-patch then in vogue?

In conclusion, I have been careful with all my four characters to avoid supplying them with any conversation, or any motive, which is not strictly on record as their own. The tempting trick of supply, apt to flourish exceedingly since the 1920's, might be defended, at a pinch, in the case where the historian and his subject share the same philosophy and, therefore, are actuated by the same fundamental principles when faced by a given problem of conduct; but even then it is a business for the poet or the dramatist rather than the biographer, for Thalia or Melpomene rather than Clio, the rigorous and knuckle-rapping maiden aunt of the Muses. On the other hand, it seems to me perfectly permissible to assume, for example, that to the drawing-room of Doña Josefa Tudó, Godoy, who found in her his only solace, would naturally bring his latest worry for discussion and consolation; that Melbourne's strange forbearance over the Lamb-Byron scandal was due not entirely to constitutional listlessness, but to active charity and pity intermingled; that in the farce of Mme de Pompadour's penitential exhibition of 1751-2 there may have been a faint streak of shame; that Potemkin may at times have believed the assassination of Tsar Peter III by his friends the Orlovs to have been, morally, a mistake. Legitimate deduction with proper safeguards is not the same thing as wanton indulgence in probabilities.

I have to thank Miss Chloë Gunn for invaluable research in the Rimsky-Korsakov archives; the Acting Librarian of the Foreign Office and the Secretary of the Public Record Office, for access to various diplomatic papers; Mr. Hilaire Belloc and Messrs. Nisbet and Co., for a passage from *Danton*; Messrs. John Murray, for permission to quote from *The Letters of Queen Victoria* and *The Girlhood of Queen Victoria*, published by them; Messrs. Longmans, Green and Co., for permission to quote from *Lord Melbourne's Papers*; Don José Brugada of the Spanish Embassy, for kindly procuring me a print of the Goya portrait of Godoy from Madrid; the Director of the National Gallery of Scotland, for the frontispiece; the Director of the National Portrait Gallery, London, for the Partridge portrait of Melbourne; the Keeper of the Prints and Drawings, British Museum, for the mezzotint of Potemkin by James Walker, Engraver to Catherine II; and, as ever, the staff of the London Library, for tireless courtesy.

D. B. W. L.

LONDON, 1948.

CONTENTS

ILLUSTRATIONS

The portraits in this book are reproduced from the originals by Boucher (National Gallery of Scotland), John Partridge (National Portrait Gallery), Goya (Academia San Fernando, Madrid), and James Walker (British Museum) respectively.

Madame de Pompadour

I

MADAME DE POMPADOUR

"In judging women I find myself always having to leave
an ample margin to note, amid the loveliest and most noble
actions, a certain tendency to deceit, or some light perfidy."

(GANIVET, *Ideario*.)

"Une petite bourgeoise,
Elévée à la grivoise,
Fait de la Cour un taudis,
Dis, dis." [1]

(Parisian street-song, *circa* 1745.)

I

IN the long list of pensions granted by Jeanne-Antoinette,
Marquise de Pompadour, at the peak of her power there is an
interesting item:

600 *livres to Mme Lebon, for having predicted to her at the age
of nine that she would one day be the mistress of Louis XV.*

This business-like recognition of a crystal-gazer's services is
doubly valuable as the key to a career, revealing not only that
efficiency which dictated Mme de Pompadour's every impulse,
but the superstition which fixed in her, as in Napoleon, a lifelong
belief in her destiny. The obscure Mme Lebon, who seems to
have belonged, unlike the Emperor's Mme de Thèbes, to the
lower or Brighton Pier branch of the profession, made a lucky
shot that day in 1730. Little Jeanne-Antoinette returned to her
dolls with a purpose. It was typical of her, years later, not to
forget her source of inspiration. But for Mme Lebon's directing

[1] Roughly: "A little bourgeois slut,
Brought up among the smut,
Is turning of the Court into a sty,
Hi, hi."

I

finger the child might never have capitalised and concentrated her brains and loveliness as suitably as she did. The Ursuline nuns of Poissy little guessed to what end their charming and popular pupil was devoting even her first dancing-lessons. "Reinette" ("Queenie"), her fond parents called her, after the custom of the bourgeoisie; not unprophetically.

Jeanne-Antoinette (1721–1764) came of a business-like family of the name of Poisson, later draped by her unerring good taste in the more decorative marquisate of Marigny. Her father was not the vulgar and socially impossible butcher of enemy legend, but an Army contractor of humble origin and rapacious ability who had acquired a sufficient veneer, while making his fortune, to ascend into those financial circles whose pride and exemplar was the current aristocracy of Mammon, that powerful clique known as the Farmers-General, *maltôtiers* or *partisans*.

La Bruyère's satire[1] and a myriad contemporary lampoons and caricatures, apart from the Abbé Coignard's outburst against M. de la Guéritaude, reveal the power and insolence of these nabobs, their often low origin, and the dislike the middle-class and the entire populace bore them. Rigaud's portrait of the eminent bankrupt Samuel Bernard, Comte de Goubert, seated regally, in his sumptuous silks and velvets and his great full-bottomed periwig, under a red velvet canopy, one haughty hand waving attention to a merchant-fleet viewed in perspective, shows how *la haute Finance* rivalled the Blood-Royal itself in splendour. The hierarchy and operations were fixed. Having advanced the Treasury a given sum a Farmer-General recouped himself from the taxes, giving his orders to sub-farmers, who gave theirs to *receveurs*, each taking his "cut," as the City would say to-day. Huge fortunes were made, also lost. Several too-hardy financiers of this type came to grief under Louis XIV and ended in the Bastille, the galleys, or—in one case, that of Grusle in 1680—on the scaffold. Occupational risks of this kind are rarer nowadays.

François Poisson, father of the future Royal Favourite and a

[1] *Les Caractères*, VI.

protégé of the brothers Pâris, princes of the Money Ring, was himself not quite in the front rank, being in his prime what we should call to-day a magnoperator in the food-market. His handling of relief-work during a plague in Provence was entirely admirable. Monsieur Poisson's luck was bad, however. Charged, when Jeanne-Antoinette was barely ten years old, with peculations involving prison and possibly the rope, he was forced to skip nimbly over the nearest frontier in the traditional big-business fashion, and retired to Hamburg under a cloud which was not dispelled till 1741, when his conviction was quashed and he was able to return; jovial, red-faced, stout, cynical, delighted at his clever daughter's progress, a perfect Black Market type.

He could reasonably congratulate her mother. Mme Poisson, *née* de la Motte, was a woman possessing "the brains of a quartet of devils," as one of her admirers in the business world remarked. She lacked morals lavishly, but her head was sound. One of Madame's principal lovers, the well-connected Farmer-General M. de Tournehem, a patron of the Arts whose portrait by Tocqué is almost as impressive as the Rigaud portrait of Samuel Bernard, was made to pay, in her father's enforced absence abroad, for Jeanne-Antoinette's education, and spared no expense. When she left her convent-school at Poissy the best singing, dancing, and deportment masters in Paris were engaged for her; her tutor in elocution and dramatic art was the eminent Crébillon *père* himself. Mme Poisson did not live to enjoy her Reinette's full triumph, but was able nevertheless to pass away in 1745 with a glad *Nunc Dimittis*, leaving behind her a whole dossier of directions for her daughter's guidance.

Before quitting this world Madame had arranged a highly creditable marriage, which took place in 1741. The young bride-groom, Charles-Guillaume Lenormant d'Etioles, son of the Treasurer of the Mint, nephew of M. de Tournehem, came of ancient and noble stock, though himself a homely figure enough, and during the preliminary negotiations declined totally to ally himself with a family whose raffish reputation was known to all

Paris. But on meeting his bride-to-be for the first time he fell, unfortunately for him, violently in love with her, and not without reason. Jeanne-Antoinette at twenty was truly a King's morsel, a fairy-tale princess straight out of the pages of Perrault or Mme d'Aulnoy: slim, supple, elegant, golden-locked, with a lovely, perfectly oval face, a dainty nose, a charming, petulant mouth, teeth of the pearliest, and a frank and delicious smile. Her large eyes were almost as magical as the eyes of Mary, Queen of Scots, apparently, and like them neither black, blue, nor grey, but a mystical, indefinable, shimmering, sparkling, ever-changing composite. To these attractions she added a gay vivacity and grace of movement and gesture, a quick intelligence, amounting to genius of a sort, and a voice so delectable, speaking or singing, that she might have been that incomparable Angélique to whom Tallemant des Réaux pays the perfect fairy-tale compliment in his *Historiettes*: "Two nightingales were found with burst hearts on the edge of a fountain where she had sung all evening." Above all, her moods, her animation, her quick flashing transitions were an enchantment. Or so say connoisseurs like Leroy, Master of the Versailles Hunt. Even her worst enemies, headed by d'Argenson, do not deny her grace, talents, and accomplishments. Within a few months of her marriage the men hanging round her panniered skirts included the distinguished philosophers Maupertuis and Fontenelle and the forty-eight-year-old Voltaire, her faithful henchman henceforward. It is clear that Mme d'Etioles possessed charms other than physical.

Her opening strategy, handicapped only by the King's absences with the army in Flanders, was to bring Louis XV within range of those devastating eyes; a task first fulfilled within a year or two of her marriage and repeated by tactful calculation. When hunting in the Forest of Sénart, Louis began to note at the meet an exquisite creature in blue (or pink) in a phaeton of pink (or blue). At length, on February 28, 1745, at a masked ball at the Hôtel de Ville, the King was accosted by a dainty vision who, after exchanging a few frivolities, doffed her mask, revealing the features of Mme d'Etioles, and fled, dropping her handkerchief, which the King picked up and threw laughingly after her. "The handkerchief is thrown," murmured the Court, raising its eyebrows.

The orientalism of the gesture is appropriate. In his thirty-sixth year Louis the Well-beloved was at intervals as satiated with the flesh as Solomon, in his last days, brooding over the splendours of his harem and meditating, with a pessimism blacker than Schopenhauer's, the vanity and vexation of all human pleasures. More weary than ever of the procession of beauties passing in and out of the Royal bedchamber—the latest, Mme de Châteauroux, recently dead, had had time to convey to *la petite d'Etioles* that she had better keep out—and sick of their caprices, the King confided his disgust to Binet, his valet-de-chambre, one evening soon after the incident of the masked ball. Binet happened to be a distant connection of Mme d'Etioles. He ventured to remind the King of the piquant new arrival of whom everybody was talking. A month later Mme d'Etioles' magnificent eyes were viewed at the Italian Comedy—soon to be absorbed by the Opéra-Comique—flashing soft fire at the Royal box. About a month after this Mme d'Etioles supped with His Majesty in his apartments at Versailles. On April 22 she supped with him again, in company with Richelieu and Luxembourg, at a party lasting till five in the morning. By the beginning of May she had left her husband, to his grief and despair, and was occupying apartments at Versailles. Between May and July, while Louis XV was again with his army in Flanders, she received a shower of notes from His Majesty, expressing considerable passion. On his return the King awarded her the title of Marquise de Pompadour, borrowed from a Limousin family now extinct and exquisitely right in every way, and in September 1745 she made her first curtsy to devout, long-suffering Queen Marie Leczinska at Versailles, in the presence of a king observed to be very red in the face.

So far the story is commonplace enough. Many an artful and pertinacious minx has attained her objective thus, even in the highest circles. But it would be unjust to Louis XV to assume that he gave in without a struggle.

Difficult as it is for anyone nourished on popular demagogic history to imagine Louis XV as possessing any good qualities whatsoever, he had, in fact, many. The traditional picture of the selfish voluptuary oppressed continually by a kind of low fever of discontent and boredom, enervated, listless, indolent, aloof— "would not one think at times," ask even the Goncourts, who have no republican axe to grind, "that he *looks on* at his own reign, as at some bad play?"—is full of falsity. Constitutional reserve, taciturnity, and affected indifference, due to an unhappy childhood and a weak will, can conceal a highly sensitive nature and a fund of good sense and kindness, which Louis certainly had; personal courage and dignity, which he also had; a melancholy clairvoyant realism likewise; odd flashes of energy and, above all, the ability to be enslaved by his passions without being duped by them. Louis XV was profligate, but not impious. Unable to comprehend this, the rugged and calvinistic Carlyle cannot withold a sneer or two at Louis' passionately penitent dying bed. Nevertheless, in a France in which religion had sunk temporarily to a very low ebb, with a bevy of worldly prelates on one hand, a rising tide of noisy atheist intelligentsia, such as bored and sickened Horace Walpole, at the other, and a fair mass of indifference in between, Louis XV retained a Christian conscience which gave him trouble over fifty years.

He did not, in fact, plunge blindly into his amour with the fascinating Jeanne-Antoinette d'Etioles. So far as habitual indecision allowed him, he made some sort of attempt at the very beginning not to submit, having been implored by the Dauphin's tutor, Boyer, Bishop of Mirepoix and a Jesuit, not to afflict his country and delight her enemies with the spectacle of the Most Christian King of France in the toils of a woman who, apart from all else, was notoriously hand in glove with militant atheists. Unfortunately Boyer's intervention merely infuriated those of Louis' daily intimates who hated the Jesuits even more than they hated religion, his perpetual bad angel Richelieu in particular.

The character of that brilliant soldier Louis-François-Armand du Plessis, Maréchal-Duc de Richelieu, illustrates one prevailing aspect of the Age of Reason which should not be overlooked. Apart from being a furious enemy of religion and morals of every kind, Richelieu dabbled, like many other European fashionables of the period, in spiritism and black magic, and was involved at least once in a celebration of the Black Mass. According to the Duc de Lévis, the great Cardinal's grand-nephew sacrificed, during another satanist orgy, a white horse to the moon. The Duke's whimsies greatly amused his protégé Voltaire, who believed in nothing at all. Richelieu was not alone in such addictions. The smartest Parisian society, the Pompadour included, ran after magicians, seers, mediums, alchemists, soothsayers, and mystical charlatans of every kind with quite modern enthusiasm, and the celebrated clairvoyante Mme Bontemps, a private soldier's wife, numbered some of the greatest names of France among her clients and was thereby protected against any annoyance from the police. Though Louis XV eschewed all evil occult gambols,[1] his character was not strong enough to withstand entirely the destructive charm of a Richelieu. It might be said, not too fantastically, that Richelieu and others of his kind pushed the King into a liaison with the Pompadour solely to score off Heaven.

They did not succeed at once. His period of hesitation and spiritual conflict lasted nearly two months. It is not a bad feat of resistance for a man of Louis' temperament.

However, the liaison began, and the Pompadour needed all her powers, physical and mental, to carry it off. An arrogant nobility could hardly overlook the insolence of a little *roturière* of the financial underworld in crashing, so to speak, into a strictly aristocratic preserve. Few great ladies could brook such an insult.

---

[1] He was interested for some time in that curious faker the Comte de Saint-Germain, who claimed to be able to increase the weight of pearls and advertised an elixir of long life; a relatively harmless warlock.

Tongues and pens of a venom only to be found in eighteenth-century France (and verses, epigrams, lampoons, pamphlets, squibs, songs, and bitter, brilliant chatter quoted in a score of contemporary memoirs show exactly what that could be) were loosed on all sides against the new favourite even before she took office. In her Royal lover's own household the frigid absolute minimum of disdainful courtesy was accorded her by the Dauphin. One or two courtiers of great influence like Maurepas, Secretary of State, and Richelieu, hardly troubled to hide their sneers. The resigned amiability of the Queen was due to her being a fount of charity and pure goodness. Outside Versailles Mme de Pompadour found little encouragement. The middle-class she came from naturally detested her, and the Parisian populace roared abusive songs, many said to be the work of Maurepas, known collectively as *Les Poissonades*, of which the alleged gutter-origin of this prostitute and exploitress was the principal theme:

> " *L'âme vile et mercenaire,*
> *Le propos d'une commère,*
> *Tout est bas chez la Poisson,*
> *Son, son.*"[1]

All these enmities she was able to defy. The far more redoubtable hostility of the Jesuits took her nearly twenty years to overcome, and it ended only with their expulsion. This, the only major defeat of her career, is profoundly interesting by reason of the fact that such a brilliant woman took so long to perceive and assess, close under the surface of easy good-breeding, that adamantine inflexibility in matters of faith and morals which is the mark of the shock-troops of Loyola and has made them so unpopular, during their Society's stormy history, with kings, favourites, politicians, careerists, Jansenists, and potentates of

---

[1] "Her greedy soul so vile,
Her gab in fishwife's style,
Everything about the Poisson's low,
Oh, oh."

every kind, and against which cajolery is powerless. Had Louis
XV been irreligious, like herself and most of the French nobility,
the Pompadour's final victory over *ces messieurs de la Compagnie*
would have arrived much sooner; but if the drifting sensualist in
Louis was on her side, his inconvenient conscience was not, and
her battle with the Jesuits, waged with such unequal weapons,
could never have been won by her without that last expedient of
physical force which always seems, at the time, so final. With
what charming naïveté does Fülöp-Miller, in his massive history
of the Society, observe that the Jesuits "neglected a really unique
opportunity of securing for their Order the protection of the all-
powerful Favourite," and that they were to pay dearly for "the
stern morality which was so mistaken politically."[1]

2

Contemplating Mme de Pompadour from 1745 to her last
day, one perceives her life to have been a fierce and perpetual
struggle—*un combat perpetuel*, her own words—without relief
or respite; as it were, the life of a lonely conquistador pushing
through dark tropical forests full of menace visible and invisible,
amid unremitting attack from all sides. Her only hold on the
King, as she well knew, was to keep him involved in a whirl of
expensive amusement, for his passion would burn itself out in
due course; and, in fact, years before the end he was as physically
tired of her as any man of breeding can allow himself to admit.
How skilfully she managed her business, even to becoming the
procuress of the Parc-aux-Cerfs, we shall observe as these pages
proceed. Her commercial instinct inspired her, at the very
beginning, to attach to her the powerful brothers Pâris, her
father's patrons, the Rockefellers and Morgans and Zaharoffs of
the period, thus relieving some of Louis XV's perpetual qualms
over ready money; together with other experts like Marmontel
and Duverney. In Maurepas' Cabinet she soon had two co-
adjutors, the Marquis de Puisieux and Saint-Sévérin, a typically

[1] VI, 13.

subtle Italian-born man of affairs. Another of her earliest allies was Cardinal de Tencin, a politician of experience and parts. And if Richelieu continued with subtle mockery to defy her, the equally hostile and insulting Maurepas badly misjudged his fair victim's capacities. Within four years of her ascent to power, after a violent scene between them, Maurepas was awakened at one o'clock one morning by a curt note from Louis XV dismissing and banishing him to his rose-gardens near Bourges. Thus Maurepas paid for his pretty gift of satire, to emerge from disgrace twenty-five years later as Louis XVI's first Prime Minister.

The Favourite was now (1749) installed at Versailles in apartments adjoining the King's. Is it possible to convey the civilised perfection of the atmosphere with which she surrounded herself, here and everywhere? A list of the gowns in which she paraded her beauty and skill on the stage of the Théâtre des Petits-Appartements at Versailles, her first experiment in amusing the Well-beloved, would make an interesting prelude if contemporary milliners' jargon were translatable; for example, her costume as Venus: *"corps et basques d'étoffe bleue en mosaïque garnie de réseau argent chenillé bleu, mante de taffétas bleu imprimé argent. . . ."* More comprehensible are the bills sent in by the Court jeweller and furnisher, Lazare Duvaux of the Rue St. Honoré, for works of art supplied to the Marquise. Lacquer and satinwood and buhl furniture encrusted with ormolu; dinner-services, vases, and clocks of China and Japan, Sèvres, and Dresden; lustres of Bohemian crystal; gold birdcages with enamelled birds; tall glass Venetian lanterns framed in bronze and ormolu; girandoles and chandeliers of silver and gilded bronze, richly ornamented; patchboxes and caskets and étuis of gold, silver, enamel, lacquer, and crystal; toilet-ware of silver, gold, and lapis-lazuli (to which attaches an amusing story told by that gallant Regency buck, Captain Gronow of the Guards, in his memoirs)[1]; watches of

[1] An eminent British Duke visiting Paris admired a fine octagonal gold bowl, engraved with the Marquise's arms, on a stand in a distant part of the Favourite's dressing-room, to which distinguished visitors were admitted. Learning of

delicate confection encased in enamel, porcelain, and precious metals discreetly gemmed; a formidable array of jades, ivories, and all those *chinoiseries* without which no great lady's drawing-rooms were complete, Celestial *magots* and "darling monsters of Japan" . . . the catalogue is eloquent of imperious profusion governed by triumphant and impeccable good taste, of its kind. Mme de Pompadour was, indeed, as she has been well called, the Queen of Rococo. Hers was the France of painters like Boucher, Vanloo, Chardin, Fragonard, Quentin de La Tour, Nattier, and Watteau, of architects like Gabriel and Bouchardon, of elaborate ornament and incomparable elegance; the languid, gracious art of a high and doomed civilisation—all French civilisation, as some think, died with Louis XVI—marvellously incarnate in this one woman's celebrity.

The Pompadour has bequeathed her name to a score of costly vanities from fans to coaches, apart from her favourite tint of rose, which the vulgar Dubarry later appropriated. She inspired, stimulated, encouraged, or financed achievement in almost every art and decorative craft. She personally conceived and established the great national porcelain-factories at Sèvres, which brought the pride of Dresden low, supervised the planning and practically financed the building of the École Militaire, and herself engraved portrait-medallions on onyx and cornaline and amethyst with more than amateur talent, which applies equally to her perform-ance on the clavecin, her horsemanship, her acting, her singing, her *savoir-faire* and, to a large extent, her political gifts. Her engravings on copper, however, are mediocre.

She may be pictured, then, moving like a golden swan over a lake of parquetry, against a background of painted Chinese paper, or damask, or Beauvais hangings, or white or gilded panelling, or walls "almost wainscoted with looking-glasses, and covered with gold," such as Dr. Johnson noted in the Paris house of

this, the Pompadour ordered a replica from her goldsmith, bearing the Duke's arms, to be sent to London. On his return the Duke found it duly facing him at a grand dinner-party, filled with soup.

d'Argenson and other mansions of the great in 1775. Her spacious or narrow rooms are lighted by elaborate chandeliers hanging from curved and gilded ceilings painted with "Loves in a riot of blue," Ledas and Venuses and Ariadnes from the brush of a Boucher or a Vanloo. Everywhere a profusion of mirrors and gilding, except in her celebrated library, which is shelved from floor to ceiling with solid manuals of history, political economy, statecraft, philosophy, both classic and of the Encyclopædic school, and law; all richly bound and nicely balanced by works on music, the theatre, and the opera, and a notable collection of romances and novels of every kind, French, Spanish, and Italian.

The costumes of her period are as rococo as the *décor*. Towards 1750 French women of quality dressed their hair high on the head and crested with ribbons, with flowing locks behind. They were considerably rouged, and wore face-patches, each of which had its name, position, and symbolism—la Passionée, l'Effrontée, la Coquette, la Majestueuse. Panniered skirts of brocade or silk with high whale-boned corsages, exposing a liberal amount of bosom, and a collarette of lace or taffetas—to be viewed in the Boucher and Nattier portraits of the Pompadour, and in a myriad prints by Chardin, Baudouin, and the younger Moreau—were worn by Society and rich middle-class women alike. Men of fashion wore coats and knee-breeches of coloured velvet; half-open brocade vests revealing richly-frilled shirts, jabots, and ruffles of fine linen or muslin; powdered perukes of several types, with or without toupets; silk stockings, white, pink, or striped; diamond-buckled shoes, three-cornered gold-braided hats with feathers, and a dress-rapier. As the Age of Reason was not remarkable for personal hygiene in any country—one thinks of Dr. Johnson's friend, the patrician rake Topham Beauclerk, who was not only dirty but verminous—men and women alike used lavish perfume, of a hundred kinds. One may complete a mental picture of one of the Pompadour's evening receptions, lit by hundreds of wax-candles in candelabra, girandoles, and chandeliers, and thronged with a brilliant, malicious crowd, by adding a regiment of powdered flunkeys in gay livery, among them the inevitable grinning, turbaned child-Negro, named frequently (like the Dubarry's dusky pet, who grew up to bring his mistress to the guillotine) Zamor. The ideal background-music to such a scene—though Mozart was not to write it until a generation later—would be the *Nozze di Figaro*: delicious, stimulating, and dry as the champagne sparkling in the tall *flûtes* of crystal engraved with the Marquise's crest, and a little heartless, like the company.

A little heartless. . . . Let us not exaggerate these things.

Everyone is familiar with the stock coloured picture, sacred to every demagogue, of France during the Pompadour's era and thence to the eve of the Revolution: the insolent luxury of Versailles, the wizened and starving peasantry everywhere gnawing dockleaves in the ditches beyond. It is, as Bainville, Funck-Brentano, Louis Bertrand, and other modern French historians have shown, grotesquely untrue, a picturesque literary fable. "Nothing," says Bainville, "is more singular than the spirit of France in the middle of the eighteenth century. Never has there been such well-being among us as then, never has life been so easy. . . . One is struck by the insignificance of what matters for complaint there were." Talleyrand's celebrated remark, half-way through the Revolution, that those who were not alive in the 1750's did not know the sweetness of living was certainly no irony, nor confined to his own class. Most critics of the fable beloved of demagogy trace it back notably to La Bruyère, whose famous glimpse from a coach-window in the 1680's of arid deserts haunted by miserable half-human shapes is typical not of France but of the atrabilious La Bruyère, in no mood at that moment to make antithetical play with the rich, smiling provinces, the stout peasant-proprietors, the prosperous rosy farmers with their carefully hidden hoards, the thriving craftsmen and artisans who made up the mass of the French people. It is not without significance, notes Jacques Bainville, that the outcries about being taxed to death raised in the 1750's come from those in rich or easy circumstances who had so far managed either to evade taxation or to cough up the absolute minimum.

Though French national finances were in no very flourishing condition following the first Seven Years War, ended in 1748, they had been in worse. The troubles of the Treasury were due, moreover, not so much to the burden of an expensive Crown (whose notions of riotous spending might well raise amused eyebrows to-day in Johannesburg, Buenos Aires, or Miami, Fla.)[1] as to the stubborn resistance of the Parlements to all measures for financial reform, an obduracy which paralysed the entire administration.[2] This was the strongly-documented case of economists of the Action Française school against Republican propagandists, and it seems worth pondering.

One may note finally, before passing on, that for all his ritual grumblings the French peasant under Louis XV, a highly popular king, was a free man, unlike some others of his degree in Europe, with a free distaste for bureaucracy and all its works.[3] Rousseau's story of being lost in the mountains and knocking at a humble cottage-door is well known. For some time the suspicious occupant refused him food and drink. He was too poor. He had nothing. Look and see! He had been stripped of all he possessed by *sacrés cochons*. Rousseau insisted, and named himself, and his unwilling host relented at length and produced on tiptoe a copi-

[1] The debts of Marie-Antoinette a generation later, after her two unhappy years of frustration and extravagance, amounted to barely £20,000.

[2] The *Parlements*, established by St. Louis, abolished by the Revolution, were not "parliaments" in the British sense, but fourteen (at this period) permanent legal bodies whose function was to register Royal decrees in Council, which thus became law, and to administer justice. The Parlement of Paris was the supreme court, and from it the provincial Parlements mostly took their lead. A Parlement could, and did, refuse to give statutory force to the Crown's taxes and other decrees. It could be dealt with finally by the summoning of a *Lit de Justice*, presided over by the King.

[3] What feudal dues survived in France in the second half of the eighteenth century were obnoxious to the peasantry chiefly by reason of the endless chicanery —exploited by a horde of petty lawyers—involved in attempts to collect (and to dodge) them. An illusion of crushing taxation derives from the fact that the same tax might bear a dozen different names, according to the province (Gaxotte, *La Révolution Française*, II, 35 ff.). The whole system had become chaotic.

ous meal, protesting that if this fact got around he was lost. The honest fellow suffered merely from what, in every age since Theocritus and probably before, is a familiar rural obsession: the dread of appearing more comfortable than one's neighbours and thereby attracting local enmities and the eye of officialdom. As Pierre Gaxotte observes, it is quite certain that on the eve of the Revolution the French peasant owned at least half of the richest soil of France.

It is therefore no starving desperate proletariat ground under the red heels of Privilege and already muttering revenge that forms the great mass of the French during the Pompadour's career, just as it is no besotted fool of a king she twists round her elegant thumb. The much-quoted "*Faites ce que veut Madame*"— "Do what Madame tells you"—uttered once to Maurepas over some trivial matter, has been developed by romancers into a kind of slogan expressing Louis XV's fundamental attitude to all State matters. What is called the *Secret du Roi* alone explodes such nonsense. It was—nobody has yet succeeded in probing it fully—a complicated system of secret service and counter-espionage, directed by Louis in person with one confidential assistant, the Prince de Conti, and enabling Louis to keep track of a large number of enemy agents (those of Prussia particularly), double-dealing politicians, foreign Court intriguers, and other menaces to France, and unostentatiously to repair his own public errors. To accuse such a man of handing over State affairs to any woman is as ludicrous as assuming, like some, his languid acquiescence in that equally-quoted piece of defeatist cynicism popularly attributed to the Pompadour, "*Après nous le déluge!*" Louis certainly perceived, towards the weary end of his sixty-year reign, the uncertain shadows flit,

> "*Announcing to the shuddering air*
> *A Darkening, and the end of it. . . .*"

Yet it was hardly possible for him to judge that certain explosive particles floating in the empyrean would combine with many others and rush suddenly together and fuse, some thirty years hence, in a thunderclap; nor could he foresee, as the most purblind history-don can foresee nowadays, such immediate causes of the Revolution as (to name only four) the financial jugglings of Necker, the untimely death of Mirabeau, the disastrous diplomatic and other blunderings of Marie-Antoinette, and the directive power of the Lodges. Such being the will of God for the French, in Louis XV's time veiled from them.

That Louis did his uncertain best for his people, as any list of his achievements demonstrates, is to-day a commonplace to the unbiased. The violent end of the long Capetian Line was no blame of his, despite the undoubtedly malign influence of the Dubarry on his final years. In his study of Danton Mr. Hilaire Belloc surveys the stupendous pageant of the Capetians in a passage of justly celebrated magnificence :

So perished the French Monarchy. Its dim origins stretched out and lost themselves in Rome; it had already learnt to speak and recognised its own nature when the vaults of the Thermæ echoed heavily to the slow footsteps of the Merovingian kings. Look up that vast valley of dead men crowned, and you may see the gigantic figure of Charlemagne, his brows level and his long white beard tangled like an undergrowth, having in his left hand the globe and in his right the hilt of an unconquerable sword. There are also the short, strong horsemen of the Robertian house, half-hidden by their leather shields, and their sons before them growing in vestment and majesty, and taking on the pomp of the Middle Ages. Louis VII, all covered with iron; Philip the Conqueror; Louis IX, who alone is surrounded with light— they stand in a widening, interminable procession, this great crowd of kings; they lose their armour, they take their ermine on, they are accompanied by their captains and their marshals; at last, in their attitude and in their magnificence, they sum up in themselves the pride and the achievement of the French nation. But Time has dissipated what it could not tarnish, and the process of a thousand years has turned these mighty figures into insubstantial things. You may see them in the grey end of darkness, like a pageant all standing still. You look again, but with the growing light and with the wind that rises before morning they have disappeared.

That Louis XV sometimes looked back on his long line thus, a little haggardly, is not unlikely. His preparation for kingship had been thorough, and the history and obligations of the ancient and enormous sacramental bond between himself and the French People would have been explained to him by his tutors even to satiety. A stronger man could have done more, doubtless, to avert that crumbling and cracking which so many observers of his reign, writing a century or more after it, have been able to detect so clearly behind the French façade even at this period. It is true, of course, that many contemporary observers of Louis XV's France smelt trouble in the air; even such frivolous foreign visitors as Horace Walpole, who did so when he was in Paris in 1765:

Laughing is as much out of fashion as pantins or bilboquets. Good folks, they have no time to laugh. There is God and the King to be pulled down first; and men and women, one and all, are devoutly employed in the demolition. (To Thomas Brand, October 19.)

And again:

Do you know who *the philosophers* are, or what the term means here? In the first place, it comprehends almost everybody; and in the next, means men who, avowing war against Popery, aim, many of them, at a subversion of all religion, and still many more at the destruction of regal power. (To the Hon. H. S. Conway, October 18.)[1]

Within the Pompadour's own circle this apostolate of wreckage was, as it were, crystallised and directed. One of her familiars,

---

[1] The most famous Parisian rendezvous of the *philosophes* and their disciples (and after them the Terrorists) was the Café Procope, in the Rue de l'Ancienne-Comédie, whose balcony still survives. Here religion was derided under the name of "Javotte," the soul being known as "Margot" and its Creator as "Monsieur de l'Etre." At Versailles the Café Amaury in the Rue de la Pompe was almost as famous, for the same reason.

Dr. Quesnay, a medical man appointed by her favour Consultant to the King, with apartments in the palace, was the leader of a discussion-group which has been since recognised as the first of those masonic and republican clubs which were to abolish the Crown and direct the Terror. Here, under the King's own roof, the end of the Church and the Monarchy was freely debated by a select circle and treated as inevitable. If Louis XV did not take Dr. Quesnay seriously, it was doubtless owing to a fondness for an undoubtedly devoted physician of amusing brusqueness, to lack of energy, and to the feeling that one crazy philosopher more or less hardly mattered. Perhaps, also, like the smart world of our own time (till recently), he found isolated specimens of the Red Intelligentsia piquant. Probably he did not know to any extent what the Favourite's intimates were so fond of discussing; or again, if he did, good-nature and weakness of will may have led him to dismiss the whole business with a shrug for the sake of peace, as he did too often. He seems to have deemed the philosophers generally more absurd than dangerous, as did habitués of the Closerie des Lilas in the 1900's, when Lenin and his friends had their nightly table there. Such misjudgments were nothing new even in Louis' time.

Voltaire, among his voluminous works,[1] recounts a revealing anecdote in this connection, related to him undoubtedly by the Pompadour herself. At a small, intimate supper-party at Versailles, those present being the King, Mme de Pompadour, the Duc de la Vallière, the Duc de Nivernais, and the Comte de Coigny, the conversation turned on the composition of gunpowder. Nobody present knew the formula. "I don't even know the composition of my own face-powder," the Pompadour admitted laughingly. "What a pity," cried Nivernais, "that His Majesty has confiscated all our Encyclopædias!" As the King was dealing amiably with this remark, the Pompadour rang the bell, with his permission. Three footmen returned shortly, each laden with seven volumes of the *Encyclopédie*. Both powder

[1] Vol. XLVIII in Beuchot's edition.

mysteries were duly solved, and the King, at the Favourite's
gay urging, raised the ban on France's most destructive publication before the party broke up.

With the sappers thus ardently at work in the very citadel of
Royalty, the routine of a Crown still absolute in theory continued.
Louis XV presided over the Council as usual, signed the usual
papers, granted and refused the usual *placets*, and conducted
ordinary State business like his predecessors. Once more the
familiar twopence-coloured impression of a yawning king
absorbed totally in pleasure and abandoning all government to
his mistress may be dismissed as fantasy. Though Louis' recurring aversion to anything decisive or violent played into the
Pompadour's hands, a weakness abetted by confidence in her
undoubted abilities, she took no step without the King's full
knowledge and sanction, and, though constantly at his elbow
when he needed her—and not otherwise, for like Lady Conyng-
ham with George IV she knew the exquisite value of absence
—never usurped his place in Council. He habitually listened
to her and consulted her on men and affairs, but he by no means
accepted all her judgments. He might bear with Dr. Quesnay
and give in good-naturedly over the Encyclopædia, but he was
well aware of the disruptive rage of her literary friends, and did
what he could to keep it in check, amid an unceasing rain of
anonymous pamphlet-attacks. Her dear Parlements, again, he
knew to be filled largely with wealthy lawyers hostile, in their dry
and pettifogging manner, to a Crown which had made and kept
France great for nearly a thousand years, and he asserted the
authority of the Executive over these also when driven to it.
And notwithstanding a few *lubies* of hers, Mme de Pompadour
reasoned and talked like a highly gifted and intelligent man. As
her capacity was at least equal to that of any public figure con-
ducting Europe's business to-day, it does not seem that the
King's habit of listening to her implies any essential abdication
from sanity.

She never bored and she was never seen to be bored. At a

period when life was such an art that even the yawn was graceful and had its place, like the nice conduct of a snuffbox or fan, in the conversation of the polite (and even more—did not that amusing rascal the Chevalier de la Morlière, self-appointed censor of the Parisian stage, kill a new comedy stone-dead by yawning with weary elegance till audience and actors alike were forced to follow suit?), Mme de Pompadour was never seen to yawn in public. Her would-be destroyers caught her off her guard, in fact, at no time. They could afford to take time off for other amusements. She continued armed, vigilant, always at high tension, perpetually on the alert, perpetually counter-attacking.

3

It was in 1751–2 that this admirable actress played her most exacting rôle. An extract from a letter of d'Argenson's in 1749 may serve to raise the curtain:

Much is being said in society about the King's wish to keep Easter. It is positively asserted that His Majesty has had a two hours' interview with Father Perusseau. . . . The Marquise weeps continuously, and her adherents [*sic*] show the greatest uneasiness.

Easter was a recurring crux in the life of Louis XV. At this great feast it was the duty of the Most Christian King of France, as of the raggedest tramp in his dominions, to confess and receive the Blessed Sacrament. Year by year Louis, whose Jesuit tutors had had such high hopes of him in youth, kept putting this duty off. Every other year or so, as Easter approached, he was racked with remorse, and on each occasion he found the Sixth Commandment too hard for him. His confessor, Father Perusseau, S.J., had stubbornly refused from the beginning to tolerate his amours, and continuously refused him the Sacraments, as was his duty. Once, during the reign of the Pompadour's predecessor, Mme de Châteauroux, Louis, falling seriously ill with fever, sent her packing and summoned his confessor; but he recovered, dismissed the priest, and took back his mistress. To her successor Perusseau was implacable likewise, refusing to have anything to do with her.

The King's symptoms of penitence in the spring of 1749 alarmed the Favourite extremely, as d'Argenson observes. They passed off as usual, however, to revive again with increased virulence two years later. This time Mme de Pompadour, in a high state of nerves, sought some means of regularising her position. While her minister, Machault, did what he could to place routine-obstacles in the way of Louis' Easter duties, she herself discovered a sudden preoccupation with her soul, and was heard to confess that since the death of her only child she had been led to take serious thought of penitence and religion. She was now observed daily at Mass in the Chapel Royal; not, as formerly, going through a boring piece of Court routine, but deeply absorbed in palpable devotion. It was murmured all over Paris that the door between her apartments and the King's had already been bricked up. But the sudden conversion of Voltaire's sceptic patroness, the theme of every Parisian salon and the joy of all the wits, did not stampede Father Perusseau, who required as a first intimation of sincerity that Mme de Pompadour should quit Versailles forthwith and for good.

She balked. She explained to the Jesuit that her relations with the King were now completely platonic. At her demand Louis himself guaranteed it. When Perusseau died, still unconvinced and unyielding, Father Desmarets, who took his place as Royal confessor, was discovered to be equally implacable. In her annoyance the Pompadour turned to another Jesuit, Father de Sacy, reported to be "easy." De Sacy certainly welcomed the opportunity of reconciling this interesting penitent. At each conference with the Favourite he merely demanded that as a first step she should return to her lawful husband, Monsieur d'Etioles; and to the surprise of every breathless onlooker, Mme de Pompadour finally accepted this condition, in apparent humility. Having taken the precaution of warning M. d'Etioles in advance that any

welcome for a penitent wife would gravely disoblige the King—
nor had M. d'Etioles by this time any intention of taking her
back at any price—she was able to report to Father de Sacy in
sad surprise that her husband totally refused to be reconciled.
"My conscience," she added, more cheerfully, "is now at ease.
Nothing more can raise any difficulties."

Father de Sacy did not concur and remained difficult, refusing
to give her absolution, insisting as the merest preliminary that the
staircase to Mme de Pompadour's apartments should be rebuilt
in such a manner that the King, who had just created her a lady-
in-waiting to the Queen, which made her residence at Versailles
obligatory, could visit her henceforth only by way of the great
salon. Her chief end being gained by her new appointment, Mme
de Pompadour grew tired of the whole imbroglio and dropped
piety as quickly as she had taken it up. The farce was played.
Nothing remained of her fervour from now on but a venomous
feminine grudge against the entire Society of Jesus, whose
French members she denounced in a wonderful private letter to
the Pope as the persecutors of a misunderstood woman humbly
striving to do her best, and the cynical instigators of all Louis
XV's debaucheries. Full vengeance was to be satisfied twelve
years hence.

Lest one should be tempted at any moment to picture a
masterful beauty, in these ensuing years of splendour, sailing
through life serenely conscious of triumph and power, it is as
well to pause again and discern the dominant note or *leitmotiv* of
La Pompadour's career. It is, notwithstanding her superb poise,
fear—fear not only of losing her precarious hold over Louis XV,
of a cloud of sleepless enemies of both sexes in and outside the
Court, of a path strewn with daily pitfalls and ambushes, but of
actual assassination. Those who saw her moving radiant and
goddesslike through Versailles galas did not see her, late at night,
closeted in her own apartments with Berryer, Lieutenant of Police,
absorbed in the reports of his innumerable spies, and studying

extracts from the public postbags and the newest lampoons submitted to her by Janelle, Intendant of Posts. It was her firm conviction that Berryer and Janelle saved her more than once from pistol, dagger, or poison, which seems not unlikely. Behind that charming mask extreme nervous tension, the Pompadour's normal condition from 1745 till the day of her death, destroyed her health, which was not good. She never knew when she might fall; and in fact she was within a fan's-length of ruin at the end of 1752, when Maurepas' successor at the head of the Ministry, d'Argenson, who hated her with a still colder, more concentrated venom, almost managed it, with the aid of his mistress, Mme d'Estrades, by throwing into Louis' arms the young and attractive Mme de Choiseul-Romanet. Marmontel shows us, as in a cynical comedy by Voltaire or Crébillon *fils*, d'Argenson and Mme d'Estrades waiting anxiously in the Minister's room for the issue of the first rendezvous in the Royal apartments. Mme de Choiseul-Romanet appears at length, flushed and breathless. Mme d'Estrades rushes towards her with outstretched arms.

"Well?"

"Yes. . . . He is happy. She is to be turned out. He has given me his word."

And an outburst of malicious joy, says Marmontel, filled the room. It was premature. The Pompadour moved swiftly. Gaining over a powerful Choiseul, then Comte de Stainville, later Duc de Choiseul and her own minister, she was able to have her young rival, whose instant demands on the King turned out to be absurdly excessive, packed from Court in a matter of weeks, and Mme d'Estrades two years later. Henceforth the Favourite took the offensive in this type of warfare and superintended the King's passing amours herself, being careful, as she said, to select "little creatures with no education, who cannot take him from me."[1]

She had actually, if we can trust d'Argenson, resigned from the Royal harem in 1751. Among the Boucher portraits of her about

[1] These were all treated with extreme kindness and courtesy, and married off with good dowries.

this period is one now in the Wallace Collection at Hertford House, that repository of so much eighteenth-century perfection. It is an alfresco scene, dated 1759. The Marquise, in a tea-rose-tinted gown of silk and lace, leans one shapely elbow against a plinth supporting a significant marble group, *L'Amour et l'Amitié*, her spaniel Iñez near her, and roses scattered at her feet. Tranquil sunlight surrounds her, or would do, presumably, if the portrait were cleaned; yet behind the marble a misty grove conveys a pervading hint of late afternoon and stealing shadows and autumnal melancholy. It would be too much to read abdication or even resignation into the Pompadour's expression; her "company" mask is on, as usual. Nevertheless, the scene has a certain faint symbolism, one might well imagine. A cool platonic breeze is perchance about to breathe over the landscape, disturbing the handsome, haughty creature's musings with a light shiver.... Yet she had many reasons for not regretting the change of 1751, if she could still keep the King.

Her wealth, derived chiefly from the normal traffic in patents, privileges, and places which is every Favourite's perquisite and a surer gold-mine than Royal caprice, was growing, and with it her cultivated, imperial rage for spending. The Goncourts place her total cost to France at about thirty-six million francs. This sum embraces expenditure on her own chateaux and estates—Crécy, Bellevue, La Celle, the Hôtel d'Evreux in Paris, the *hermitages* at Versailles, Fontainebleau, and Compiègne—and on such Royal chateaux as Choisy and other places which she redecorated and furnished for the King, employing an army corps of architects, builders, sculptors, painters, gardeners, specialists of every kind. It is for economists to decide, so far as they ever decide anything, how far this outpouring of gold was useless extravagance and how far it benefited the French, as it obviously did. The artists and craftsmen of France soon had reason to bless her ardent, nutritious, and of its kind, exquisite taste. As she attached the Arts to her, so she attached Literature, counting among her admiring friends and protégés such figures as Voltaire, Marmon-

tel, Diderot, d'Alembert, Buffon, and even, to some extent, the
prickly and paranoiac Rousseau. By 1756 she had many of the
military and lesser nobility on her side also, having almost single-
handed established the École Militaire for five hundred orphans
of officers of noble birth.

All this did not mollify the clergy, the higher nobility, and
the mass of the nation, who saw in her merely a common
prostitute enriching herself at the public expense; and not only
herself but her family, whose fortunes she established with
admirable affection. Her Papa, the cynical old profiteer, was
created Seigneur de Marigny, and her brother Abel—a highly
presentable type, elegant, full of good sense and modest charm,
greatly liked by Louis XV—Marquis de Vandières and later
Marquis de Marigny, having meanwhile filled the lucrative post
of Director-General of Works. As for her only child, Alexandrine, her daughter by d'Etioles, the Pompadour had only just
succeeded, after three attempts among the higher peerage, in
arranging for her betrothal to the Duc de Pecquigny when
Alexandrine died at the age of ten; a bitter blow to a mother who
adored her.

Such is the Favourite's position *circa* 1756, surrounded by
violent hate and braving it with sweet audacity. The word *nous*,
linking herself and the King, is perpetually on her lips. "We shall
see." "We shall be at Compiègne." Ambassadors and Ministers
pay her the extravagant deference mistresses are usually paid.
In her apartments at Versailles the strictest etiquette is enforced,
and when she receives formally she alone is seated. Her furnishings, appointments, and liveries are likewise quasi-royal, and in
the Versailles theatre and the Chapel-Royal she occupies a
private box. This calculated ostentation aroused no revolt at
Court. If brother Abel dropped his handkerchief in the Gallery
of Mirrors, dukes tracing their ancestry back to Charlemagne
hastened smilingly to pick it up. It was the era of the mask, we
may recollect. Dissimulation was a fine art, and the general
decline in honour and morality enabled the smoothest flattery

and the most poisonous slander to trip from polite lips with normal alternation.

The Marquise had so far made her power felt only in domestic affairs. In 1756 she was to launch into *la haute politique* and enter on the international stage, defying Frederick the Great and dragging France (as vast numbers of her enemies have cried) at the heels of Austria into a disastrous war.

4

When, six months after ascending the throne of Prussia in May 1740, Carlyle's hero Frederick-William II, later surnamed "The Great," signified curtly to Europe at large that he regarded the Pragmatic Sanction as a scrap of paper and forthwith invaded and annexed the Austrian province of Silesia—*more Teutonico*, the morning after a Court ball, with a last-minute ultimatum to Maria Theresa, and hardly in that "fit of amnesia" attributed to him in Mr. Bentley's admirable clerihew[1]—it was clear to the French that the disastrous foreign policy of Cardinal Richelieu in the previous century was bearing fruit. The Prussia Richelieu had so wilfully backed against Austria was rising from the huddle of small German States, and already, with its small but formidable force of intensively trained (though by no means invincible) military automatons, bent on dictating to all Germany and ripe for pillaging Europe.

In January 1756, Great Britain, at war with France for the past two years, was the first to recognise the Prussian power by concluding a military alliance at Westminster whereby Frederick's status and recent acquisitions were recognised to begin with. Where could France turn now save to Austria, whose existence was equally threatened by Britain's new ally?

For some time Maria Theresa's Chancellor, Prince Kaunitz, had foreseen the storm, and urged that necessary alliance for accepting which Louis XV has been so fiercely denounced by

[1] In Frederick's own words, actuated by "desire of glory, and even curiosity."

lovers of the Essential Boche. The decisive part played by Mme de Pompadour in bringing this alliance about has naturally invited still more abuse, and explanations for her admirable performance are not wanting. Feminine spite, aroused by the arid Prussian intellectual whose widely-quoted nickname for her was "Cotillon II," as if she were a horse, who never referred to *la demoiselle Poisson* without a Voltairean sneer, and whose agents tirelessly vilified her all over Europe; the vanity of the bourgeoise flattered at attaining contact, even at second-hand, with the great imperious Maria Theresa; a vulgar ambition to shine in Europe's eyes by meddling in the field of high international diplomacy—her enemies have made due play with all these motives. Even if they are all contributory, the fact is that this clever woman practically made up her mind that an Austrian alliance was inevitable some time before the King and Council did, with the result that when the subtle Kaunitz arrived in Paris from Vienna, soon after the Prusso-British treaty, he had no difficulty in gaining the ear of Mme de Pompadour according to his intention.

Prince Wenceslas Anton Kaunitz-Rietberg, Maria Theresa's prop and stay, is the perfect diplomat of romantic fiction, out-shining even Talleyrand. With his elegant, spare figure, thin hawk-nose, high-arched eyebrows, firm chin, and pale, cold, searching eyes went a genius for affairs which only fools dazzled by his easy, attractive conversational gifts could avoid discerning. Kaunitz was, in fact, the strong, silent man who chatters continually, with a purpose; a fop affecting many eccentricities, such as wearing three shades of wigs and washing his teeth at table, and perpetually probing the minds of those around him; a powerful freemason, a formidable character with an intelligence like a Toledo blade and a patience inexhaustible. He knew when to flatter and how to wait. A Franco-Austrian alliance was by no means a ripe plum ready to fall. Hereditary French dislike of Austria, dating from the time of the Emperor Charles V, and hatred of the Favourite were inspiring opposition in the Council, which wanted no war in any case. Having made his point to Madame and assured himself that Louis XV, at the moment still weighing the matter, would shortly come round, Kaunitz retired and left the field to the Austrian ambassador, Starhemburg.

A trifle decided it at length, as often happens. A certain Marquise de Coislin, who had recently attracted the King's notice, looked suddenly like ousting the Pompadour completely. A bold stroke of self-assertion was needed, the Pompadour made it, and Starhemburg was shortly able to inform Maria Theresa that negotiations could be opened with the Favourite. The magnificent and irreproachable Hapsburg had naturally no intention of stooping to personal contact with a cocotte, however clever, and the Imperial acknowledgment, three years later and via Kaunitz, in the shape of a diamond-encrusted miniature of Maria Theresa set in a costly lacquer escritoire, was merely the reward a great lady may make a maidservant through her major-domo. Nevertheless, it was Mme de Pompadour, assisted by the Abbé de Bernis, her new Minister for Foreign Affairs, who actually conducted and concluded the alliance-negotiations.

A fatal air of frivolity, created by hostile pens, hangs around the whole procedure; the atmosphere of a Lancret picnic on cool shaven lawns, figures in rich silks and satins playing at Blind Man's Buff, flirting in swings, exchanging persiflage with exquisite languor by marble fountains crowned with Cupids and Graces. Actually it was a wholly calculated and serious business. De Bernis, outwardly a typical powderpuff Court abbé of the period, all red heels and mocking epigrams, was a man of strong sense and discernment, convincedly anti-Austrian. Madame de Pompadour, as we have realised, was no fool. Starhemburg was a man of intelligence and experience. The opening conference between these three at Mme de Pompadour's little house called Babiole, in the park of Bellevue, on September 22, 1755, was as devoid of amusement as any assembly of the plenipotentiaries of what are ironically called the United Nations to-day.

Louis XV, having sanctioned the procedure, trusted with confidence to Madame's brains. De Bernis was doubtful, and to win him over took Starhemburg and the Favourite some time. The Babiole conference was succeeded by others at the Luxembourg Palace. The treaty which finally emerged to be signed at Versailles turned out to be surprisingly advantageous to France. In exchange for military assistance to Austria, she secured an extended frontier in the Low Countries from Ostend to Chimay, all Austrian territory, the rest being created an independent state under Louis XV's nephew, the Infante of Parma. The schemes of Prussia were further checked by giving the strong-point of Luxembourg to France, with the fortress of Mons. Poland, coveted equally by Austria, Prussia, and Russia (a contracting party to the Franco-Austrian alliance), was declared an hereditary monarchy. Silesia was declared once more Austrian property, and Prussia was split up in advance between Poland, the Elector-Palatine, Sweden, and Saxony. The French received the treaty with acclamations, and the Pompadour's headaches—the battle over details had been long, and the Council, headed by her foe d'Argenson, obstructive—were amply rewarded. A long congratulatory letter from Kaunitz preceding the Empress's gift, and no mean testimonial in itself, sealed the Favourite's triumph. "It is entirely to your zeal and wisdom, Madame, that all that has taken place so far between the two Courts is due. . . ." Behind Kaunitz loomed the aloof, majestic, maternal figure of the Hapsburg, likewise approving.

The war—a gentlemen's war—began in 1756, promisingly enough for France, with dashing Marshal Richelieu's landings in Minorca and Corsica and the capture of Port-Mahon, clearing the Mediterranean and irritating the British Government so profoundly that it had Admiral Byng shot on his own quarterdeck with full naval honours. But that was practically all, apart from one or two very minor successes. Frederick the Great, having invaded Saxony without a declaration and forced the Saxons to surrender after the battle of Lobositz, went on to invade Bohemia.

In the next year he beat the Austrians at Prague, and was beaten by them at Kölin so heavily that when the Austrians marched on Berlin—their Russian allies having meanwhile given Frederick's General Lehwaldt a thrashing at Gross-Jaegendorf in East Prussia—the great Frederick burst into tears, flourished the poison-phial he carried with him in the Nazi manner, and apparently even meditated buying off Mme de Pompadour with the principality of Neufchâtel. But the tide was soon to turn. At Rosbach on November 5, 1757 Frederick routed a mainly-French army under Soubise with such crushing and humiliating brilliance that "a Rosbach rout" became a French proverb. Thus Frederick wiped off the capitulation to the French, two months previously, of the Anglo-Hanoverians at Klosterseven, for the generous terms of which Richelieu was (and is) severely blamed. A subsequent Prussian victory at Leuthen drove the French back to the Rhine.

Meanwhile things were going gravely for France overseas. After a gallant resistance Montcalm succumbed at Quebec, Lally-Tollendal in India. In the Royal Council Bernis insistently urged Louis XV to cut his losses and retire from the war. Bernis was overruled, chiefly by Choiseul, till recently ambassador at Vienna and now about to replace him, and amid the Pompadour's forebodings France continued the war, to meet more disaster in August 1759 at Minden, where a small British force under the Duke of Brunswick defeated Marshal Contades in a victory which still adorns the caps of three British regiments with commemorative roses once a year. After one or two more bad setbacks for the Prussians (Hochkirch, Kunersdorf) and another bout of suicidal despair, Frederick emerged victorious from the final campaign of 1762, when cretinous young Tsar Peter III abandoned his allies, on the eve of his murder ; providentially for Frederick, who could not have gone on much longer. Austria gave up then, and France had no option. At sea she had suffered more than on land, despite the aggressiveness of Choiseul on taking over the Ministry. A projected descent on

England in 1759 fizzled out with Hawke's victory in Quiberon Bay, and the British fleet held France completely blockaded. A naval expedition to Ireland was a failure. By the peace-treaty of Paris (1763) France signed away practically her entire colonial empire, including Canada, Louisiana, and the left bank of the Mississippi, most of Senegal, and all her possessions in India except Pondicherry, leaving Britain undisputed mistress of half the world.

Of all these disasters Rosbach rather than Minden rankled most deeply in the French soul, from now till the rise of Napoleon. It is extremely difficult to get oneself "in the picture," in modern military jargon, of such a reverse from a study of contemporary colour-prints, in which battles all seem ordered like a gavotte. There, under rolling white and dirty-yellow billows of cannon-smoke, is the many-coloured advancing array of the French line, for whose tough files-on-parade Godard d'Aucour, in his jovial *Académie militaire* (1745), did what Kipling was later to do for Victoria's rankers. Each infantry regiment has its own coloured tight-fitting *justaucorps*, vest and breeches: blue for the Guards, red for the Suisses and the Mousquetaires, white, green, amaranth, and other colours for the regiments of Artois, Picardy, Champagne, Burgundy, and the rest. They advance in triple rank and parallel alignment, like a Dutch tulip garden, with well-floured heads and stiff pigtails under cocked or mitred hats, carrying musket with fixed bayonet on the shoulder and sword at the side. The hussars and dragoons, with their short fur-trimmed cloaks and horsehaired casques, prance in neat formation in their proper place. The artillery is parked and ranged with equal neatness. To and fro caracole impeccable staff officers. On a symmetrical hillock in the left foreground Soubise and his generals gesture towards the Prussian generals, far away on theirs, and the tinted Prussian troops in the middle distance advance in the same stiff formation as the French. Nothing in the artistic convention of the period conveys any hint of that confusion, disorder, indecision, and bloody muddle which is inseparable from nearly every battle in history except Austerlitz, and from Rosbach in particular.

Rosbach was a major rout, and its effect on the French, notes Bainville, peculiar. Mixed with public rage and humiliation was a rising note, encouraged by the philosophers, of bitter comparison between luxurious Gallic inefficiency and the simple spartan virtues of the Prussian Superman, a state of mind lasting till nearly 1870 and profiting Prussia not a little. Actually the French generals, like the French people, had little enthusiasm for the war, and the loud publicity campaign by the intelligentsia in favour of the Philosopher-King of Prussia, Voltaire's ex-crony, had had its effect long ago. Almost every intimation of France's decaying spirit from this period may be traced back directly to the Encyclopædists.

All this time Mme de Pompadour had been involved in a whirl of religious and political strife at home.

The root of the trouble, Clement XI's Bull (or to be pedantic, Constitution) *Unigenitus*, which condemned the Jansenist heresy on September 8, 1713, was creating unrest in the 1750's among a sizable minority of the French clergy and laity still infected with that sour virus, Gallican in grain, and above all hostile to the Jesuits. By this time the issue had been enlarged and confused by two new allies for the Jansenists: the Parlements, whose lawyers were obstructing national finance and defying the Crown whenever possible, on Voltaire's own admission, and the philosophers and their following, who yearned to destroy not only the Jesuits but the Church as well. Like the Jansenists, the lawyers were on the whole rabidly Gallican, anti-Jesuit, and *frondeurs;* like the philosophers, they had more or less turbulent tendencies. The position was further complicated by a decree of the Archbishop of Paris depriving finally-recalcitrant Jansenists of the Last Sacrament and by a revolt of the clerical majority, with half the nation, against a new tax laid on all property by Machault, Minister of Finance, who owed his office to Mme de Pompadour.

It is not necessary here to unravel all the tangled threads of this trouble, except to note that the main revolt against Machault's *vingtième*, chiefly abhorrent by reason of its apparent permanency, was headed by the Parlements and États[1] of Brittany and Languedoc, backed by the Parlement of Paris, and that in 1757 Machault had to make concessions. Eight years later the Parlement of Brittany was to refuse further taxation and, after being summoned to Versailles and reprimanded by Louis XV in person, to resign in a body, thus reviving a struggle which ended in 1771 with the overhauling of the entire judicial and financial system. It would be a mistake to read into this turbulence of Brittany an excess of idealism, or even a hint of Breton separatism. Meetings of the États of Brittany, held at Rennes, were a regular and eagerly awaited diversion for the smaller rustic nobles and gentry, who had little amusement in their lives but hunting. Between the sessions there was feasting, dancing, duelling, gambling, and other relaxations. The Bretons, moreover, paid far less in taxation than any other subjects of Louis XV.[2] It is possible that a large amount of the intransigence of the États and Parlement of Brittany was due merely to Celtic high spirits.

At this time, then, the Crown was faced with trouble from half a dozen quarters, and the intelligentsia, rubbing their hands, doubtless saw the end of the régime in sight. But it was not due yet. With unaccustomed energy and patience Louis XV at length, having brought about a religious truce with the aid of Pope Benedict XIV, asserted his authority over what even Voltaire called "the astonishing anarchy of the Parlements", and the Parlement of Paris, their leader, which had lately extended its

---

[1] The *États*, or deliberative assemblies, one for each province, established by Philippe IV and abolished by the Revolution, theoretically represented the Three Estates. By the eighteenth century they had lost most of their power and were under the control of their provincial Governors, though they sometimes asserted themselves against Governors and Parlements equally. The *États-Généraux*, representing all France, were not called at all between 1614 and 1789—a lapse which became one of the chief causes of the Revolution.

[2] Waquet, *Histoire de la Bretagne*, 1943.

powers to dictation in theology, had its teeth drawn. But in the late 1750's the Crown was still giving way, and Louis, at the Pompadour's urging, allowed—reluctantly, in his need for money—Choiseul, Minister of State, to participate in that international Masonic offensive against the Jesuits which forced Clement XIV ultimately to dissolve the entire Society; Choiseul's ministerial brethren in the service of the Lodges being Kaunitz in Austria, Aranda in Spain, and Pombal in Portugal.[1]

The Paris mob divined without difficulty the driving-force behind Choiseul and the King, and fresh insults were bellowed in the streets against the *coquine du Roi*, whose womanly tears over the expulsion of "these honourable men" deceived nobody; not that the mob was ready to shed its blood for the Parlement, still less for the Society, against whom popular feeling had been skilfully worked up, but because the mob correctly guessed who had been setting the country by the ears to serve private vengeance, with the aid of her devoted Voltaire, who surpassed himself on this occasion and revelled in mischief, as a stream of pamphlets records.

So the Jesuits were expelled at length from France (August 6, 1762), save for a minority who joined the secular priesthood, and, like the rest of the Society ten years later, found a refuge in Germany and, oddly enough, in Russia, since Catherine II and Frederick the Great admired their educational system and were equally charmed to defy the Papal Brief of 1773. They did not return to France as a body till 1814, by which time their archenemy Voltaire, who had always kept up friendships in the Society, had made a Christian end, summoning a Jesuit confessor for that purpose.

The Favourite's triumph secured a position which had once more been gravely menaced. In January 1757, following Damiens' attempt to assassinate a well-loved King and Louis' repentance on what seemed to be his dying bed, she had actually packed her baggage. But Louis recovered, and she remained: it

[1] Fülöp-Miller, VII, 11.

was d'Argenson who was dismissed a little later, after a lethal scene between these deadly enemies in which she delivered her ultimatum. "Either you or I, Sir. . . ." She remained, and increased her share in public affairs with more aplomb than ever, even to outlining military strategy to Marshal d'Estrées—on a fan, runs a too-picturesque story—and personally intervening between the Parlements and the Crown. There is a long interview, quoted in Richelieu's memoirs, between the Favourite and the President of the Parlement of Paris, showing with what extraordinary skill she could handle such matters, what knowledge of her subject, what authoritative yet diplomatic ease. The President, abashed and charmed, left her presence admiring.

In Choiseul, with whom she replaced Bernis in November 1758, she had what seemed the ideal instrument. This gay, ugly little diplomat possessed considerable powers of mind, a natural audacity and precision, a perfect cynicism, no morals worth mentioning, intense energy, and a good-humoured malice which altogether made him redoubtable and, with the masses, highly popular. He lived at such a lavish pitch that his butler, after glancing round the Duchesse de Choiseul's drawing-rooms any night, would add fifty or eighty covers to the supper-table. Choiseul's birth and connections made him the equal of the highest blood in Europe, and he was a prominent Freemason. His inclinations were towards a permanent Franco-Austro-Spanish alliance against the Nordic Bloc; at home, towards an aggressive alliance of what would to-day be called the forces of the Left against what would be called those of the Right; all completely consonant with the policy of the Pompadour. It has been claimed for Choiseul that he hastened the Revolution. The claim can be made for half the ruling class of France, but it was the middle-class who planned and carried it out.

5

As the war dragged humiliatingly to its close, with the defeats of Minden and Warbourg and Filhingshausen following

Rosbach, and the worse disasters in America and India, with the French fleet driven from the seas and the Treasury bleeding to death, Mme de Pompadour was fully aware that her dream of *la gloire*, and the capture of the admiration of Europe and posterity as one of the figures of history, was swiftly fading.

She was even more aware that her romance with Louis had declined into something which was not even what the French call nowadays *un vieux collage*. When yet another dangerous young rival clouded the horizon in the 1760's, a Mlle de Romans of mysterious, languorous charm, who captured the King without difficulty, the Duchesse de Mirepoix, one of the Favourite's few intimates, summed up the situation bluntly and reassuringly. "Princes are creatures of habit. You know all his moods, you know all his stories. He need not put himself out or have any qualms about boring you. Why should he ever find the courage to destroy all this in a day?" Though vanity suffered from the knowledge that she was no more than a piece of Royal furniture, the Pompadour's strong intelligence was able to accept this consolation, since she retained her power. But she was wearing herself out. Her health, which had never been normal, had not been improved by drug-stimulants and a sequence of miscarriages. As she drove herself more and more fiercely, her early chest-weakness developed into anæmia and a tubercular condition, with increasing fevers and exhaustions. Her beauty began to leave her also; her complexion yellowed, her perfect shape vanished; she grew thin and began to plaster her face with red and white. But her spell remained, as her enemies reluctantly admitted. The thousand daily activities of her feverish life, from drafting a State paper for the King's approval to deciding the design of a silver salt-cellar, continued as before. Choiseul in particular needed a firm directing hand. He had become inclined to dictate and domineer. In 1758, despite France's losses in the war already, he had taken a more aggressive line and furnished, by treaty with Austria, a French army of 100,000 in Germany for the duration.

The Favourite's vast correspondence reveals her fatigue, her disillusions, and her energy simultaneously, and flits among a hundred topics. Ribbons, fans, battles, fainting-fits, building projects, duels, pictures, Parlements, jewellery-sales, the Encyclopædists, the Court, the British, the Prussians, the army, the navy . . . her letters run the entire gamut from chiffons to high policy. To discern the woman behind the majority of them is not very easy, since she so rarely takes her mask off. To *mon cher Papa* she is affectionate, grateful, and commonplace. To her brother Abel (*frérot*), she is equally affectionate and full of sisterly counsel. ("If one confined oneself to being amiable to people one liked, one would be detested by most of the human race.") Of her little daughter Alexandrine, *Fanfan*, she writes like any fond mother to the child's grandfather—who adored her equally, as cynics will—on teething-troubles, indigestions, and kindred topics. "I think she is getting much plainer. Provided she doesn't grow really frightful (*choquante*) I shall be quite satisfied. I am far from wishing her a dazzling face—such a thing only makes an enemy for one of the entire female sex, which, including their male friends, makes two-thirds of the world." As indeed Fanfan's Mamma should know.

She had one other confidant, Mme de Lutzelbourg ("*grand' femme*"), to whom she could likewise chatter without affectation:

I saw Mme de Crèvecœur to-day, *grand'femme*. I don't think she has anything nasty to say to you about me.

I hate your Lutherans to death for loving the King of Prussia. If I were in Strasbourg I should be fighting all day long.

Send me the gown quickly, since you think it's nice. I have some embroidery ideas for it. Send it to Janelle by the first post.

Mme de Pompadour is no Sévigné at any time, and does not deal in epigram or whimsy. Even to Mme de Lutzelbourg she could be oddly formal, as shown in a letter written in April 1759, after the Marshal de Broglie's success over the Hanoverians at Mons:

The battle has given me great pleasure. M. de Soubise had made his dispositions so well and chosen such a good field that we couldn't be beaten. My only regret is that he was not there, and that the King detained him. . . . Do not worry over the journey to Lyons; I shall run no risks. If the confidence with which the King honours me were not proof against fifteen days' absence, it would be ill founded, and I could not flatter myself with it. I shall take a rest during that time at St. Ouen. . . .

She is, of course, a convinced Anglophobe. "Those villains will not wait for you, Sir, I terribly fear," she writes to d'Aiguillon in September 1758, "for I am quite certain you will give them a superb beating." A reflection on Lord Lovat's execution (1747) in a letter to the Marquise de Saussaye contains another bouquet to British address:

No one could die with more courage. Of course he was a Scot; they know how to fight and die. Thus are all Prince Charles's friends sacrificed one after the other. The English do not know how to forgive.

She curiously echoes George II, voicing his contempt to Lord Hervey. England is the land of "roast-beef and insolence"; the English have no taste in any of the arts of life; the best thing in England is their horses. George III's Ministers have only one gift, that of deceit; Pitt is a trickster and a comedian, and so forth. Mme de Pompadour vastly prefers the redskins of the Great Lakes:

I like those honest savages. . . . They so generously offer us the *right hand of gallant youth* that we must be careful not to refuse.

Though I do not approve of eating the dead, one must not quarrel with these honest folk over trifles. I trust this alliance will be of more use to France than the foolish embassy to Siam which Louis XIV made so much fuss about. . . .

The faint smack of Voltaire is more strongly apparent in some of her reflections on religion, which any sceptic would approve.

But the celebrated and touching anecdote of Mme de Mailly, *qui s'est faite dévote*, moves even this cool heart. To get to her seat for a sermon in Notre-Dame some time after her conversion, Mme de Mailly had to disturb a whole row of chairs. An onlooker exclaimed brutally: "Here's a lot of fuss over a whore!" "Sir," said Mme de Mailly gently, turning to him, "since you know me so well, grant me the favour of praying God for me." On which Mme de Pompadour comments: "A most respectable woman. If my failings, or my stars, make me commit similar faults, I trust I shall repent like her at the end."

To the Marquise de Fontenailles she unbosoms herself on Court life very early in a letter which seems to me, as to better judges, too good to be true, but is interesting nevertheless as a period-piece:

I am quite alone in the midst of this mob of lordlings (*petits seigneurs*) who loathe me, and whom I despise. As for most of the women, their conversation gives me a sick headache (*migraine*). Their vanity, their lofty airs, their meannesses, and their treacheries make them insupportable. I don't tell them so, but it makes me no more happy. . . .
Louis XV has five hundred apes around him every day when he rises from bed, but they rarely make him laugh. He is hardly less melancholy than I.

Her fallen enemy d'Argenson receives a note of smooth regret with a sting of mockery in it:

Your own example, Sir, reveals that good qualities often attract more hatred than bad ones. They tell me you are bearing your exile with more courage and patience than a stoic. I am not surprised, since I know you. I would willingly give you an ostrich for your device, with the motto: "*There is nothing too hard for the strong to digest.*"

With ambassadors and generals and princes like Mirepoix, Nivernais, Clermont, Condé, and Marshal Saxe, she discusses diplomacy, politics, and strategy with marked authority. Thus, after the French success at Johannisberg on August 30, 1762, she writes to the Prince de Condé in a temporary flush of good spirits:

M. de Boisgelin came to me at Choisy. I asked him to detail for me on the map the happy action of the 30th. He explained to me very clearly, and to everyone else in the room, the various attacks which were made, with time and place, and told me in detail what I will now tell you in brief. . . .

A précis of the battle follows, showing how clearly she could assimilate such matters. Condoling with the Comte de Clermont over the defeat at Crevelt, she displays her perpetual tact:

Who are the fools of officers, Monseigneur, who have mishandled your troops and turned what should have been one of the finest of operations into the most unfortunate one in the world? My consolation is in the good morale of the Army, which makes me hope you will take your revenge in a manner to make the enemy long regret having dared to attack Frenchmen commanded by a grandson of the great Condé. . . .

In that same year, writing to the blunt old Marshal de Noailles in a fit of depression and begging him for advice on the situation, she received a reply from that warrior which has been held suspect. Even if unauthentic, it must have represented his true feelings:

You ask me for advice, Madame la Marquise, and you flatter me, for it is something new to find myself consulted in my old age. But what use would my advice be? It will be taken for an imbecile's, since I advise amputation of every limb so far attacked by gangrene. Unfortunately the noble parts are affected, and a cure is difficult.

Yes, Madame; the head of the nation is corrupted, and thence come our disasters. . . .

Exactly the retort such a man would make, regardless of fear or favour; and if genuine, it must have given Mme la Marquise food for meditation. Whether several other items of her later wartime correspondence as printed by Barbé-Marbois, steeped in gloom and flavoured with a taste of dust-and-ashes curiously recalling those chapters of Proust's interminable novel describing the Duchesse de Guermantes' salon in its final phase, are authentic or not, I am in no position to decide. Her habitual and desperate attempts to fight despondency and stimulate the military leaders in their trials are possibly a strong argument against them. Typical extract, from a letter to the Duc d'Aiguillon about the time of the fruitless project for invading England:

To be beaten is merely a misfortune; not to fight is a disgrace. What has happened to our nation? The Parlements, the Encyclopædists, etc., etc., have utterly changed it. . . . We shall have to abandon all thoughts of glory. The extremity is cruel, but I believe it to be the only one. Do not be as discouraged, Sir, as I. Your zeal and attachment to the King, etc., etc.

Doubtless the sigh over the Encyclopædists, her admired friends and protégés, alone stamps this letter as a forgery. Whether another one, written to d'Argenson, is authentic or not, it seems worth quoting as an indication that Madame, or whoever may have counterfeited her style in 1747, can take a modest seat among the prophets:

I regard this alliance with the Russians as of most dangerous consequence. . . . That nation will soon be in a position to turn on its masters, and will become formidable. It may not be impossible to see a new deluge of barbarians, issuing from the caverns of Siberia and commanded by a new Attila, inundating Europe. God save us from it!

So the war was lost, and in the autumn and winter of 1763, after France had signed away her empire, the Favourite was observed to be so worn and haggard with melancholy and increasing illness, though striving valiantly and pathetically to impose on all beholders her wonted poise and sparkle, that Choiseul, her right-hand man and, for a time, lover, observed to one of her ladies-in-waiting that he feared Madame was likely to die ere long of sheer chagrin.

Choiseul was not far wrong. Disappointment, weariness, increasing sickness and exhaustion, and broodings over her share of the responsibility for the French disasters—all hers, as her myriad enemies were vigorously proclaiming—at length brought a breakdown, hastened by her considerable money worries. For if she had acquired avidly she had spent regally, not only on herself but on public works, the École Militaire especially. Since the lavish Royal New Year gifts had ceased, round about 1750, and her pension had dropped gradually from 24,000 livres a month to some 4,000, she had been forced more than once, surrounded by priceless possessions, to meet pressing bills by her winnings at the card-tables and the sale of jewellery.

When the Court went to Choisy in February 1764 she kept to her apartments as much as possible, forcing herself to appear in public when it became unavoidable, like a sick soldier answering the drums. On February 29 she was put to bed by her women with inflammation of the lungs, high fever, and blood-spitting. Five weeks later she rallied—assisted by the sincere anxiety of Louis XV and a surprising wave of public sympathy, the first she had ever known—enough to be removed to Versailles. A relapse occurred in April, and she summoned her courage to meet death, painting her haggard face with care and suffering her considerable pain with firmness. On April 13 she summoned the Curé of the Madeleine and received the Last Sacrament with calm resignation and apparent sincerity, having written to her husband for forgiveness. Early in the morning of the 15th she died, after addressing the priest, as he was leaving, with a flash of her old vivacity. "One moment, Monsieur le Curé. We'll go out together."

In a storm of wind and rain on April 17 her body was conveyed to Paris for burial, passing under the King's window. From the balcony Louis watched the cortège out of sight and turned away with tears—"the only tribute I can give her," he said to Champlost. She was buried, according to her own wishes, without pomp, by her child's side, in the Church of the Capucines in the Place Vendôme, pulled down in 1806 and now covered by the Rue de la Paix. Her share of the vault had been acquired some years ago from the illustrious La Trémöille family, whose ancestor was the comrade-in-arms of St. Joan. A titter from her enemy, the bitter Princesse de Talmont, the Queen's cousin, was only to be expected. "The great bones of the La Trémöilles will be agreeably astonished to find themselves jostled by the ribs of a fish (*Poisson*)."

Her will, opening with the devout and penitential formulæ still prevailing, adequately remembered her servants, her relatives, her half-dozen friends, and the King, to whom she left her Paris mansion, occupied to-day by Presidents of the Republic. Exquisitely of the period, as the Goncourts remark, is the bequest to her friend Buffon, the naturalist, of her three best-loved pets— a parrot, a dog, and a monkey—with instructions to care for them tenderly; which the great Buffon did, till all three died of old age. It would seem that these pets surrounding Buffon in his study at Montbard were soon the only tangible reminder of her feverish and dazzling existence. On the fly-leaf of a volume of her correspondence of the 1774 edition lying before me is written in English, in a delicate small contemporary hand:

There was neither Monument nor Epitaph to her memory, at least not in 1776, when last I viewed the spot.—J. C.

The sale of her treasures lasted a year and drew the virtuosi from all over Europe. She herself was forgotten, as the gentle Queen remarked with a sigh, completely, at once, and by all.

6

"She loves money and disposes of every place," remarked the laconic Papal Nuncio, Mgr. Durini, during the Pompadour's lifetime, in a phrase which many historians have adapted for her missing epitaph. Cold, heartless, dry, sceptical, devoured by cupidity, a true *petite bourgeoise* in her haggling and meddling and mean ambition—such is the verdict (1878) of Jules and Edmond de Goncourt, who were not notable for charity at any time. *La caque sent toujours le hareng*, says an old French proverb; the herring-keg stinks always of its contents. Cynical Papa Poisson's pride in his Reinette was fully justified, cry all her enemies in chorus.

Kinder judgments have been forthcoming from more recent observers, who balance Mme de Pompadour's inherited love of money—not avarice, nevertheless—with her magnificent patronage of the Arts, the splendour and courage with which she played her difficult and dangerous rôle, the undoubted value of her friendship to the King. No doubt a just appraisal must include all this. Moreover, she symbolises for ever the beauty and elegance of all her incomparable period, much of it her own creation.

One not uninteresting psychological possibility concerning her seems to me to have been curiously overlooked by critics favourable and unfavourable. She had marked dramatic talent, and had been trained by Crébillon. At her first appearance on the stage of the Théâtre des Petits-Appartements, she was so fascinating as Elmire in *Tartuffe* that Louis XV congratulated her as "the most charming woman in France." Many other successes of the kind followed. Might it not be that, like so many born actresses, she was acting all the time, that her career was one long exciting drama with herself as heroine, that she came soon to the point, as so many actresses have done, when the actual world seems fantastic and the real one is the one of make-believe? This solves nothing much, perhaps, yet it might explain some of the Pompadour's unfailing poise amid all her dangers. Her business sense would remain unaffected (a striking parallel case is Rachel, than whom no great actress more consciously inhabited the lofty enchanted world of Racine, and none more fiercely clawed her gold). The essential *cabotine* in Mme de Pompadour may be as significant as her streak of bourgeois cupidity, who knows?

However this may be, it is certain that no member of the bourgeoisie has ever risen so high and acquired and spent so much. The middle-class—especially the French middle-class—has many virtues, however restricted its horizons, however frequently its motives lack nobility. In England, where it is now being slowly taxed to death, its rise to power in the early years of Victoria filled Melbourne, as we shall observe, with forebodings. He despised, even more than its smugness, its materialistic standards, which were those of the Pompadour, though her unbourgeois passion for art and beauty differentiates and perhaps redeems her.

That a perpetual obsession with money has a degrading effect not merely on the soul but on the features was a commonplace long before Marinus van Romerswael painted his remarkable panel, now in the National Gallery, of two usurers at their calculations; a pretty object-lesson. Thus must the business men of Florence have looked on returning to their counting-houses after driving out Dante Alighieri. From the many existing portraits of the Pompadour it is plain that her comely face was never thus affected; but her nature was certainly calculating, and she knew few generous impulses, as her handling of appeals from the Bastille alone reveals. Even her love for her only child is linked with determination to make a dazzling alliance at all costs. What she did for her father was affectionate, and she was undoubtedly fond of her brother; yet he also was part of her schemes, though he steadily refused to make any of the glittering marriage-contracts she planned.

As a favourite by choice and career she has three distinctive marks: self-possession, courage, and a relentless tenacity. Beauty, her initial asset, would never of itself have made her virtual mistress of France for twenty years. Her successor, the Dubarry, made a poor showing enough. The explanation of the Pompa-

dour's hold over Louis XV is a strong unscrupulous will, illus-
trated not only by the sequence of rivals, male and female, she
defeated but, notably, by the incident of the secret papers of
1763, which throws light on the King's character as much as hers.

The *Secret du Roi* has already been mentioned; that private
switchboard of underground information whereby Louis XV,
who knew his weaknesses and detested them, was able frequently
to repair blunders and lapses and to counteract the effect of
promises wrung from him against his better judgment, and those
concessions and surrenders for the sake of peace which were part
of his, as of most men's, life. Its operation was, as we have noted,
a secret shared only with Conti, whom the Pompadour loathed.
One day in June 1763 Louis XV summoned Tercier, one of his
trusted familiars, and in extreme agitation told him that a few
nights earlier, after supping *tête-à-tête* with Mme de Pompadour,
he had dropped off to sleep in his chair; that he had subsequently
discovered highly confidential papers, locked in a cabinet of
which he alone kept the key, and on his person, to be in disorder;
that he strongly suspected Madame of having taken this opportunity (possibly she had prepared the way at supper) of abstract-
ing the key and going through his correspondence; and that the
most urgent and watchful discretion was in consequence to be
impressed at once on the Chevalier d'Éon, then on the eve of
starting for London with the French Ambassador, Nivernais,
"whom I have every reason to believe is entirely devoted to the
Duc de Praslin and to Mme de Pompadour." I can find no
evidence that Louis ever accused the Pompadour of this perfidy.
If he thought it politic, doubtless she was too clever for him—
though never clever enough, still less the stupid Dubarry after
her, to penetrate the *Secret du Roi*—and her hold was too strong.

The secret of this hold we have sufficiently perceived. Its long
duration is no great mystery. Beginning with attraction of the
flesh, it merged into a bond of pure habit. The initial or erotic
phase, indeed, did not last overlong. With all her charm and
beauty Mme de Pompadour possessed a temperament of

fundamental coldness, freely acknowledged to one or two feminine intimates, often with apprehension and in due course almost with despair.

That her influence did not cease with her lover's satiety is nothing remarkable. The French have always ranked clever women above the finest dolls, and in the catalogue of France's notable women very few are flaming beauties by any standard. One may recall incidentally that it is a habit of the Whigs who have cornered official British history to hold James II of England up to additional scorn for preferring his mistresses plain. If James were not blacklisted by the Whigs for obvious reasons, if James had been a Dutch usurper addicted to *moeurs spéciales*, he would undoubtedly have been lauded for esteeming feminine intelligence above mere prettiness. As for Mme de Pompadour, she was not only well worth listening to on most topics but, almost to the end, highly agreeable to contemplate, so Louis' bondage can hardly have been very burdensome. It has been suggested that, apart from all else, he endured her out of a kind of weak fear that if discarded she might commit suicide. If this were an additional weapon in her armoury, the Pompadour was certainly not above using it without compunction. However she kept her place, in fact, she kept it. She is the Favourite *in excelsis*, unique in her kind.

And so, though years before her death the King had ceased to love her, and she knew it, he could not snap his silken chain. Domination of weak men by clever and ruthless women is nothing new in human relationship, and doubtless thousands of Louis XV's subjects were in a similar plight. But in his case the issue was the welfare of France, and it was fortunate that the Pompadour's private ambitions coincided for the most part with national requirements and her zeal for the King's service. There seems no doubt that the principal charge against her, that of dragging France into a disastrous and costly war, is unjust. The alliance with Austria was inevitable, she made it at Louis' order, and she managed, indeed, to get very good terms out of Starhemburg. The stubborn continuance of the war after a sequence of defeats is another matter, since she was chiefly responsible for Choiseul's policy; but it is difficult to see what France could have gained by abandoning the struggle midway. Even her part in the expulsion of the Jesuits might be susceptible, perhaps, of a little deflation, since her personal spite against the Society was not so powerful as the enmity of Choiseul and of the Parlements, who held the financial whip-hand. She certainly pressed on Louis the final money argument, but it is difficult to see how he could have coped with the Parlements otherwise.

So Mme de Pompadour remains Exhibit A for all feminine careerists. Her most modern imitators, the ladies rustling behind the politicians of the late Third Republic in its last corruptions, on the eve of the Second World War, merely lacked all her qualities. There seems no reason to believe that in our grim new Utopia there is no place henceforth for a second Pompadour of genius. It is true that since her time women have assumed complete equality with men, but a woman of intelligence could overcome even this handicap. One may reasonably conjecture that the Pompadour of the future will not be a dazzling vision dispensing power openly in a blaze of limelight, but a small bespectacled creature of sinister efficiency, shielded from publicity, unknown to the mob, and controlling a secret police of skill and dimensions and ruthlessness never dreamed of by the Marquise or Berryer her faithful aide.

She, too, will be an object of pity to the charitable, but unlike the Pompadour, this Favourite of the future will bequeath to posterity no legacy of beauty, alas.

Melbourne

II

MELBOURNE

" Dear Lord M! . . ."

(Queen Victoria's Journals, *passim*.)

"I can understand your physical-force men, but as to your
moral-force men, I'm damned if I know what they mean."

(Lord Melbourne to Sir Rowland Hill.)

I

"MACLISE and I are raving with love for the Queen,"
wrote emotional young Mr. Charles Dickens to his friend
T. J. Thompson in January 1840, on the eve of the Royal wedding. Dickens was not the only smitten one. Three-quarters of
the nation was yearning likewise over its girl-Queen, and had
been, barring one or two tiffs, in this condition for nearly three
years.

It is hardly possible to avoid remarking (as has possibly been
remarked before) that the Accession of June 1837 presented a
décor to the British people wonderfully reminiscent of their
favourite Christmas pantomimes. The great Mr. Nelson Lee,
whom Thackeray visualised pacing Brighton front on a summer
morning, revolving "the idea of some new gorgeous spectacle of
faëry," might himself have conceived it for his Drury Lane
production the following December. The Demon's Cavern had
vanished. Britannia's wicked uncles, from George the Fourth
down to the sinister Duke of Cumberland, had popped down
their several trapdoors in red fire. The Comic Baron, in the person
of that kindhearted testy old buffoon William IV, had just
rolled off the stage, arm in arm with the Fairy Carabosse. To a
soft pizzicato of fiddles and a trilling of flutes and bird-calls the
Grand Transformation Scene had shimmered into reality in a
haze of lacy, silvery magic, like a Keepsake illustration, revealing

49

a vista of sparkling fountains and sunny lawns, blooming flowers and marble pavilions; a delicious background, in soft primary tints, for the Fairy Queen, now poised tiptoe in the centre and beckoning all the winged virtues to Albion's shores with an imperious wand.

A rather plump, rather plain, but exquisitely graceful and utterly good little vision it was that held the stage; a fairy with prominent Hanoverian blue eyes and a determined little chin, infinitely appealing in her girlish innocence. And benign and watchful, beaming respectfully in the wings, waited the Good Uncle, ready to trip on at his cue and join Britannia's Fairy in a melodious duet; "Lord M.," William Lamb, second Viscount Melbourne, Her Majesty's first Prime Minister, prime favourite, unwearied mentor, oracle, and friend from the day of her accession till his death in 1848.

At Victoria's accession Melbourne was fifty-eight, Her Majesty eighteen. Lytton Strachey's brilliant improvisations on Victorian themes, greatly admired in the restless 1920's, lack nothing save, perhaps, as a recent critic has remarked, a stronger tincture of that truth for which Strachey never cared very passionately. Even his most skilful disciples in debunking Victorianism demonstrate that the urge to destroy cannot completely immunise the toughest against certain restful, nostalgic enchantments. The scenes amid which Melbourne moved so long, and with such unfailing poise, the background of the "great world" between the Regency and the fourth decade of the nineteenth century, have for some of us unfortunate heirs of Victorianism a dewy magic, an almost poignant glow.

So solid, so serene, so spacious, so gracious, and so immutable was that English world that one can scarcely believe it could vanish like a dream at almost the first blast of World War I. Its tall inhabitants pace, calm and unhurried, over mossy carpets in airy, florid apartments; stepping in the fragrant hush of summer evenings from the French windows on to wide stone terraces and smooth ancestral lawns, coolly approving infinite purple vistas of rolling parkland, immemorial oaks, elegant deer, glassy lakes, white and winding avenues. Of the great country-houses behind them the furnishings are magnificent and cumbersome as the table-silver, and often of a hideous beauty. Armies of servants, housed in top-floor barracks, trot up and down endless staircases and through endless corridors at regular intervals with hot-water jugs, and very often hip-baths; or stand to attention, stiff and proud in plush and powder, in lofty vestibules; or exact from each other, in the servants' hall, a more jealous precedence than that of their masters and mistresses dining above. Battalions of gardeners cut and roll the velvet turf, rake and gravel the endless avenues, tend the hothouses. Platoons of grooms and underlings feed, rub down, and exercise the pampered occupants of enormous stables. The lightest touch on a heavily-embroidered bell-rope brings instant and obsequious service.

Chesney Wold in *Bleak House* is no bad picture of a patrician country-house of the 1840's, framing a mode of living which differed in no wise from that of forty or fifty years before and after it. Many memoirs have shown how little this atmosphere and background changed down to the Oriental invasion under Edward VII. In town those same tall, cool personages inhabited tall, cool mansions in Mayfair and Belgravia during the London Season with the same effortless poise and nonchalance. The drawing-room of Zenobia, queen of Tory society in *Endymion*, with its haughty mistress on her sofa, extending her hand to be kissed by blue-ribboned dukes and ambassadors, while a dozen smoothly gliding flunkeys hand ices and sherbets, is a typical salon of a typical great lady of the 1830's, when Melbourne was at the Home Office. Except for the costumes, it might be a leading politico-patrician drawing-room of any subsequent year down to the end of Victoria's reign. Life was calmly splendid and established for the ruling class for all time, exactly so.

Disraeli's last *roman à clef* supplies the perfect light orchestral accompaniment—like a selection from Donizetti at a Tory hostess's rout—to this world. Though Melbourne himself, like Wellington, is glimpsed only once or twice, distantly, allusively, fleetingly, and under his own name, much of high Early Victorian society parades through these pages under very thin disguises, from Palmerston (Roehampton) and Rothschild (Neuchâtel), Lady Jersey (Zenobia) and Queen Hortense (Agrippina), down to Mr. Poole (Mr. Vigo) of Savile Row, the eminent tailor, by no means the least impressive figure in this gallery nor the least important, since he lent Prince Napoleon some thousands in the 1840's to attain his throne. *Endymion* is, indeed, a document offering not only an Opposition commentary on current politics by an expert, but a highly instructive social background. We learn, for example, that the London of Melbourne's prime was a damnably dreary place, the most melancholy city in Europe since Regency wickedness had been driven underground.

It had, one might almost say, only two theatres, and they so huge that it was difficult to see or hear in either. . . . There were then no Alhambras, no Cremornes, no palaces of crystal in terraced gardens, no Casinos, no music-halls, no Aquaria, no promenade-concerts. Evans's existed, but not in the fullness of its modern development [*Endymion* was published in 1880], and the most popular place of resort was the barbarous conviviality of the Cider-Cellar.

The gay metropolitan bachelor, unless eligible for Almack's—later Willis's—or White's, or Boodle's, or the Reform, or the Athenæum, was thus in dismal case; nor had the dingy insignificant West End streets, rich in mud and horse-dung under the gas-lamps, with their hordes of blue-faced beggars and crossing-sweepers, much to offer the connoisseur of enlivening spectacle, though from 1830 onwards Mr. Shillibeer's reckless new omnibuses with their howling "cads" were apparently a great solace and diversion to fast men of the type of Mr. "Soapy" Sponge. The middle-class Londoner of the 1830–40's, according to Disraeli, found his chief evening relaxation in "religious and philanthropic societies"; and having discovered what some of these were like one may be forgiven a shudder, in concert with the objects of that appalling charity.

In the slums, which lacked even those ghostly vestiges of a merrier England still haunting rural festivities and fairs, the gin-palaces flaring big and bright and frequent relaxed the metro-politan lower classes all too thoroughly. As for the great world, it had no real need of any London amusements but those of its own making, and its tireless round of dinners, receptions, routs, parties—including, says Greville, "morning parties extended into the night"—and balls, thronged and glittering and orchid-aceous behind those gloomy and well-guarded façades, amply satisfied it. In Disraeli's novels unseen fiddles mingle gaily with the chatter and the pop and foam of the champagne; feathers curl with languorous elegance over fair dazzling shoulders; the epigrams tripping from dainty or whiskered lips match the prevailing diamonds for sparkle and are often as good as Oscar Wilde's (which they strangely resemble) a little later; or, if it comes to that, as some of Melbourne's own. For example:

My lord always liked Paris—the only place he ever did; but I am not very sanguine he will go; he is so afraid of being asked to dinner by our Ambassador.

He said I ought to belong to the Athenæum. . . . They rejected me and elected a bishop. And then people are surprised that the Church is in danger!

I declare that when I was eating that truffle, I felt a glow about my heart that, if it were not indigestion, I think must have been gratitude.

One never sees a pottle of strawberries now. I believe they went out, like all good things, with the Stuarts.

On the whole, Lord Montford [Lord Granville] was, for him, in an extremely good humour; never very ill; Princedown was the only place where he was never very ill; he was a little excited, too, by the state of politics, though he did not exactly know why.

All these personages have a costly exquisite gloss, as if grown and preserved carefully under glass like the hothouse fruit and flowers on their tables. Never a heartache among any of them, one might imagine sometimes, but for the faint sardonic smile on their historian's sallow, subtle, and remarkable features.

These Olympians nevertheless had their secret troubles, which Thomas à Kempis could have warned them were inevitable had they ever heard of him. Melbourne himself is a notable example. Sprung from professional middle-class stock (his forbears were lawyers) ennobled only in 1815, he was to begin with not quite sure of his own birth. In the great world it was widely murmured that his father was not Sir Peniston Lamb, first Viscount Melbourne, but George Wyndham, third Earl of Egremont, F.R.S., the great eighteenth-century Mæcenas and patron of Turner. Melbourne was perfectly aware of this rumour. One day, towards the end of his career, at Brocket Hall, noting Landseer glancing with involuntary curiosity from a portrait of Egremont to his host's features, Melbourne calmly observed, "So you've heard the story, have you? It's a damned lie, for all that. But who the devil," added Melbourne pensively, after a pause, "can tell who is anybody's father?" From which it might be perhaps deduced that he himself occasionally had doubts. Yet this was nothing to the two resounding scandals, one of them literally Byronic, in which he was involved before Victoria's accession. He outlived both with ease.

2

William Lamb, whom it will be convenient to call Melbourne henceforth, though he succeeded to the title only in 1829, was born on March 15, 1779, his mother being Elizabeth, the clever and beautiful daughter of Sir Ralph Milbanke of Halnaby, Yorkshire.

It was to her brains and energy that Sir Peniston, her husband, with his great inherited wealth, owed his post of gentleman of the Bedchamber to the Prince Regent and, a little later, his viscounty. She turned Melbourne House—now Albany, off Piccadilly, and then possessing a ballroom with a ceiling by Cipriani—into a Whig salon, of which Fox became the oracle and the Regent and his most brilliant intimates habitués, drunk or sober, one of its eminent drunks being Sheridan. Lady Melbourne combined charm and intelligence, to which her son owed much, with exquisite tact and few scruples, and was indeed as perfect a hostess as her friend Madame Récamier. At the age of eleven William, the second son, was sent to Eton, and endured the historic savageries of that foundation with admirable fortitude, managing, amid all the floggings, bullyings, and uproar, to acquire a solid classical culture and a real passion for literature (as he said blandly in later life, if you really wanted to read at Eton there was nothing to stop you). From the Sixth Form he went up to Trinity, Cambridge, and displayed no great promise, apart from winning the declamation prize with an essay fondly entitled "The Progressive Improvement of Mankind," an illusion derived from France and rapidly gaining ground.

Normally he would have proceeded from Cambridge to make the Grand Tour, like all other youths of his rank; but we were at war with France, and the ancient civilised tradition of allowing harmless travellers from an enemy country to move about during a war more or less as they pleased had been killed by the French Revolution, which destroyed so many international courtesies. Scotland was deemed by Lady Melbourne a good alternative. In 1798 young William was accordingly despatched, with his younger brother Frederick, to Glasgow University to sit under John Millar, Professor of Comparative Law. There was no Cantabrigian lotos-eating under dour Professor Millar. William's letters at this period to his mother, whom he loved and admired, have been described as priggish. No doubt the raw, rarefied air of Glasgow was responsible.

On his return to London in 1800 Lady Melbourne consulted her friend, Lord Egremont, on William's future. Egremont suggested the Bar, to which William, a rather languid, diffident, personable youth, was duly called in Michaelmas Term, 1804, and completed one Northern circuit. On the death of his elder brother Peniston in January 1805 he gave up the Bar forthwith. It bored him, and he was moreover deeply in love with a very desirable and disturbing *partie*, Lady Caroline Ponsonby, only daughter of the great Whig Earl of Bessborough. To this attractive, appalling creature, with her piquant and vivacious face, her devilish temper, her mop of curly golden hair "shingled" in the fashion of the 1920's, her soft, lazy drawl, her large, appealing hazel eyes, her complete inability to tell the truth, her generous impulses, her considerable talents, and her unbalanced mind, Melbourne was to owe years of misery. Nevertheless they were married in June 1805, the wedding-day being enlivened by a spectacular fit of hysterics from the bride.

The dowager Lady Melbourne was well satisfied. Though her stingy husband refused to fix William's allowance at more than £2,000 a year, she was able, with Fox's help, to get him into Parliament for Leominster, and he duly took his seat, among Fox's supporters, in January 1806, the year of Austerlitz and Trafalgar. At their apartments in Melbourne House the young couple had already begun to entertain that haughty high Whig society into which young Melbourne had now married, which was headed by the Cavendishes and the Russells and knew no master in Heaven or earth save, perhaps, the sublime Brummell, at this period also a guest at Melbourne House. In the Commons Melbourne could exchange nods on both sides of the House with relations, relations-by-marriage, and relations of both, exactly as in Mr. Belloc's early Parliamentary satires. But notwithstanding the cosy family atmosphere of politics, Melbourne's Parliamentary début was a failure. His opinions were advanced and he was apt to vote against his party, with whom he was accordingly unpopular. He looked beyond Fox for an apostle of reform and opposed the war, and at the general election of 1812, when Lord Liverpool became Prime Minister, he lost his seat, owing to his support of Catholic Emancipation, and retired into private life with a shrug for the next four years.

The young Lambs meanwhile were living in reasonable harmony. Despite recurring temperamental storms Lady Caroline allowed her husband to read with her and to improve her somewhat sketchy education generally, especially along classical lines; her own talents lay in the direction of music, caricature, horsemanship, and general diablerie. They were sharing Melbourne House with the dowager, who already had had occasion once or twice to rap "dear Caro" on the knuckles for reckless flirtation, and in six years they had three children, two of whom died in infancy.

It was at an evening party on March 25, 1812, a fortnight after the publication of *Childe Harold* had swept the town off its feet, that Lady Caroline met Byron and received the *coup de foudre*. The pale, plump young poet, with his dark, luminous eyes, his insolent, melancholy beauty, his hyacinthine curls, his Satanic charm, his sinister ancestry, his Luciferian pride, his interesting limp, and his aura of nihilist disillusion, was less violently smitten. But from his Calvinist upbringing he knew himself, as M. André Maurois has pleasantly remarked, to be "predestined to an ardent and guilty life," and subsequent philosophical and romantic conversations at Melbourne House with Lady Caroline, a fascinating and completely undisciplined talker, and her clever mother-in-law, who became Byron's intimate friend and future confidant, swiftly took their predestined course, as Society was breathlessly anticipating, and turned in the Affair of the Season.

In the primary stages Byron had gloomily warned Lady Caroline, in the ritual Byronic manner, against that "fallen spirit," himself. He might as well have warned a typhoon. It was, moreover, too late. Lady Caroline hurled herself at him with all the violence of her half-crazy temperament, to the vast amusement of her world. *"Vénus toute entière à sa proie attachée,"* quoted the better-read of the aristocracy with relish. Showering passionate letters on him, exacting a continuous crescendo of emotional intensity, visiting Byron's lodgings by night in boy's costume, even—when the Corsair, in due course, grew inevitably sick of her—writing to his valet, Lady Caroline showed that public opinion meant nothing to her; and she was not to be shaken off, even by being removed to Ireland for a space by her mother, Lady Bessborough.

Within six months Byron revolted. Having assured Lady Melbourne in September 1812 that "I wish this to end . . . I am tired of being a fool," and complaining of "the destruction of all my plans last winter [*sic*] by this last romance," he dismissed Lady Caroline with elaborate emotion. The effect was disagreeable. To Francis Hodgson Byron wrote in February 1813;

The Agnus [Lady Caroline] is furious. You can have no idea of the horrible and absurd things she has said and done since (really from the best motives) I withdrew my homage. "Great pleasure" is, certes, my object, but "why *bitch*, Mr. Wild?"[1]

With a postscript:

The business of last summer I broke off; and now the amusement of the gentle fair is writing letters literally threatening my life.

At a ball at Lady Heathcote's in July 1813, meeting Byron and being slighted by him, the "Agnus" stabbed herself with a fruit knife, whether accidentally is not certain. She had already burned her collection of Byronic verse, portraits, rings, locks of hair, and other mementoes in the park at Brocket Hall, while village girls dressed in white and trained for the purpose danced round the pyre, chanting "Burn, fire, burn!" with mystical incantations of Lady Caroline's own. In 1815 she was still writing to him. In July 1816 she published an anonymous novel in three volumes entitled *Glenarvon*, in which Byron, very thinly disguised as Lord Glenarvon, is the destroyer of a virtuous British home.

[1] An allusion to a domestic fracas in Fielding's *Jonathan Wild*.

To Tom Moore Byron conveyed his impression of this work of art in a postscript to an impromptu rhyming-review of the season's literary successes;

> *"I read 'Glenarvon,' too, by Caro Lamb—*
> *God dam!"*

His lordship added in a subsequent letter to Moore, "The picture can't be good; I did not sit long enough." He had some time ago set Lady Caroline down in his diary as "mad, bad, and dangerous to know." More recently he had expressed himself equally critically, and perhaps a trifle caddishly, in a valedictory verse which, when it appeared in print after his death, can hardly have pleased any of the Lamb or Bessborough clans:

> *"Remember thee! Ay, doubt it not!*
> *Thy husband too shall think of thee!*
> *By neither shalt thou be forgot,*
> *Thou false to him, thou fiend to me!"*[1]

He had married Anne Isabella Milbanke in January 1815, and *Glenarvon* was Lady Caroline's last broadside. Her frenzy subsided, and she returned to more normal amusements, such as bareback-riding, personal tuition at Astley's Circus of the King's Champion at George IV's coronation, Bohemian parties, wild canvassing for George Lamb in a Westminster election, organ-recitals and causeries for guests specially wakened at 3 a.m., more novel-writing, and the philosophy of William Godwin. At a masquerade at Almack's in August 1820 she appeared as Don Juan and was carried off shrieking by devils. "It don't surprise me," wrote Byron to John Murray from Ravenna. "I only wonder she went so far as '*the Theatre*' for '*the Devils*,' having them so much more natural at home."

And Melbourne?

He behaved through all this turmoil with a pity and a for-

[1] *Occasional Pieces*, 1812–24.

bearance at which few of the worldly have been unable to sneer. His constitutional indolence ("no backbone!") and that pose of elegant indifference he always cultivated must be added, no doubt. Of the three courses open to him under the social code— to kill or maim Byron in a pistol-duel, to demand a bill of divorce, or to separate from his impossible wife—he took none. He nearly made up his mind to a separation in 1819, when Lady Caroline's gambols, which would fill pages, had driven him almost mad. "Nothing is *agissant*," wrote Lady Granville to a friend in 1815, "but Caroline-William in a purple riding-habit, tormenting everybody." "Cherubina has been outdoing herself in absurdity," wrote Lady Cowper to Frederick Lamb four years later. "She will really make William the laughing-stock of the country. . . . William all the time miserable, fretted to death, flying into passions continually, and letting her have her own way." A deed of separation was drawn up. Lady Caroline charmed and petted her husband out of it; for she still had intervals of grace and sanity and gratitude, her heart was not bad, and he was still in love with her.

Byron's death at Missolonghi in March 1824, followed, three months later, by Lady Caroline's curiously macabre accidental encounter, as she was coming out of the gates of Brocket Hall for her morning ride, with the poet's funeral cortège on its way to Newstead, brought on fresh brainstorms and a climax. Legal separation was at last decided, and four years later Lady Caroline, who had taken energetically to brandy and laudanum, died at Brocket Hall, at the age of forty-two. Towards the end she expressed contrition for hurting her husband so much, and his response was affectionate and magnanimous. But his domestic trials—his only surviving child, a son, weak-minded from birth, lived until 1836—embittered Melbourne for years, fortified as he was by the stoic wisdom of the Classics, and established in him a cynicism, mellowing as time went on into playful sardonic whimsy, in its way irresistible.

3

It was a rich, warm night at the beginning of August (year not stated, but plainly 1827) when a gentleman enveloped in a dress-cloak emerged from a club (obviously White's) at the top of St. James's Street and, half-way down that celebrated eminence, encountered a Tory friend in the Cabinet and engaged him in that amicable altercation about "taking refuge in Canning" which so aptly opens the first chapter of *Endymion*—to which we may now say hail and farewell—for any observer of Melbourne's career. For like Mr. Sidney Wilton, Melbourne also took refuge in Canning, greatest of Whig-Tories,[1] and thus began his career at last.

He had returned to the House in 1816 as member for Northampton, saying and doing nothing very memorable for the next few years. But Canning had begun by about 1820 to take shrewd note of the ability behind this highly intelligent backbencher's pose of indolence. In 1825 Melbourne lost a safe Hertfordshire seat, owing chiefly to his Radical opponent's skilful exploitation of the Byron scandal as a political issue, and retired once more. Two years later Prime Minister Canning ("just the man for an age of transition") brought him into Parliament again and immediately appointed him Chief Secretary to the Lord-Lieutenant of Ireland. From now until Queen Victoria's accession will be a crowded ten years in Melbourne's life. Since they do not concern our purpose, save as a formative period, they may be briefly dealt with.

In 1827 the giant figure of Daniel O'Connell was dominating the Irish scene, and striving with magnificent oratory to dispel rankling Irish memories of the recent blood-bath of 1798 and to wean his desperate fellow-Catholics from the planning of more risings to political action. Like Yeats three years before

[1] The Whigs began calling themselves "Liberals," and the Tories adopted the name "Conservatives," in 1828. I have used their more historic and descriptive labels throughout.

the Easter Rebellion of 1916, O'Connell might well have cried to the Irish:

> *"Romantic Ireland's dead and gone,*
> *It's with O'Leary in the grave."*

And like Yeats, he would have been wrong.

There is no need to recount the long tale of slavery or to review that "barbarous debilitating policy" which aroused the indignation of Dr. Johnson. By Melbourne's time the Penal Laws were in many ways relaxed, though even yet no Catholic could sit in Parliament or fill any public post, and the mass of the Irish remained in subjection and misery. Melbourne, like most of the advanced of his time, was strong for the emancipation of what, in England at least, was a small, obscure, harmless, and obviously dying body of eccentrics. His stay at Dublin Castle, that fortress-nest of Government jobberies, taught him a great deal about the Irish Question. He would have learned more had not Canning died within six months and the dithering Goderich taken his place as Premier, to be swiftly succeeded by the aged Iron Duke, Catholic Emancipation's most dogged opponent. Shortly after his recall to London Melbourne, with Palmerston and other members of the small and derelict Canningite group, came to terms with the Duke and voted with him against the repeal of the anti-Catholic Test and Corporation Acts, thereby demonstrating one aspect of Melbourne which is unpleasing and universal, namely, a recurring preference for expediency over principle. In February 1829, on his father's death, he succeeded to the title, and in November 1830, accepted the Home Secretaryship from the new Premier, Earl Grey.

Many shoulders, including Greville's, were shrugged in Pall Mall over Melbourne's appointment. His languid deportment deceived the know-alls, not for the first or last time. Within a month Greville was admitting that "he has surprised all those about him by a sudden display of activity and vigour, rapid and diligent transaction of business for which nobody was prepared."

And the starving agricultural rioters and Chartists firing hay-stacks and breaking machinery all over Kent, Sussex, Hampshire, Berkshire, Wiltshire, Surrey, and the North were the first to feel his hand. Melbourne's technique was to call out the troops and to refuse, except in a very few cases, to interfere with the sentences of hanging and transportation passed on the ringleaders by the Special Commission which duly tried them.[1] For this he has earned for ever the just execration of the proletariat, whom he vastly preferred, nevertheless, to the smug and rising bourgeoisie. The case of the "Tolpuddle martyrs," those six admirable Dorset pioneers of Trade Unionism whose deporta-tion to the hell of Botany Bay might have been remitted, perhaps, for something less savage had a nervous King and Cabinet not been so terrified by tales of secret oaths, Jacobin agents, and a national class-war, damns him above all else. To Melbourne a Trade Union was not precisely a seditious conspiracy but a body "perfectly legal unless accompanied by illegal acts"; a nice distinction.

He met the rioting over the Reform Bill (Third Edition, 1832), that middle-class Magna Carta, with equal implacability, holding troops in reserve and keeping the restive mob in order. He deserves at least one good mark, however. At the angelic Lord Shaftesbury's instigation he pushed through a Bill limiting child-labour in the factories, in the teeth of Britain's strongest com-mercial interests.

In July 1834 Grey resigned, and Melbourne was ordered by William IV—reluctantly, for the King did not care for him—to form a Government. He received the command with customary nonchalance, describing the Premiership to Young, his private secretary, as "a damned bore." Greville sums up the misgivings of the clubs:

Everybody wonders how Melbourne will do it. He is certainly a queer fellow to be Prime Minister, and he and Brougham [Lord

_____
[1] Only one Lancashire millowner was murdered.

Chancellor] are two wild chaps. . . . I should not be surprised if Melbourne was to arouse his dormant energies and be excited by the greatness of his position to display the vigour and decision in which he is not deficient. Unfortunately his reputation is not particularly good; he is considered lax in morals, indifferent in religion, and very loose and pliant in politics.

And Greville proceeds to relate an anecdote charmingly illustrative. On being assured by Melbourne that office was a damned bore, Young, "a vulgar, familiar, impudent fellow," cried: "Why, damn it, such a position never was occupied by any Greek or Roman, and if it only lasts two months, it's well worth while to have been Prime Minister of England!" "By God, that's true," said Melbourne. "I'll go."

Four months turned out to be his limit. The dictatorial caprices of the Sailor King proved too much even for Melbourne's polished stoicism, and he had difficulties with his colleagues as well; most markedly with the overbearing and overheated Brougham, his Lord Chancellor, that great Scotch bag of illusions and windy chimeras, and with Lansdowne, his Lord President of the Council, whose ruffled feelings over the omission of two protégés from the Irish Poor Law Commission had to be soothed with a Garter. Very shortly afterwards Viscount Althorp, Melbourne's Chancellor of the Exchequer, that honourable and tightly-buttoned-up man of whom O'Connell once remarked pensively that "nobody has yet been able to discover whether his Lordship wears a shirt or not," resigned and ascended to the Upper House on succeeding to the Spencer earldom. The dismaying effect of this on Wellington and the Tories may be viewed in *Coningsby*. To Melbourne it came as pure relief. His brief and trying exercise of power had somewhat disillusioned him. He resigned forthwith, declining a Royal offer of an earldom and the Garter with graceful thanks; though, as he subsequently admitted, "there's no damned nonsense of merit about the Garter."

Having seen the Duke, his successor, go out, Melbourne

shrugged and strolled back into office at the Royal command in April 1835, after Grey had declined to carry on, and remained Prime Minister for the next six years; chiefly, as one of his intimates said, to oblige his friends.

It is convenient to pause here a moment to survey the England which Melbourne now surveyed in his mind's eye as he gazed musingly out of his Downing Street window.

The national theme-song, so to speak, was a loud, feverish, infinitely touching choral act of faith in Progress and the new Machine-god. Blake's dark Satanic mills were growing in number and blast-power, and the Midland and Northern countrysides were swiftly being defiled with chimneys, furnaces, railwayworks, slag-heaps, refuse-dumps, and all the raw stinking horror of the new industrialism, as more and more Coketowns and their slums rose above the horizon, the forerunners of those belching Midland hells we know to-day. For a comprehensive view of the appalling scarecrow-parade of victims, even so early, of Progress and Industry I commend the strong-nerved reader to Chapter XIII ("March Past") of Miss Edith Sitwell's *Victoria of England*, on which a later Dante might profitably have drawn for a new Malebolge. Two early Factory Acts (1831, 1833) had reduced child-labour under the age of eleven to a forty-eight-hour week, but sensible employers could safely disregard this. In the Black Country and other mines there was no nonsense about regulations, and half-naked women and children of tender age slaved in wet and darkness twelve hours a day (in Scotland, fourteen) in the service of masters of stern probity, with moral and Benthamite apophthegms booming incessantly from their glossy whiskers; for labour was dirt-cheap, and praise ascended daily to the Machine-god from his ministers.

> "*We thank thee most earty
> For mercies to date . . .*"[1]

[1] Ralph Hodgson, *Hymn to Moloch*.

Meanwhile Brougham's Society for the Diffusion of Useful Knowledge was alleviating the misery of the serfs with free lectures and cheap pamphlets proclaiming the marvellous new gospel of Science and its ushering in of inevitable Millennium. Over the pastoral southern countryside, not yet harmed except by railways, still echoed the thunder of the great Cobbett, now a sick old man of seventy-three and due to die this year (1835), leaving behind him his *Political Register*, those *Rural Rides* which are an English classic, and a confused conviction among the populace that to denounce the flogging of British soldiers by German mercenaries of the Crown, as Cobbett did in 1810, was a pleasure too dearly bought at a £1,000 fine and two years' imprisonment.

Slavery (Negro) within the Empire had been technically abolished. The Poor Laws had been "reorganised" and made more hateful. On the other hand, Mr. Angerstein's collection of Old Masters had been bought by the Government and the National Gallery established to satisfy public craving for Art. To those of the proletariat who had time for reading the Library of the British Museum, an institution founded by a State lottery in the reign of George III under the auspices of the Archbishop of Canterbury and others, was likewise open.

One could quote a dozen far more vital instances of the contemporary "march of mind," so evocative of the satire of Peacock. The case of the Rev. Dr. Folliott's cook, absorbed in a tract on hydrostatics written by Lord Brougham and published at sixpence by the Steam Intellect Society, dropping gently off to sleep, overturning her bedside-candle, and nearly burning the Doctor's house down, will occur to all Peacock-lovers immediately. Nor could there be omitted from any such list examples like the beginnings of compulsory education for the children of the poor, nor yet Mr. Robert Owen's design for a new moral world based on the formation of that "British and Foreign Consolidated Association of Industry, Humanity, and Knowledge" which so signally failed to turn out to be what the public wanted.

All this yeasty new ferment in British life, and the emergence of a horde of Reformers, Improvers, Utopians, Radicals, Chartists, Trade Unionists, and other trouble-makers accompanying it, affected the majority of the ruling class not at all. Except for that very few interested in the game of politics, and for a handful rendered pusillanimous by an un-English imagination, like the baronet in Tennyson who was shown a Chartist pike and

> "... *shudder'd, lest a cry*
> *Should break his sleep by night, and his nice eyes*
> *Should see the raw mechanic's bloody thumbs*
> *Sweat on his blazon'd chairs* ..."

—except for such as these they hunted in the Shires, went racing at Goodwood and Epsom, shot and fished in Scotland and Yorkshire, sailed at Cowes, and danced, dined, gambled, made love, and yawned through the London Season as usual, serene and splendid. Their attitude towards the Industrial Revolution, if they took any attitude, was more or less that of Sir Lester Dedlock towards Mr. Rouncewell; magnificently disapproving, "opposing his repose and that of Chesney Wold to the restless flights of ironmasters," connecting the new industrialists vaguely with Wat Tyler and torchlight-processions of mobs in some universe too far away to be real. And as few of them ever met Mr. Rouncewell, the leisured rhythms of patrician existence in town and country continued as if separated from the bubbling and boiling of the lower orders by interstellar space. An entry in Charles Greville's journal for July 1, 1836, conveys a charming selective nonchalance towards even his own world. "At Stoke for three days; divine weather, profusion of flowers and shade, and every luxury; nobody there of any consequence." As a frequent guest of the Yorks at Oatlands, and at other house-parties thickly studded with Royalties and ambassadors and duchesses and the topmost *gratin*, the snobbish Greville's standards were perhaps abnormally high. At all events his phrase, demonstrating that in the greatest houses there were people who had no existence for Mr. Greville, implies an abyss between the great world and the mass of the nation which was hardly plumbable or bridgeable.

There were, of course, a few members of the ruling class who bridged it. But noble eccentrics consumed by a Franciscan love of the poor, like Lord Shaftesbury or Harriet, second Duchess of Sutherland, were even rarer than noble eccentrics who danced the antic hay as vigorously as Melbourne's Lady Caroline. The high State clergy were more concerned with the goings-on at Oxford, where a youngish Fellow of Oriel had in 1833 begun publishing some highly subversive pamphlets called *Tracts for the Times*. Such things did not interest that Erastian-agnostic aristocracy to which Melbourne belonged. He himself was a liberal epicurean, "a quietist of the school of Fénélon," as he gravely explained in due course to Queen Victoria, with fantastic inaccuracy; though if he ever made the famous remark attributed to him, "Nobody has more respect for the Christian religion than I, but really, when it comes to intruding it into private life . . . !" he was doubtless indulging that characteristic whimsicality and talking "off the record." His episcopal appointments ("Damn it all—another bishop dead!") were in harmony with his easy views, and he got into sore trouble early in his Premiership with what Oxford called the Two-bottle Orthodox[1] by giving the Regius Professorship of Divinity to the latitudinarian Dr. Hampden. He would undoubtedly have appointed Disraeli's Dr. Comely, that smooth and silky divine who quoted Socrates in preference to St. Paul and rejected "all symbols and formulas" as unphilosophical, with equal insouciance.

Though not actually of the Beau Monde—his culture was far too broad and deep—Melbourne was now moving in its midst with genuine pleasure, and especially in what journalists call Clubland. Among the distinguished ghosts which haunt Pall Mall after midnight and frighten those clubmen who have

---

[1] Newman, *Apologia*.

homes to return to, his should certainly loom largely, for next to Brooks's round the corner he loved the Reform, that impressively classic edifice, founded in 1836 to commemorate an event with which he had been so intimately connected, and he had no grave objections, so far as I can discover, to the Athenæum, the Oxford and Cambridge, the Travellers', or either of the Service clubs which decorate that still-dignified thoroughfare, though I can see his shade lounging rather hurriedly past the R.A.C. Melbourne was, in fact, with his tall, elegant figure, his handsome, open, genial features, and (when not moody or abstracted) his easy and whimsically amusing conversation, a most agreeable man of the world and the phœnix of clubmen. And something more. At Holland House, Kensington, the Whig Temple of Fame,[1] where the only British hostess in history comparable to Mme de Rambouillet ruled her famous salon with absolute and capricious authority, Melbourne's laughing fellow-clubmen at Brooks's would hardly have recognised the talker who in that brilliant headachy atmosphere could quote Bossuet and St. Jerome as freely as Shakespeare, and Sappho as easily as Scott, and could at times outshine Macaulay, or even Sydney Smith. Next day, dining with a friend like Lord Sefton, Melbourne might be (as Greville once encountered him) in "roaring spirits," or, if he sat next to some attractive and intelligent woman, one of the gayest and most fascinating of cavaliers; or quite equally, and in other company, silent as a dumb-waiter, or damning like a Guardee. The many facets of his social personality have baffled more observers than one. A basic melancholy was accurately perceived by Bulwer Lytton:

"His mirth, though genial, came by fits and starts;
The man was mournful in his heart of hearts."

Moreover, one could never be certain how far his cynicism was simply playful. That often-quoted story of him told by

[1] Oil-bombed in October 1940.

69

G. W. E. Russell affords a typical instance of this offence to the serious. While Melbourne was Home Secretary a small boy was taken into his room in Whitehall, and Melbourne, who liked children and ached for his son, chatted with the child most charmingly, finally asking him if he saw anything round him he would like to have. A bright thick stick of red sealing-wax was the instant choice. "That's right, my boy, begin early," said the genial Melbourne, seizing and adding a bundle of new quill pens to it. "All these things belong to the public, and your business must always be to get as much out of the public as you can." It was, as Russell observes, the authentic voice of the Victorian ruling class. How far it was a pure joke, how far it was a shaft of acid satire directed at himself and his kind, who can say? Whistler should have quoted it when he urged Tom Taylor, Civil Servant and *Times* Art Critic, to "set your house in order with the Government for arrears of time and paper and leave vengeance to the Lord," for Bureaucracy past, present, and future has the same guiding principle.

Melbourne was, then, frequently disconcerting to the sober-minded, including Lady Canning, who thought he "wanted *caractère*." The well-known story of his reception, again as Home Secretary, of a delegation of the Society for the Abolition of Capital Punishment is yet another instance. Half-way through the proceedings Melbourne became absorbed in blowing a feather about, and fired off a succession of mild quips. As he had taken the trouble to read up the Society's case thoroughly the night before, this frivolity was probably merely a protest against the whiskered dull. Thus he remained an enigma to many. Greville, who admired his culture, was greatly puzzled at "the mixture of bluntness, facility, and shrewdness, discretion, levity, and seriousness which, colouring his mind and character by turns, make up the strange compound of his thoughts and actions." Such a complex character, enhanced by that deferent, sunny charm he knew so well how to wield, was soon to prove irresistible to the prosaic yet romantic young daughter of

Edward, Duke of Kent, now finishing her education at Kensington Palace under the Baroness Lehzen and a cloud of tutors.

This same charm, expended for preference on women, got Melbourne into nasty trouble in the spring of 1836, when a violently unpleasant character named the Hon. George Norton, a brother of Lord Grantley, brought an action—the equivalent of a modern divorce suit—against his wife Caroline for "criminal conversation," asking for damages and naming the Prime Minister as co-respondent.

It has been adjudged by many a case of attempted blackmail, political or otherwise. Melbourne had for some time been in the habit of dropping in of an evening, on his way home from Whitehall or the House, at Norton's house at Storey's Gate, Westminster, to chat for an hour with handsome, clever, unhappy Mrs. Norton, a granddaughter of Sheridan, a poetess described by Lockhart as a female Byron, and the original of Meredith's Diana of the Crossways. Nothing could have been more blameless, apparently; but long before the case was brought into court it had become the scandal of the age.

"John Bull fancies himself vastly moral, and the Court is mighty prudish," noted Greville in his diary on May 11, "and between them our off-hand Premier will find himself in a ticklish position." As it turned out, Melbourne, who was gravely perturbed, found a great deal of weighty opinion on his side. The Sailor King breezily rejected his offer to resign before Norton *v.* Norton and Melbourne came on, and the aged Wellington hastened to assure him, on behalf of the Opposition, of active sympathy. At the hearing the only evidence implying misconduct in the faintest degree was given by a relay of discharged servants, so Melbourne's counsel, Sir John Campbell, Attorney-General, had little difficulty in blowing it to pieces; especially as Norton had never objected to any of Melbourne's visits, it appeared. One inspiration of Norton's counsel is deservedly celebrated. Admitting that three brief notes from Melbourne found in Mrs. Norton's escritoire afforded no proof of guilt, he added: "There is, however, something in them which may aid you, gentlemen of the jury, in forming an opinion as to the nature of the intercourse existing between the parties." The notes were as follows:

> I shall call about half-past four or five. Yours,
>
> MELBOURNE.

> How are you? I shall not be able to come to-day, I probably shall to-morrow. Yours,   MELBOURNE.

> No House to-day. I shall call after the Levee, about four or half-past. If you wish it later, let me know. I will then explain about going to Vauxhall. Yours,
>
> MELBOURNE.

Has this not a faint but unmistakable flavour? Dickens's parody appeared in one of the monthly instalments of *Pickwick* later the same year. The jury in Norton *v.* Norton and Melbourne found for respondent and co-respondent without leaving the box, and though Mrs. Norton wished to proceed further and vindicate herself completely, she was persuaded by Melbourne, with some difficulty, to drop it. Melbourne himself emerged from the case with William IV's congratulations and a practically spotless toga.

The Court from the next year onwards was going to be more than "mighty prudish." It says much for his qualities that the Norton case—together with the case of Brandon *v.* Brandon and Lamb, non-suited some years before and, according to the gossip Creevey, not involving the co-respondent in any blame worth mentioning—did not disqualify the Prime Minister from becoming the adored mentor of a virginal Queen, a lifelong dragon of propriety. Or more accurately, perhaps, one might conclude that the faint aura of adventure surrounding Melbourne increased his appeal for Victoria. As Mr. Sinclair Lewis has succinctly phrased it, "women love heels." Melbourne, no heel in any sense, was a woman's man, nevertheless. His lifelong interest in women undoubtedly added lustre to his slightly tarnished halo in those prominent girlish blue eyes, though Victoria would equally undoubtedly have died rather than admit it.

Old King William died on June 20, 1837. Early the same morning his eighteen-year-old niece, Princess Alexandrina Victoria, only daughter of Edward, Duke of Kent, was proclaimed Queen of England, and Melbourne's masterly performance simultaneously began.

4

There are two recognised schools in the technique of bullfighting: the classical School of Ronda and the flamboyant School of Seville. So, one might say with all respect, does the method of Melbourne with Queen Victoria contrast with his successor Disraeli's. Doubtless Melbourne had the advantage. Though far from malleable, the youthful Victoria was as susceptible to the glamour of her first Prime Minister as any schoolgirl doting on the visiting French master, as her artless diaries reveal. By the time she came to Disraeli the Queen was, if the phrase may be excused, a far tougher proposition; more sophisticated, more imperious, less impressionable, more accustomed to dealing with politicians, more conscious of her power, and brandishing inconsolable widowhood like an oriflamme. The subtle Jew had a more difficult task than the skilful Anglo-Saxon. The outrageous flattery Disraeli lavished on his "little Faëry" would have been impossible to a man of Melbourne's temperament, in any case. In terms of music, the one is Liszt, the other Bach. To each his laurel.

The girl whom Melbourne found himself detailed to charm, guide, tutor, counsel, and mould during her first critical years of reigning over the British People was not a very complex character at any time, perhaps. She had strong native good sense, but her intellect was mediocre, despite a very sound education.

The grace and poise of her dumpy little body were always exquisite, her voice musical (in infancy she exercised also what Max Beerbohm has called "the perfect lungs for which the House of Hanover is most justly famed"), and her manner for the most part unaffectedly amiable in private and public, well deserving of Mr. Jorrocks's tribute a few years later. "A werry nice little 'ooman, and keeps a pack of stag-'ounds." She had been well-drilled in deportment, but she lacked the lighter social gifts, and though she laughed with all her teeth at dear, kind, amusing Lord M.'s quips she was quite humourless.

One aspect of her character was markedly Teutonic. Her father had managed to blend genuine philanthropy and enlightened ideas in his civilian character with a sincere belief, as Colonel of the Royal Fusiliers, in the "cat" as the cure for all military misdemeanour. One of his men, a deserter ordered 999 lashes, died at the flogging-post. Another, sentenced to death for mutiny and desertion and marched in his grave-clothes to the gallows, with Edward, Duke of Kent, heading the cortège and the regimental band playing funeral marches, found himself reprieved by Royal clemency at the very last moment, and quite likely, as Miss Sitwell suggests, went mad. It is therefore, perhaps, no surprise to find Queen Victoria, who had a German governess for twenty years, much perturbed at the proposal to abolish flogging in the Army in the late 1870's. One of Melbourne's first recorded remarks concerning her is that "she would not hesitate to sign a death-warrant if the culprit deserved it."

To this and other disciplinary foibles Victoria added, unlike most of her subjects, an essential goodness, a simple and shining evangelical piety which illuminates her entire existence, and of which Melbourne became first aware at her Coronation, when she was sincerely shocked to find a light collation served in the Chapel of St. Edward the Confessor and the altar of that once-famous shrine turned into a snack-bar laden with wine-bottles, fruit-stands, and sandwich-dishes. For the rest, the Queen possessed natural dignity, enormous conscientiousness and devotion to duty, great industry and attention to detail, a strict sense of responsibility, and in fact most of the virtues whereby good little girls escape the fate of the naughty little boys in *Strüwwelpeter*. Her heart was warm and she was naturally affectionate; capable in her teens, even, of discreet high spirits. Her musical taste was sound and her drawing (as all the art-critics agreed) showed genius; though whether, as one of them cried in ecstasy, she would have been "the first female Artist of her time" had she not been Queen of England may be open to doubt. Her obstinacy has become historic, her frosty flashes of dictatorial temper likewise. She came to the throne modestly determined to rule, and a Constitution, unique in history, which provided for sovereigns who reign without ruling was one of the first puzzles Melbourne had to explain to her.

On the eve of accession she had already shown her spirit. What might have been, in any other Court but a Hanoverian one, foredoomed to banality, a palace-plot of Ruritanian vivacity had enveloped her towards the spring of 1837, the conspirators being her restless and voluble mother, Victoria, Duchess of Kent, and the Duchess's Comptroller, a bustling intriguer named Sir John Conroy. The scene was Kensington Palace, then as now a dullish retreat enough, with its dark Grand Staircase, painted by Verrio and Kent, its interior browns and ochres, and its hauntings by the boredom and melancholy of Mary II and Anne; though one would not hastily quarrel with the praise accorded it by a connoisseur like Sir Osbert Sitwell for "sedate good manners," and especially for the mingled boldness and repose of its Orangery.[1] The Palace had at least one bright and Barriesque corner. Up to the recent war the visitor found Queen Victoria's nursery quarters, gay with chintz and exhibiting her beloved dolls, still faintly echoing the *glockenspiel*-chimes of a happy childhood.

Conroy's influence on the Duchess of Kent, who had been tentatively appointed Regent in the event of William IV's dying

[1] *The Scarlet Tree.*

75

before Victoria's legal coming-of-age, was considerable. The old King hated her. His violent and unexpected attack on "a person now near me," in a speech at a Windsor dinner-party in September 1836, still lingered in the memory of a hundred embarrassed guests. "I have no hesitation," the trying old man had boomed loudly, "in saying that I have been insulted—grossly and continually insulted—by that person"; after which indecent exhibition (Greville) the Duchess ordered her carriage at once, and would barely consent to patch up a formal reconciliation next day. According to Greville, the very simple essence of the Kensington Palace Plot was an attempt by Conroy and the Duchess to establish the Regency automatically on William IV's death, on the grounds of Victoria's youth and inexperience. Whether, as one story goes, the young Princess, refusing firmly to co-operate, was imprisoned by "Mama" in her bedroom and released only by having a note slipped by a trusted servant to Lord Liverpool, who happened to be visiting the Palace at the time, does not seem fully proved. Beloved Uncle Leopold, King of Belgium, who had long since begun writing to her those letters of advice which became a lifelong habit, himself could extract no information from her. Since one of Victoria's first acts on accession was to exclude Mama from participation in all public affairs and to banish Conroy from her presence with a baronetcy, in place of the peerage he was expecting, it may be deduced that something unpleasant had happened. It was some years before the long-standing breach between Victoria and her touchy and difficult mother was completely healed, and their old affection restored. The Queen's tears over the Duchess's grave were remorseful and genuine. Her father's considerable debts she had paid immediately on assuming the Crown. Filial duty was another of her virtues.

To Melbourne, with his hard-won knowledge of women and the devilries of which they can be capable, his new pupil's character did not present any insuperable difficulties. Her youth and innocence were a cordial to a lonely elderly widower whose only surviving child, a hopeless mental case, had died in the previous year. As Greville accurately remarks, Melbourne was "a man with a capacity for loving without having anything in the world to love." The Queen's emotional, flattering, possessive admiration of him from the beginning was a more direct stimulant, and called forth all his considerable skill at charming during the six hours a day he spent, on an average, and at this period, in her company. As for what Greville calls her "peremptory disposition," Melbourne was aware from the beginning that it might create trouble. He trusted to his powers to cope with it, and his confidence was in the main not deceived. Years later the Queen was to complain bitterly of Mr. Gladstone's habit of "addressing Us as if We were a public meeting." Melbourne lacked the Gladstonian platform-habit and the Gladstonian unction as totally as he lacked the Oriental bravura of Disraeli. As a tutor his sense of humour, his worldly polish, his gently cynical, non-obtrusive doubts of the divine inspiration of the Whiggery he professed, his intimate knowledge of Society, his gift for amusing anecdote, and his entire lack of pompousness, priggery, and pedantry all combined to make his daily discourse on British history and the Constitution almost as pleasant as his conversation in Her Majesty's drawing-room. Victoria was fortunate in her first and greatest favourite and she knew it.

Her diaries are full of him from the day after her accession. First impressions:

Monday, 19th June. . . . At 9 came Lord Melbourne, whom I saw in my room, and of course *quite* ALONE, as I shall always do all my Ministers. He kissed my hand, and I then acquainted him that it had long been my intention to retain him and the rest of the present Ministry at the head of affairs, and that it could not be in better hands than his. He then read to me the Declaration which I was to read to the Council, which he wrote himself and which is a very fine one. I then talked with him some little longer time, after which he left me. He was in full dress. I like him very much and feel confidence in him. He is a very straightforward, honest, clever, and good man. . . . At about 11 Lord Melbourne came again and spoke to me upon various subjects. . . .

In July Melbourne's manner strikes the Queen as "honest, frank, and yet gentle . . . He talks so quietly. I always feel peculiarly satisfied when I have talked with him. I have *great* confidence in him." The panegyric repeats itself in page after page. By January 1838 Melbourne has become "Lord M.," and his view that the climax of *Hamlet* is "awkward and horrid" and that our national Bard's Richard III is "a horrid man" is carefully recorded. By now Lord M., apart from daily private audiences and regular notes of instruction and advice, is a nightly habitué of the Drawing Room, enduring the boredom of those artless symposia with exquisite gallantry and discoursing on his cushions with mellow avuncular grace, though apt to fall asleep now and again, "which," comments the Queen fondly, "is always a proof that he is not quite well." He is now the Indispensable.

Thursday, 1st February,—This was the first Council that I have yet held at which Lord Melbourne was not present, and I must say I felt sad . . . as I feel a peculiar satisfaction, nay I must own almost *security*, at seeing him present at these formal proceedings, as I know and feel that I have a *friend* near me.

In March he is approving a new gown ("very pretty," and "does very well"). "He is so natural and funny and nice about *toilette* and has a very good taste, I think," notes the Queen, who has long since begun to accept him as an oracle. If Lord M. looks through the newspapers and says there is nothing in them, there is nothing in them. Blue, he settles, is an unlucky colour. He opines that the Irish Tithes Bill is a very good one; "so do I." Poor Henry VIII was a great man; "those women bothered him so." Everything is explained by Lord M. "like a *kind* father would do to his child; he has something so fatherly and so affectionate and kind in him, that one must love him. . . ." He has become, in fact, the Queen's ultimate and infallible authority on all things, from Crown prerogatives to sudden death by lightning, which is "sublime."

But even so early the docile and affectionate pupil was to surprise her beloved mentor with that will of her own. The episode is worth extracting from its setting, like the central cairngorm of a Balmoral brooch.

In February 1838, the Queen broached to Lord M., lightly and allusively, that matter of impending marriage which was of immediate importance to herself and the nation. Indefatigable Uncle Leopold of Belgium (she mentioned) had expressed extreme alarm over a visit to London during William IV's last years of the Prince of Orange and his two sons, for the last person Uncle Leopold desired his favourite niece to marry was a Dutchman. Lord M. replied to her smoothly that when sounded by the Prince of Orange on that occasion, he had informed him that the British Government had, in principle, no more objection to a Dutch *parti* than to "any other prince in Europe." One may well imagine a pregnant pause after this tactful lead. The Queen did not respond. She knew what was going on, and had the matter well in hand. Mama and Uncle Leopold had been busy behind the scenes for some little time, not without her entire connivance and approval. At this very moment her handsome and virtuous cousin, Albert of Saxe-Coburg, whom she had met and adored in childhood, was being groomed for stardom, as Hollywood would say, by Baron Dr. Stockmar, Uncle Leopold's right-hand man, that walking encyclopædia and future power behind the British Throne.

The byplay continues through 1839. In April, Lord M. hints that cousins are not very good to marry, and that "those Coburgs" are not very popular. The Queen asks innocently why she need marry at all for the next three or four years. In July she remarks with a sigh that Prince Albert and his brother Ernest are coming to England. It is really very tiresome. Far too many relations have been coming over. She really doesn't want to see Albert very much. The whole subject of marriage is an odious one. . . . Did Melbourne never realise that her mind had been firmly made up for some time and that nothing was going to prevent her marrying Albert? Apparently on August 6, after admitting to her laughingly, and after much hesitation, that he did not care for the idea of a Coburg connection, he received his warning. The prominent blue eyes became suddenly frosty. *Much* as the Queen loved her country, and *much* as she desired to serve the public good, surely dear Lord M. should realise that "her own liking was one of the principal things?" Even then he seems not to have grasped it, by all accounts.

On October 10, after some vexatious dallying in Brussels, the Royal cousins arrived in London. Albert was *beautiful*, the Queen discovered to her joy. His delicate mustachios, his slight and decorative whiskers, his broad shoulders and slim waist, his dashing but decorous technique in the Waltz and Galop were all noted in her diary with enthusiasm. A day or two later she informed Lord M. what half Society had guessed already, namely, that she had changed her mind about marrying, and on October 13 she announced to him, and to Uncle Leopold by letter likewise, her irrevocable decision. Greville's summing-up shows how completely contemporary opinion assumed that the Favourite had been led by the nose, though one may still be permitted a few lurking doubts. Says Greville:

The Queen settled everything about her marriage herself, and without consulting Melbourne at all on the subject, not even communicating to him her intentions. The reports were already rife while he was in ignorance, and at last he spoke to her, told her he could not be ignorant of the reports, nor could she; that he did not presume to enquire what her intentions were, but that it was his duty to tell her that if she had any, it was necessary that her Ministers should be apprised of them. She said she had nothing to tell him, and about a fortnight afterwards she informed him that the whole thing was settled.

An acidulous outburst from the Press, heralded some time before by a reference in a *Times* leading article of December 1838 to the British nation's distrust of "that unwelcome foreigner, Leopold, the Brummagem King of Belgium," culminated in a *Times* leader of February 10, 1840, noting the unpopularity of the House of Saxe-Coburg but hoping glumly, nevertheless, that Prince Albert might be able to retrieve for Her Majesty "much of what (we speak with frankness but with all respect) she has forfeited in the hearts of the most loyal, enlightened, and virtuous of her subjects, through her unhappy bias towards persons and principles which are hourly undermining the deep foundations of her Throne."

The Times added with a strong shudder:

Let any honest impartial eye take a survey of the Court of Queen Victoria—that Court which a mercenary and profligate, a contemned and odious Administration has, for its vile purposes, surrounded her—and then answer us whether her new Consort will find there a faithful sample of the dignity and character of this realm?

Those Byzantine corruptions at Court for which *The Times* was blushing embraced nightly classical music, round-games and charades, quadrilles and country-dances, draughts and teetotums, and even battledore and shuttlecock, in which the sinister Favourite himself had been known to take part as late as 11 p.m. Rarely has the essential decadence of Whiggery been more thoroughly exposed.

So the determined little Queen married her Albert, who introduced fish-knives and the Christmas-tree to England; and the London populace bawled rude, half-friendly songs about sausage and sauerkraut; and the Royal pair, after an awkward start, were divinely happy, as all the world knows; and the Consort behaved perfectly; and the pride of the English in being part of the Teuton race lasted almost till the eve of the first World War (1914).

5

Long before this happy consummation of girlhood's dreaming and his own inevitable eclipse, Melbourne had had to extricate the Queen from one or two embarrassments which sent her stock down with the nation considerably.

The new reign had very early met stormy weather. In Canada official bungling had brought about a joint revolt of the Upper Province, inhabited by Scotch Presbyterians, and the Lower Province, inhabited by French Catholics.

The handling of this affair by the Lieutenant-Governor, Sir Francis Head, evoked such criticism that he hurried back to London to see the Prime Minister, who received him at morning, characteristically, in his dressing-room, and continued shaving while Sir Francis anxiously developed his defence. At length Melbourne wiped his razor and delivered judgment. "But you see, Head," he remarked genially, "you're such a *damned odd fellow*," which was apparently true enough. The solution was to send out Lord Durham as High Commissioner to settle the trouble, which he did very badly, inviting an almost apoplectic attack by Brougham in the Lords, to which the mildness of Melbourne's defence was so remarkable that he felt bound to justify it to some of his critics. "If I had said anything, the fellow would have gone stark, staring mad"; which was also, relatively, true. Durham's ensuing resignation, to be succeeded by the more capable Sydenham, did Melbourne's Government no good, and ensuing troubles over the forcing of the hated Poor Laws on Ireland, together with growing proletarian restiveness at home over the new horde—how tiny by modern standards!—of factory inspectors and Poor Law bureaucrats, weakened it still further. Tory reaction under Peel was already on the horizon.

More clouds loomed simultaneously. The Chartist movement was spreading. The activities of the Ecclesiastical Commissioners were discontenting the Anglican clergy. The Irish, comparatively quiescent under Daniel O'Connell's influence, still had sporadic outbreaks against their more oppressive landlords of what the conqueror somewhat pompously described as "agrarian crime," but was often nothing more than shooting. Only the British bourgeoisie—what Melbourne, looking down his nose, called "the middle-class Dissenters," growing daily more fatted, complacent, and powerful—was content. He himself was still preoccupied, when not in the House or at Downing Street, with the daily tuition of his Sovereign, and had failed signally to convince her that her statutory five minutes over the wine after the ladies have withdrawn from the dinner-table is not sufficient for men of the world.

Behind the Queen, until he left to conduct Prince Albert on his educative Continental tour, hovered Baron Stockmar, Uncle Leopold's man, helping unobtrusively. Melbourne does not seem to have resented this profound and studiously self-effacing, yet pervasive, German pedant. Stockmar—"Stocky" to the Queen in girlhood—had come to England in the reign of George IV as private physician to beloved Uncle Leopold, who lived many years at Claremont, near Esher, before attaining the Belgian throne in 1831. On Victoria's accession the doctor, now a Baron, joined the Court in "a private capacity" and became a consultant, behind the scenes, of encyclopædic information, at the service of Queen and Ministers alike; a Professor of Things in General (*Allerley-Wissenschaft*), like Herr Teufelsdröckh.

It is true that Baron Stockmar's qualifications were impressive. He had a mind, as W. B. Yeats said inaccurately of H. G. Wells, like a sewing-machine; perfectly co-ordinated, awesomely efficient, terribly well-informed, rigidly correct, bleakly uncompromising, totally disinterested, typically Prussian, and devoted to the Anglo-Teuton Entente. Still less, apparently, did Melbourne resent beaky, vociferous Baroness Luise Lehzen, the Queen's adored governess since 1824, a relatively unwhiskered but equally assiduous shadow behind the Throne. The British public resented Stockmar and Lehzen impartially—Melbourne had very early to deny publicly that Stockmar was the Queen's private secretary—and took with a bad grace to both these Nordic guardian angels.

In February 1839 a very unpleasant happening jolted Lord M. out of his humdrum Palace routine. One of the Queen's Ladies of the Bedchamber reported to him in great agitation that "everybody" was saying that Lady Flora Hastings, one of the Duchess of Kent's ladies, was in what the Victorians called, not with invariable accuracy, "an interesting condition."

As the ladies of the Royal entourage, like those of Catherine de Médicis (whom Queen Victoria so oddly resembles in a duodecimo way) were presumed to be vestal virgins, and were not allowed to walk on the Terrace at Windsor without escort,[1] a fine scandal was looming. Melbourne learned from the Royal Physician-in-Ordinary, Sir James Clarke, that Lady Flora might or might not be pregnant. Sir James had been refused permission to examine her, and had his autocratic doubts. The scandal grew. On February 17, Lady Flora's own physician certified that her condition was due to an internal tumour. Poor Lady Flora, who had been extremely vocal over a "conspiracy," naming the Baroness Lehzen, accepted her colleagues' apologies and the Queen's own shocked regrets, but the affair now had become a party and a public question. The Press raged, and the Tory *Morning Post* especially distinguished itself on the topic of the essential purity of British womanhood and the baleful influence at Court of noisome Whigs.

While this uproar was still in progress, a major political crisis blew up over conditions in Jamaica, where slavery had been all but abolished in 1833 and the planters were cynically exploiting the "interim period" before complete emancipation. Melbourne's majority in the House fell, and he had to advise the Queen, to her dismay, to have recourse to the Tories, with the Duke of Wellington as a counterbalance to Sir Robert Peel, whom Her Majesty disliked intensely, and whose cold, nervous formalism

[1] Melbourne's ruling, highly resented by the Maids of Honour.

of manner (how unlike dear Lord M.'s!) offended her. Peel was duly given an audience at Windsor before forming his Ministry, and over a very reasonable request of his another storm broke.

Peel had requested Her Majesty, as was his plain right, to show her confidence in his Cabinet by replacing some of her more prominent Whig ladies, such as Lady Normanby, by Tories. Immediately the Royal features tightened. The Royal brow grew dark. The Royal eyes bulged. Certainly not! The Queen would not change *any* of them. Peel mumbled and retired, and the ancestral Duke of Wellington hastily replaced him with a great-grandfatherly appeal to Her Majesty's prudence. The Duke fell back, routed likewise, and Peel declared that in the circumstances he was unable to form a Government.

An urgent note from Melbourne came to the Queen. He implored her not to allow personal feelings to dominate her. She scribbled an agitated reply, promising to take the excellent advice of "a father to one who never wanted support more than she does now." But next day she changed her mind and refused totally. The atmosphere became electric. Hurried consultations took place between the politicians. A perfect snowstorm of notes descended on the Queen from Lord M., and on him from her. At a Cabinet meeting on May 10 Melbourne read aloud two of his latest missives from the Queen, eloquent of anguish and sleepless nights and voicing pathetic dread at the possibility of being deprived of all her friends and "surrounded by spies." The pulpy hearts of the statesmen, soon to yearn with the rest of England over the deathbed of Little Nell, were touched. An official note was drawn up for the Queen to sign, accepting Peel's withdrawal.

All this time Lord M. had been under the impression that Peel had asked for the removal of all the Queen's Whig ladies, instead of two or three. It came to the same thing, she pointed out when he brought this to her notice. Lord M. seemed a trifle startled. "I must submit this to the Cabinet," he said. Her Majesty's diary-note of the end of their conversation is terse and tight-lipped.

Lord M. said we might be beat; I said I never would yield; and would never apply to Peel again. Lord M. said, "You are for standing out, then?" I said certainly. I asked how the Cabinet felt. . . .

The Cabinet, whose spokesman was Lord John Russell, was practically solid for standing by its little Queen, it appeared. That night she attended a State Ball at Buckingham Palace, danced quadrilles with the visiting Hereditary Grand-Duke of Russia, later Alexander II, with the Prince of Orange, and with Lord Mulgrave, exchanged a smiling, trivial word or two with Melbourne, noticed Wellington and Peel looking "very much put out," and "left the ballroom at a ¼ past 3, much pleased, as my mind felt happy."

She had won. After a long session the Cabinet decided to remain in office and humour her. "Her Majesty's confidential servants," ran their communiqué, "are prepared to support Her Majesty in refusing to assent to the removal of the Ladies of her Household, which Her Majesty conceives to be contrary to usage, and which is repugnant to her feelings. . . ."

Usage! No wonder the little Queen was radiant, though Melbourne resumed office without much enthusiasm. "Nobody thinks I want to stay, do they? I have to think of the poor fellows who have to put down their broughams." A typical Melbournian *boutade*, and possibly sincere. The Cabinet's surrender to chivalry got a bad Press. The *Morning Post* snarled in its best Eatanswill manner that "the female tyrants of Buckingham Palace have again seized hold of the Royal Victim, whom they had released a moment from their foul and poisonous grasp." . . . A real poison-cloud, figuratively, was almost immediately to blot out the brilliance of the Royal triumph. Poor Lady Flora Hastings died of her tumour within two months of Melbourne's resumption of power, and a storm of vituperation broke over the Throne. Pamphlets of incredible scurrility (such as *The Palace Martyr* and *A Voice from the Grave of Lady Flora*

Hastings) flooded London. Though the Queen was not personally attacked, Baroness Lehzen came in for ferocious abuse as "a low-born foreign woman"—she was a highly respectable Hanoverian pastor's daughter—"of most forbidding aspect,"—her homely features were far from repulsive—directly responsible for Lady Flora's tragedy. Melbourne himself did not escape. The Court was plunged in dismay and foreboding, the Queen's growing popularity vanished, and the breach between Victoria and her Mama, which Wellington had been recently trying tactfully to heal, was widened; for the excitable Duchess had taken Lady Flora ostentatiously under her wing, and this dreadful affair was just one more bitterness added to what she considered a brimming cupful of her daughter's slights.

Sixty-one-year-old Lord M., it was noted afterwards, seemed to have aged palpably. The Hastings ordeal had shaken him. It is hard to believe he was not aware that a handsome and earnest young German princeling, now adding the final touches to his grooming for the Consortship, would shortly step into his place. In any case he was losing his zest for the routine: the daily office in Whitehall, the daily business in the House, when he had to be there, the daily instructional hours with the Queen, the evening Drawing Room, with its decorous ritual of conversation, round-games, music, and innocent boredom.

Melbourne was feeling distinctly tired. He had been heard at Holland House lately complaining of his health, though talking as urbanely as ever. His Government owed its lease of life to a Court squabble and could not stagger on indefinitely. Lord John Russell was beginning to come to the front, partly owing to his own abilities, partly to the fact that Melbourne had lately been spending more time at the Palace than in the House. As for Lord M.'s health, it was perhaps time that he took more care of it and did not eat so much (the Queen had commented in her diary on this). And if he was changing, so was she. Some of her first girlish freshness and eager response had gone. She was becoming harder, more intent on getting her own way; it was becoming less easy to restrain her, as half smart London knew. "By God, I'm at it morning, noon, and night!" Melbourne said wearily to Greville about this time, when Greville complimented him suavely on his skill as a brakesman.

As yet, the Queen was certainly envisaging no parting. In the early summer of 1839 she had noted in her diary:

Friday, 24th May.—This day I *go out of my* TEENS and become 20! It sounds so strange to me! I have much to be thankful for; and I feel I owe more to *two* people than I can ever repay! My dear Lehzen, and my dear excellent Lord Melbourne! I pray Heaven to preserve them in health and strength for *many, many* years to come, and that Lord Melbourne may remain at the Head of Affairs, not only for my own happiness and prosperity, but for that of the whole Country and of all Europe; and lastly, that I may become every day less unworthy of my high station!

A slight coolness between her and Uncle Leopold was in progress, following a recent note to Prussia by Palmerston, Foreign Secretary, hinting very strongly that Great Britain was disposed to back Holland rather than Belgium in the event of any Continental trouble. Uncle Leopold had taken recently to grumbling and touting for his niece's affection more than usual. He clearly saw the elegant shadow of Albert of Saxe-Coburg looming over his future as Victoria's most intimate mentor, as he had himself arranged. She really could not be too upset over Uncle Leopold. Prince Albert's foreign tour with indefatigable Baron Stockmar was over, and the Baron's final report to Uncle Leopold on his candidate was, it seemed, more than satisfactory; the Prince was high-minded, devoted to duty, and a foe to idle frivolity.[1] In September 1839 Albert arrived in England with his brother Ernest, as we have already noted, and conquered its

[1] Though the Prince did not lack a sense of humour. Several practical jokes attach to his adolescence—e.g. from the Royal Box in Coburg Opera House he once sprinkled the house with capsules of sulphuretted hydrogen, and at a Court ball he filled a lady's cloak-pockets with soft cheese. In later years he and the Queen would laugh heartily at a footman's tripping over a mat, or the quaint antics of her terrier.

Queen without difficulty. It could not be long before Dear Lord M. declined automatically into Poor Dear Lord M.

6

"Youth! Youth!" murmurs the indulgent Oxford wine-merchant in *Zuleika Dobson* as Lord Dorset's dinner-party across the street begins to get under way. So must Lord Melbourne's inner voice have murmured to him, rather sadly, as he discussed her marriage plans with the Queen in the autumn of 1839. "A very fine young man," Lord M. agreed. "Very good-looking." She wanted her Albert created a Field-Marshal, "just like Uncle," at once; anyhow, a Royal Highness. And Parliament must provide for him properly. Lord M. said he would mention it to his Cabinet. Victoria took his hand and said impulsively that he was *so* kind, *so* fatherly about all this.

One can imagine rather a wry smile on Lord M.'s lips. What are elderly charm, utter absorption, incessant devotion, indulgence, gaiety, finesse, knowledge of the Constitution and the world, and all the rest of it to the bright face of a popinjay of twenty-one? His weariness was patently increasing. At twenty-five past six one November afternoon he came to the Palace in "a strange costume, that is to say, light white and grey striped calico trousers, with very large shoes. I feared I had interrupted him in his sleep, which he wouldn't allow, but which I think *was* the case." Lord M.'s valet could doubtless have confirmed, if bribed, with private evidence of elderly testiness over the interrupted after-luncheon nap, elderly sighs at the dressing-table, elderly groans, while awaiting the carriage, at the winter dark, the cold, the daily grind, the overhanging sense of finality, and perhaps futility.

The Queen announced her engagement to the Privy Council. On her round left arm she wore a miniature of Prince Albert, set in diamonds. It would be very surprising not to read that Lord Melbourne's eyes were filled with tears, since Early

Victorian eyes filled with tears on every possible emotional occasion. All England's eyes were full of tears, but in the House the Tories were simultaneously behaving just like Radicals; not merely over vexed questions like the Prince's style and precedence, but over his annual allowance. What was his religion, they were asking to begin with? Was he a Papist? Certain Saxe-Coburgs had perverted, to use the official Victorian word, to Rome not long ago. Or was he, as was equally hinted, an infidel, like so many German Protestants, especially in Prussia? Stockmar having testified to Melbourne concerning the purity of Prince Albert's Lutheranism—a system practically indistinguishable in the Communion Service, he pointed out, from the usage of the Book of Common Prayer—the debates on the Prince's allowance proceeded, with a certain acrimony. Eventually the sum was cut from £50,000 a year, which the Government had requested, to £30,000.

If Prince Albert, "shocked and exasperated" (King Leopold), took this rebuff in due course with the philosophical reflection that not all the British, perhaps, were as enchanted by the Royal choice as Stockmar thought—he did not mind about the money —the little Queen and Uncle Leopold were both furious. At the same time, and despite her lyrical adoration of him, Victoria had already given her beloved clearly to understand which of them was to hold the reins. At her bidding he resignedly accepted an English secretary, English gentlemen-in-waiting. His future as a lonely, unpopular, heel-clicking foreigner occupying an honorary stool by the Throne—in the first gush of excitement Victoria had toyed with the idea of having him created Consort by Act of Parliament, till an anguished cry from Lord M., "For God's sake, Ma'am, let's hear no more of it!" dissuaded her— seemed fairly grim. We may reflect again that the Prince, by no means passionately smitten, was already feeling the snaffle. "You forget, my dearest love, that I am the Sovereign," Victoria had written to him after the mildest of arguments over their honeymoon plans.

To Uncle Leopold she observed, emphasising her recent full agreement with the Cabinet that "Albert should *not* be a Peer," that "the English are very jealous at the idea of Albert's having any political power, or meddling with affairs here—which I know from himself he will *not* do." One may judge that the matter had already been discussed with Albert thoroughly, and had been, perhaps, mainly a monologue. Gently but firmly the Beautiful and the Good was being shown his place, once and for all. The fact may have assuaged Lord M.'s feelings to some slight extent as he lounged on his sofa at the Palace, benevolently watching the affianced pair playing at Tact, Fox and Geese, or "that game of letters out of which you are to make words . . . great fun," or making Islay, the Queen's Scotch terrier, sit up to beg for Lord M.'s glasses, in his amusing way; that is, if Lord M. had not by this time dropped into snoring oblivion, as was becoming his wont.

During the marriage-ceremony at the Chapel Royal, St. James's, on Monday, February 10, 1840, Lord Melbourne in his stiff gala uniform, holding the Sword of State, was very much affected, the Queen noted, and continued so at the reception at Buckingham Palace, where she and Prince Albert drank a glass of wine with him. Just before the departure for the two-day honeymoon at Windsor he had ten minutes' light conversation with her, was teased about his smart coat, kissed her hand, and said, "God bless you, Ma'am" ("such a kind look!"). As the small, radiant figure in the dainty white bonnet trimmed with orange-blossom and the white-silk pelisse edged with swansdown drives away with Dearest Albert, handsome, open-faced, impeccably *sanglé* in his waisted frock-coat, stiffly doffing his beaver to the cheering multitude, one may picture Lord M. going a little creakingly and slowly, a little bent and moody, to his carriage. The Queen had reminded him gaily as they parted that he was to dine with them at Windsor in three days' time. It would never be the same any more. However affectionately and gradually, he was to be relegated to the background of Victoria's existence, and the process had begun that morning. As Melbourne smiled good day to the sniffling Lehzen on leaving the Palace, he may have reflected acidly that this powerful crone, with her ageing parrot-face and her neat moustache, her shrill perpetual chatter and her passion for caraway-seeds and her hold over the Queen, was now as superannuated as he (he was wrong). A nice pair of relics! Two battered old discarded Royal toys, fit only for the nursery cupboard at Kensington Palace. . . .

Lord Melbourne was certainly feeling jaded. There is no record, so far as I know, of his deriving the faintest amusement, at the beginning of this year 1840, from the prosaic romance (highly diverting to Society) of two elderly turtle-doves styled by the irreverent Creevey "old Sussex and Ciss Buggin," or, more briefly, "Suss and Ciss." At the age of sixty-seven Augustus Duke of Sussex, one of the Queen's more seemly, intelligent, and existent uncles, had provided "dear little Vic"—Creevey again—and her Minister with a nice pair of headaches on the very eve of the wedding. The Duke had twice defied the Royal Marriage Act (12 Geo. III, c. 11) by marrying, without the Privy Council's permission, Lady Augusta Murray and, after her death in 1830, Lady Cecilia Buggin, née Gore, who had lately changed her un-musical widowed surname by Royal licence to Underwood. Two complicated questions now preoccupied the Queen; firstly, whether Lady Cecilia could possibly be recognised at Court, and secondly, whether the Duke's precedence—as the eldest surviving son of George III he came immediately after the Queen—could be transferred to Dearest Albert.

The romance of Suss and Ciss seems to have bored Melbourne not a little, though he liked the Duke, a favourite of all the Whigs. On April 1 the Queen and he compromised on the first question. Lady Cecilia was gazetted Duchess of Inverness, one of her husband's titles, without Royal rank or precedence, though she took care to insist on both outside the Court. The Duke solved the second question by agreement. The faint comedy atmosphere overhanging the business was increased by a *Times* correspondence, started in April by an indignant gentleman signing himself "A TRUE CONSERVATIVE AND A LOVER OF JUSTICE" and demanding why the Duchess of Inverness had not been created Duchess of Sussex. The dash of old-time Regency devil-may-care blending in this imbroglio with the hopeless Victorian respectability of the parties would have amused Melbourne considerably, I think, in earlier years, and perhaps inspired a *mot* or two for private circulation at Brooks's. But now he was feeling his age, and he perceived his usefulness coming to an end. And his damned valet was waking him too damned soon after luncheon. . . . Well, the Palace was a home for him yet, superannuated or not.

It would be unfair to assume that the Palace had practically replaced the House in the Prime Minister's cosmos. Though Lord John Russell was rapidly displacing him as a public figure, Melbourne was constantly on duty and could take the credit for pushing through Rowland Hill's penny-post innovation in 1839, as well as an Elementary Education Bill to which the Established Church, having almost a monopoly of what elementary schools there were, had shown some antagonism. The Government had recently to some extent been reshuffled, with Russell taking the Colonies, and strengthened by the inclusion of the Whig historian and bravo, Macaulay, as Secretary for War ; so far as a gentle cynic like Melbourne could deem his side strengthened by a man with Macaulay's naïve faith in the divine mission of Whiggery. Macaulay's noted oratory was an asset, but Melbourne's Government was plainly on its last legs, and Melbourne himself was clinging to office chiefly, as once before, in order not to let his friends down.

Rejoining the Royal pair at Windsor after the honeymoon, he perceived Prince Albert to be brooding over his position; feeling acutely lonely, finding Victoria's "dearest Angel" a cipher in his own household, whereas Lehzen the insufferable was daily consulted by the Queen about everything domestic, superintending the Privy Purse and even dealing with the Queen's private correspondence. The Prince's evening chess already bored him unspeakably. He yearned to invite approved literary and scientific celebrities to Court and to recreate the Weimar of Goethe's time, but the Queen disliked and feared the intelligentsia. Even the world-famous Dickens was not received at Buckingham Palace till 1870, the year in which the Queen was prevailed on to offer him a baronetcy, the year of his death; on the occasion of which reception she was able, as a fellow-author, to present him with an inscribed copy of *Leaves from the Journal of Our Life in the Highlands* in exchange for a richly bound set of Mr. Dickens's complete works. She did not, as Melbourne tactfully puts it, "like conversation to be going on in which she could not take her fair share," and no doubt she shared the customary public illusions concerning the nature of the conversation of literary men, its subtlety, loftiness, and brilliance. Melbourne adds, quite rightly, that Victoria was "too open and candid to pretend to more knowledge than she possessed," which makes one more reason for respecting her.

On June 10, 1840, a lunatic fired a pistol at her as she was driving with her husband past the Green Park. The little Queen's steely courage—she was four months gone with child—aroused enthusiastic national admiration and set British sentiment flowing Crownwards once more. A month later Melbourne was able to pilot through Parliament a Bill appointing the Consort Regent in the event of Victoria's death before her heir attained the age of eighteen; a concession which raised the Consort's spirits to some extent.

Lord M. had taken a sincere liking to his supplanter, a feeling mingled with genuine pity for the Prince's discontent, futility, and frustration. Like Queen Anne's oafish mate from Scandinavia a century and half earlier, Victoria's idol was not proving easy to put across, as purists say nowadays. Though he did not solve his conversational problems, like Prince George of Denmark, by attaining a permanent and almost Buddhistic state of glassy alcoholic contemplation, Prince Albert, like his predecessor, had a formidable foreign accent and a limited vocabulary. His manner was rigid and frigid, his conversation (unlike Matthew Arnold's) wholly serious, his gestures stiff. He was morbidly conscious of being a mere appendage, to use a no more realistic word, to the British Throne, and his passion for virtue was demanding an impossibly high standard in his personal suite. "This damned morality will ruin everything," Melbourne is reported as growling in a testy moment. But he esteemed the Prince's considerable qualities justly, and praised them to the Queen. To Baron Stockmar, now hovering more pervasively than ever—the Consort's *éminence grise*, as Lehzen was the Queen's—Melbourne still took no dislike, oddly enough, though he knew that Stockmar was indefatigably coaching the Prince for power and inoculating him with ambition, amply and quite admirably fulfilled.

Perhaps Lord M. had now ceased to care very much about anything. Our infamous Opium War with China seemed to be ending successfully. There had been a crisis with France in 1839–40 over a revolt against the Sultan of Turkey and an invasion of Syria by what Melbourne called "that old ruffian" Mehemet Ali, Pasha of Egypt, backed by Thiers; but the jaunty Palmerston had handled it less recklessly than other crises. Louis-Philippe had dismissed the bellicose Thiers, France had fumed and calmed down before an Anglo-Prusso-Russo-Austrian coalition, and a British fleet had burned Acre and Beirut and brought about the fall of the Egyptian swashbuckler and a wave of Anglophobia across the Channel. At home agitation against the protectionist Corn Laws was increasing.[1] Melbourne was now inclined very reluctantly to favour more moderate duties, though not repeal, and was facing much criticism for changing his mind.

It was the Corn Laws which brought Melbourne's Government down at last on August 28, 1841, when Peel took over. In

[1] The Corn Laws of 1828 established a "sliding-scale" whereby, if British wheat was selling at (say) 62s. a quarter, a duty of 24s. 8d. a quarter was imposed on imported corn. If the price of wheat reached 73s. a quarter, or famine-price, the duty on imported corn fell to 1s. a quarter. Radicals damned the whole system.

one of his last speeches Melbourne characteristically pointed out
that if there was any disappointment in the country over Whig
measures during the past six years, "it does not arise from the
vicious principle or the ill working of those measures themselves, but from the wild, unfounded, and exaggerated expectations which were indulged in and anticipated." To which the
tartest of footnotes would seem to be the verse of Winthrop
Mackworth Praed (*d.* 1839) on the policy of the Melbourne
Ministry:

> "*To promise, pause, prepare, postpone,*
> *And end by letting things alone;*
> *In short, to earn the people's pay*
> *By doing nothing every day.*"

But even Praed could not accuse Melbourne, who had six
Acts to his credit, of being a visionary. He had, indeed, a great
horror of that species, and thought the Utopian Messiah Robert
Owen a perfect fool and a pedlar of moonshine.[1] Perhaps he had
never cared for dreamers to any extent since Byron's time.

He bethought himself now of assisting the awkward Peel with
advice on handling the Queen, and asked Greville to pass it on.
"She is not conceited; she is aware there are many things she
cannot understand, and she likes to have them explained to her—
elementarily, not at length and in detail, but shortly and clearly.
Neither does she like long audiences. I have never stayed with
her a long time." To the Queen likewise her retiring Mentor
addressed a few tactful words, particularly on making up her mind
fully before a decision. She was beginning to shiver, however
intermittently, over the approaching hour of inevitable parting;
partly because of her enduring affection for Lord M., partly
because she still had that violent dislike and dread of Peel which
was to merge on closer acquaintance into the warmest of friend-

---

[1] Though in a freakish mood he presented the eminent Socialist at Court
in 1839, defending himself by saying that Owen, who was going abroad, had
asked to be presented, as an asset on the Continent; "and in order to get rid
of him, I said yes."

ships. The sun and centre of her existence was Dearest Albert, but she was determined, as she told Peel when he arrived for his audience, never to break off her correspondence with her dear Lord Melbourne.

Peel agreed. It was not precisely what a new Prime Minister would have suggested, but he agreed. Lord M. took his official leave of the Queen in due course. She was "dreadfully affected" for some time afterwards. But if she could no longer have his daily visits, she had his letters, which continued in a steady stream. *Absolute confidence* in Sir Robert Peel, wrote Lord M., was essential; yet before long Peel began to note opinions and judgments expressed by the Queen which had an unfamiliar, or rather a familiar, ring. This kind of thing could not go on, and Peel took steps. Stockmar was brought in to remonstrate, through an emissary, Anson, with Lord Melbourne for making a speech in the Lords identifying himself with the Opposition while still the Queen's confidant. Lord M.'s urbanity suddenly broke down and he swore violently. "I only spoke on the defensive, which Ripon's speech rendered quite necessary! I cannot be expected to give up my position in the country! Neither do I think it to the Queen's interest that I should!" But he could not deny that his present correspondence with Her Majesty was irregular, and unfair to Peel. Stockmar, always the man for order, urged that after the Queen's next confinement, now approaching, he should drop it. Melbourne agreed and duly informed the Queen, who was far from amused. A couple of weeks after the birth of Albert Edward, later Edward VII (November 9, 1841), his letters were resumed. Again Stockmar protested, and got no reply. The letters continued, but Lord M. ceased by degrees to touch on current politics and diverged into topics of a harmless kind: the weather, Shakespeare, and the musical glasses.

7

His retirement—though he reappeared to lead the Opposition in the Lords, with fluctuating interest and energy—restored him to his clubs, his library, and his friends, who were many, including a little circle of affectionate intimates like his brother, Lord Beauvale, and Lord Hatherton, and (till her death in 1845) Lady Holland, and Lady Palmerston, and the "lounging, pert, and voluble" Palmerston himself, whose hair-raising tight-rope performances as Foreign Secretary were to inspire the German tribute:

> *"Hat der Teufel einen Sohn,*
> *So ist er sicher Palmerston;"*[1]

and of whom Rothschild was to remark drily that he had "the inconvenient gift of causing every stock in Europe to fall without consulting us."

Of one group of old friends Melbourne had seemingly had enough, save in small doses. He was tired of the brilliant self-conscious circle at Holland House, much as he esteemed its dictatorial hostess; though on one occasion, being ordered by Lady Holland to change his seat at table, Melbourne had walked out on the spot with the words "I'll be damned if I'll dine with you at all." To Lord John Russell he wrote in September 1840, rather grumpily: "The talking at Holland House is irremediable. They can't help it, and they are not themselves aware how much they talk."

Such a sidelight on those illustrious chatterboxes is interesting, even if the boredom of a weary ageing man may have blunted his appreciation of their performances. The great days of Holland House were certainly over by this time; the days when the omniscient, interminable Macaulay ("Macaulay, you talk too much!" Lady Holland had once snapped), the ever-sparkling Sydney Smith, the poetic Rogers, the fascinating Byron, and such other distinguished guests, among a score, as Nelson, Talleyrand, Palmerston, Thiers, Scott, Luttrell, and Moore, won Lady Holland's salon a European reputation. A comparatively recent

---

[1] "If the Devil has a son,
He must resemble Palmerston."

débutant, young Mr. Charles Dickens, was noting this change from 1840 onwards. The first-floor apartments where the wits and the great (Whigs exclusively) assembled on Saturday nights were now dark and vacant. Macaulay was becoming a political bore, Sydney Smith in his seventies was crippled with gout, Lady Holland herself was often abstracted and depressed, though still levying tribute on her landowning guests for game and venison. Mortality, in fact, was hovering over what Mr. Jorrocks's sporting friend, Mr. Bowker, would call the Premier Wags, and Melbourne was sensitive to atmosphere. Exhibitionist and competitive talking moreover had never greatly amused him. I doubt if his shade haunts the gaunt and ruined shell of Holland House to any extent to-day.

A close friend and, when out of town, correspondent of his decline was the still-charming Mrs. Caroline Norton, whose co-respondent he had been in 1836, and whose volumes of poetry—especially *The Dream* (1840) and *Aunt Carry's Ballads*, a children's book—were found in every British middle-class home. One of her poems, now embedded in *The Oxford Book of English Verse*, had a particular vogue among tender hearts:

> *"I do not love thee!—no! I do not love thee!*
> *And yet when thou art absent I am sad!*
> *And envy e'en the bright blue sky above thee,*
> *Whose quiet stars may see thee and be glad. . . ."*

Mrs. Norton's outcry against child-labour, *A Voice from the Factories*, and her later connection with the Woman Movement were not quite so popular with the bourgeoisie. Yet the comfortable middle-class of this period was not so universally materialistic and selfish as Melbourne deemed. When young Mr. Ruskin, travelling in Switzerland with his valet and his courier in 1845, wrote home to his father, the wealthy City merchant, after contemplating the *Alpenglüh* at Chamonix and finishing an excellent *soufflé* and a half-bottle of Sillery, remarking how sad he felt at the thought that "so few are capable of having such enjoyments," Ruskin meant it, as he later tried to prove in practice. The hearts of many of Mrs. Norton's large public were equally sound. George Meredith had yet to add her as Diana of the Crossways to his gallery of somewhat overpowering heroines. I believe dogged Meredithians rank Diana even above Clara of *The Egoist*.

A mild paralytic stroke visited Melbourne in October 1842. It did not disable him, but it affected the elegance of his gait and the brightness of his eye, and he grew more and more addicted to long, unaccustomed silences, though he could still be heard communing with himself on his settee at Brooks's, a habit of his. Lounging in the Carlton Club windows at their traditional pastime (as the middle-classes then firmly believed) of tearing women's reputations to shreds, the Tories with pitying eyebrows watched him straighten up on approaching and strive to recapture his old nonchalant saunter, as Lord Hatherton once saw him. Reclining in the windows of the Athenæum, setting the populace (as to-day) a good example but taking no active interest in its affairs, like the saints of the Low Church Heaven, a more dignified type of club-member watched Melbourne pass from the Reform with dragging step towards Whitehall and the House of Lords, and turned with a sigh to order tea and toasted muffins. A witty *Punch* cartoon on his retirement in 1841, showing him gazing despondently at a portrait of himself at his peak, with Wolsey's plaint under it—"Farewell, a long farewell," etc. —had already conveyed to the vast majority of clubmen the fact that their late Prime Minister was no more the public figure he once had been, though doubtless *Punch's* effort involved some tedious explanations at the United Service Club. And now, towards 1845, it was plain that his faculties were beginning to fail. A pathetic obsession that he was still of use to the country and the Queen, and might be called back to office at any moment, still persisted. Her Majesty continued to write to him at intervals; kind, chatty letters, eagerly looked for.

BUCKINGHAM PALACE,
3rd April, 1845.

The Queen had intended to have written to Lord Melbourne from Osborne to thank him for his last note of the 19th, but we were so occupied, and so delighted with *our new* and really delightful *home*, that she had hardly time for anything; besides which the weather was so beautiful, that we were out almost all day. . . .

The sea of the Isle of Wight (adds the Queen) is so blue and calm that the Prince has compared it to Naples. Portsmouth and Spithead are close at hand, which will please the Navy. The children are all well; the Queen has just had a lithograph made from a little drawing by herself of the three eldest, which she will send Lord Melbourne with some eau-de-Cologne. Fanny and Lord Jocelyn dined last night. The Queen hopes Lord Melbourne is enjoying the fine weather, and concludes with the Prince's kind remembrance.

Longer letters came to her in reply; all, like hers, in the third person, beginning with the invariable formula "Lord Melbourne presents his humble duty to your Majesty, and thanks your Majesty very much for the letter of," etc., etc., and retailing much the same kind of chit-chat. Even to less august correspondents Melbourne was never a letter-writer in the showy tradition of a Swift, a Walpole, or a Lamb, and very little of his whimsicality gets into what correspondence of his I have read, which deals mainly with State business and is sober to a degree. In a letter to Lord John Russell in 1841 on the Civil List a glint of the essential Melbourne is perceived, perhaps:

The list of applications which I have comprises Mrs. James, widow of the writer of the Naval History; Leigh Hunt, distinguished writer of seditious and treasonable libels; Colonel Napier, historian of the war in Spain, conceited and dogmatic Radical and grandson of a duke; Mr. Cary, translator of Dante, madman;

Sheridan Knowles, man of great genius, but not old nor poor enough for a pension. Say what you think ought to be done. . . .

And even more in another letter to Lord John, in the same year:

Just a hint that Plumridge seems to me to be rather an ass. What business had he to second that old fool Burdett's motion about Warner?

He cannot have been greatly cheered by the Queen's last (published) letter, in the March before his death; a perturbed missive, bewailing the latest revolution in France—"the rabble armed—keeping the Government in awe—failures in all directions, and nothing but ruin and misery!" It was nevertheless still an assurance of her care and affection. He could hardly expect very much now that her public duties, her husband, and her regularly expanding nursery were absorbing all her considerable energies. His old co-favourite, Baroness Lehzen, had departed in a gale of tears in 1842 for her distant Hanoverian home-town of Bückeburg, where she lived till 1870, a shrivelled, virtuous old witch out of *Grimm's Fairy Tales*, surrounded, like the traditional retired Victorian housekeeper, by portraits of her late mistress of every shape and size. With Lehzen also the dutiful Queen kept up a correspondence till the end. "She had devoted her life to me," runs Victoria's obituary entry, "from my fifth to my eighteenth year, with the most wonderful self-abnegation, never even taking one day's leave. After I came to the throne she got to be rather trying, and especially so after my marriage, but never from any evil intention. . . ."

Of poor Lord M. the Queen had long since confided to her diary: "The dream is *past*." Yet he lingered on, talking volubly between his silences, embarrassing Palmerston's dinner-guests one night by describing how he had lain awake half the night before, deciding what advice he would give Her Majesty if the Government went out. In July 1846 Lord John Russell, on becoming Prime Minister, had the delicate task of reminding him that his health prevented his taking office. The old man sighed and agreed. "You have judged very rightly and kindly in making me no offer." Two months earlier there had been a final flare-up, as of a dying candle, of his political activity. As a conclave of Whig noblemen, summoned by Lord John at Lansdowne House, sat debating Peel's decision to repeal the Corn Laws at last, the bent and shuffling figure of Lord Melbourne was shown into the room, to the surprise of all. He listened for some time to the discussion, then gave his opinion in a quavering voice. "My lords, it's a damned thing, but Peel has done it, and the consequences are that you'll all have to vote for it." Which they did.

About a year before his death Melbourne discovered that he was in financial straits. The Queen at once lent him a considerable sum, which his heir subsequently repaid. In the autumn of 1848 one of the London newspapers published (in the public interest) a letter of the troublous Reform Bill period written by Home Secretary Melbourne's private secretary, the "vulgar and impudent" Young, to Colonel Napier, discussing aspects of the situation in facetious terms. Its publication proved harmless enough, but poor old exhausted Melbourne took it hard and, according to Greville, never recovered from the shock.

His last public appearance had been made on the 25th of the previous May, when he voted in the Lords on the Jewish Disabilities Bill. His handwriting was now quite illegible. On November 21 Queen Victoria mentioned, half-way in a letter to Uncle Leopold: "You will grieve to hear that our good, dear old friend Melbourne is dying. . . ." The sad event brought the Queen many recollections, "though, God knows!" she added, "I never wish that time back again." She had certainly grown up.

Lord Melbourne died at Brocket Hall on November 24, 1848, at the age of sixty-nine, and his brother succeeded to the title, which became extinct five years later. "Though not a *firm* Minister," wrote the Queen in her diary, "he was a noble, kindhearted, generous being." What is now the city of Melbourne on the Yarra River in Victoria, Australia, was named after him in 1835.

8

Lord Melbourne stands somewhat above the other three Royal Favourites adorning these pages by natural reason of superior intellectual gifts and deportment. Moreover he did not rise to power, as they did, by amorous intrigue, though I have no doubt any smart psycho-analyst could speedily discover a buried sexual element of some kind in his blameless paternal affection for the young Queen; possibly a Cenci-complex.

Such pokings in the Freudian garbage-heap need not concern us. What is of final interest in Melbourne's technique is that it died with him. Disraeli, as we have briefly noted, employed a quite different method, and the enigmatic John Brown, the Highland gillie, whose eerie influence over Queen Victoria from the 1850's onwards is so remarkable, a different one still; a gruff, rugged, hairy, almost bullying technique, astonishingly assisted by that habit of copious weeping, tottering, and occasionally falling down which, as Miss Sitwell has engagingly observed, the cynical were wont to attribute to "causes other than grief."[1] Perhaps the secret of Good Brown is somehow connected with that *baroquismo* which we shall encounter in the career of Don Manuel Godoy, though Brown certainly increased his claim on the Queen's affections by saving her from the youth with the unloaded pistol in February 1872.

The extent to which Melbourne employed and enjoyed his charm consciously and deliberately is not known, but may be readily conjectured. Every virtuoso of his kind, like every good actor, has a varying degree of narcissism in his nature, and like Oscar Wilde is bound sooner or later to fall in love with his golden voice and his powers of enchantment. When the charmer

[1] Accurately, as appears from an excellent monograph (*Queen Victoria's John Brown*, by E. E. P. Tisdall, 1938).

is an elderly man of the world and the charmed a young and impressionable girl, and a Queen to boot, it must be impossible to avoid a certain complacency in one's hours of private meditation. Lord M. had of course no opportunity of viewing himself in the flattering mirror of Her Majesty's diaries. The mellow cynicism of a lifetime would probably have protected him from over-conceit on contemplating this bequest to posterity—or would it? He was only human.

One more essential factor in his success, distinguishing him also from the other Favourites in this book, may be noted. He had no serious rivals, for Stockmar kept strictly to his consultant post and the influence of Lehzen was that of the dear old fussy nursery-governess, operating in a totally different sphere of the Queen's existence. No jealous courtier tried to oust Lord M. from his place. Nobody accused him of any malpractice or misdemeanour, still less any poison-plot. Even the raucous Tory Press of the period never attacked him *as a favourite*, except on the occasion of the Hastings scandal, when it bespattered the Queen's entourage with mud quite impartially. His influence over her was recognised as beneficial and irreproachable and even invaluable, and is so still. For this reason Melbourne may be said to have missed one of the keenest pleasures of a Royal Favourite's career, namely the pleasure of detecting and checkmating the moves of the envious and the hate-filled, the need for perpetual alertness, sharp wits, a smiling mask, and a ready tongue.

No doubt Melbourne would have welcomed this necessity with relief more than once as he drove sleepily home after a more than usually leaden evening in the Drawing Room of Buckingham Palace. No other dashing member of Brooks's could have endured this part of Melbourne's duty one-hundredth as long. Perhaps his more serious-minded fellow-members of the Reform, where the classic atmosphere of Caracalla's Baths is even to-day strongly impregnated with a flavour of Liberal improvement and high endeavour, like the ghosts of dead Gladstonian breakfasts, would have found the nightly Palace routine more bearable. It is on record that in the Queen's presence Melbourne uttered a "damn" on only one occasion, in his last years, at the Windsor dinner-table, and on the topic of the repeal of the Corn Laws. "Ma'am, it's a damned dishonest Act!" ejaculated the old man. The Queen, who was to freeze genial Mr. Ambassador Choate from the United States with a single glance fifty years hence for merely remarking "Your daughter's looking fine to-night, Ma'am," dismissed this awful impropriety with an indulgent laugh, and only when poor dear Lord M. persisted in repeating it did she beg him to say no more on the subject. For a man whose speech was normally (as the *Dictionary of National Biography* observes with shrinking delicacy) "interlarded with oaths," the effort of restraint in the Royal presence must have been often heroic.

One final observation. In her youth the Queen was a Whig by heredity, training, and inclination, making Melbourne's initial work easy. Had he had to deal with her a few years after her marriage, when she became a Free Trader because Dearest Albert was a Free Trader, those hours of instruction would not have proceeded so smoothly, perhaps. The cards were stacked for him perfectly from the beginning, and as the world goes, Melbourne had little to complain of once the last disagreeable echoes of the Norton case had died away.

As the world goes. . . . The glittering Duc de Grammont in Rostand's play expresses the after-taste of renown quite adequately:

> "*Voyez-vous, lorsqu' on a trop réussi sa vie,*
> *On sent—n'ayant rien fait, mon Dieu, de vraiment mal!—*
> *Mille petits dégoûts de soi, dont le total*
> *Ne fait pas un remords, mais une gêne obscure.* . . ."[1]

[1] "Don't you see, when one has made too great a success of one's life, one feels—though, God knows, one has done nothing really bad—a thousand tiny self-disgusts; not amounting to remorse, but to an obscure unease..." (*Cyrano de Bergerac*, Act V, Scene 2).

This *gêne obscure* Lord M. certainly knew in his dragging last days at Brocket Hall, brooding over Cicero's *De Senectute* or muttering, as he was more than once heard to do, some lines from *Samson Agonistes*:

> *"So much I feel my genial spirits droop,*
> *My hopes all flat; nature within me seems*
> *In all her functions weary of herself,*
> *My race of glory run, and race of shame,*
> *And I shall shortly be with them that rest. . . ."*

He was not a student of Thomas à Kempis, as we have noted.

III

GODOY

"He made the Court of Madrid one of those places to which
the indignant muse of Juvenal conducts the mother of Britan-
nicus."
(BOURRIENNE, *Memoirs of Napoleon*.)

"My sole enjoyment, my only pleasure was to do good, to
perform something useful or honourable for my native land."
(GODOY, *Memoirs*.)

I

IN a shabby room up four flights of stairs behind the Passage
de l'Opéra, Paris, in the year 1835, a tall old exiled Spaniard
with ironic, humorous eyes, a smile of great charm, and the
remains of striking comeliness finished dictating, to a cleric of
his acquaintance, his long-deferred reply to the most furiously
protracted chorus of loathing any fallen statesman has ever had
to endure, perhaps.

To children playing in the Tuileries Gardens the old man was
known, with some affection, as "Monsieur Manuel"; to the rest
of Europe—so far as any still remembered him, apart from Lord
Holland—as Don Manuel Godoy, Prince of the Peace, Grandee
of Spain, Duke of La Alcudia, ex-Prime Minister, ex-Captain-
General, ex-Grand Admiral, a Queen's paramour, a King's
favourite, a daring adversary of Napoleon (who once called him
a genius), and, fifty years before, the most powerful and possibly
the richest man in Spain; now a pensioner on Louis-Philippe's
charity at 6,000 francs a year, a fate so hard and so picturesque
that he might almost have deserved it.

That Godoy by no means deserved his fate by the world's
standards—and what more melancholy than the fall of a once-
gorgeous rocket which continues to fizzle on for half a century in

loneliness and oblivion to its end?—is now claimed by many. But he has his enemies still.[1] Spanish enmity, like Spanish friendship, love, piety, and impiety, is ardent, mystical, and profound, deriving directly, as has been often remarked, from the Roman Africa of St. Augustine and St. Cyprian; and enmity from one quarter or another enveloped Godoy practically without a break from his scandalous rise to power in 1792 to the day of his death in 1851, and does so to-day. His career covers sixteen years, his exile forty-eight; and since the roots of his enduring unpopularity are undoubtedly in the manner in which his fortunes began, we may profitably examine this point immediately.

Adultery as the first step to success, though not unusual, is not essential even to-day; still less such of its allied industries as enabled handsome young John Churchill, for example, to lay the foundation of the Marlborough fortunes. In the case of Don Manuel Godoy, several factors were against his securing public approval. The *ménage à trois* in which a husband and his wife's lover become dear lifelong friends is a hackneyed theme of comedy; but the Spaniard is sensitive on the point of honour, and the Queen was already sufficiently notorious. However amusing such an arrangement in the House of Bourbon might seem to liberal wits in the Madrid chocolate-houses, the Godoy-Maria Luisa-Carlos IV triangle ceased to amuse the laxest Spaniards when it became the jest of Europe; and this notwithstanding a general relaxation of morals and manners in Spain, as elsewhere, at this period, labelled by Eugenio d'Ors "baroquism." It happened on the wrong side of the Pyrenees.

In addition, Godoy was a needy provincial, a nobody, sprung from that impoverished rustic-noble stock which is a natural feature of the Spanish as of the Highland-Scottish scene. As his native place was Badajoz in Estremadura, the province of pig-breeders, he was naturally nicknamed El Choricero, the Pork-Butcher, all his life. His serenely handsome presence was a

[1] And he gets very poor marks from the dons of the *Encyclopaedia Britannica*.

continual irritant, not only to less decorative politicians and goaded rivals around him but to the nation at large.

Spain at this period was weary and easily irritated. *Baroquismo* is, among other things, that reaction which attacks imperial nations fatigued by sustained spiritual and physical effort. Greece, Rome, Byzantium, France, and more recently Great Britain have all experienced it. Having discovered, evangelised, colonised, and exploited so much of the New World with such superb vigour during the fifteenth, sixteenth, and part of the seventeenth centuries, Spain had begun the eighteenth by being dragged by the French Bourbon into the War of the Spanish Succession, which lasted thirteen years and deprived her of Gibraltar, Minorca, and the Spanish dominions in Flanders and Italy. For such losses the subjection to the Spanish Crown of the turbulent Catalans and Aragonese by Felipe V was hardly a recompense. Two unprofitable adventures in the 1730's, due to the beldame Isabella Farnese of Parma, Felipe's consort, failed to recover Gibraltar, Sardinia, and Sicily, and lost Spain a naval force off Cape Passaro.

Thirteen years of ensuing peace and prosperity under Ferdinand IV had been followed by an operational alliance (1778) made by the popular dictator Carlos III with France in support of Britain's rebellious American colonies. Having recovered Minorca and Florida and stamped out Algerian piracy, Spain in the 1780–90's sinks, as it were, into temporary torpor, wrapping herself in her cloak behind the wall of the Pyrenees and brooding over dead fires. The dominion of the seas—the Armada fiasco of 1588 was of course far from being the disaster to Spanish imperial arms and pride that British schoolboys are induced to believe— had passed long since to England, the dominion of diplomacy to France. The treasure of New Spain had been frittered away with the lives of Spaniards, wrote the historian José Cadalso in the 1790's, in ventures perfectly alien to Spanish interests. Thanks to Cardinal Richelieu, the old Spanish dream of a strong, re-united Catholic Europe had vanished, and with it had gone by degrees the old high-minded austerity of Spanish manners, to be succeeded among the leisured classes by languor, scepticism genuine or affected, a craving for amusement, and a general feeling that Heaven had abandoned its favourites. The day of *gesta Dei per Hispanos* was done.

In the eyes of Europe during most of this century Spain is a sphinx walled up. To that long, indefatigable procession of British nobility and gentry making the Grand Tour—as to all Englishmen, save Beckford and Twiss, before the advent of the gorgeous liar Don Jorge Borrow—the Peninsula was as unthinkable as Tibet for travel purposes, and duly avoided; even by the energetic Archdeacon Coxe, who travelled so widely and disapproved of so much. It is therefore tempting to assume for the whole of Spain at this period the atmosphere and pulse-beat of that remote little Andalusian cathedral-city in which Alarcón places his delightful comedy, later to inspire Picasso and De Falla, of *The Three-Cornered Hat*, set in the Godoy period; a little city so devout, drowsy, and sedate that even the perpetual bells seem waking from and returning to siesta, from prime to compline. The temptation must be firmly resisted. In every Spanish city of any size from Madrid downwards there were clots or groups of what we should call to-day the Left intelligentsia, enthusiastically Voltairean and natural propagandists for the French philosophers and revolutionaries. The province of Biscay in particular, notes Salcedo Ruíz, was a hotbed of Encyclopædism and irreligion which the young of the wealthy merchant-families of Santander imbibed from education abroad.[1] In some of the religious Orders—overcrowded, as Godoy remarks, and not infrequently by men with little or no vocation—"liberal" tendencies were noted also. In the Inquisition itself there were active infidels like Llorente. It must be added that the outbreak of the Revolution and the Terror sobered many Spanish hotheads down and altered their views. The immense majority of Spaniards of every class were fiercely hostile to Jacobinism at all times, despite the

[1] *La Época de Goya*, III, iv.

Jacobin agents who swarmed in the Peninsula from 1789 onwards, as throughout Europe.

On the throne during the period we are about to contemplate is the stout, long-nosed, lethargic, dull, but by no means imbecile or uncourageous Bourbon, Carlos IV. His much-younger wife, Maria Luisa of Parma, unbeautiful but vital, a collector of cats, jewels, and young men, is a byword for roving amours. The rigid monotony of the Court is mitigated by the Spanish aristocracy in a myriad frivolities. No more extravagantly wayward great lady than Maria del Pílar Teresa Cayetana, thirteenth Duchess of Alba, treads the eighteenth-century stage, and no imperious great lady (her principal enemy being the Queen, and to a lesser extent Godoy) more democratic in her waywardness; for the distinctive mark of Baroquism in the latter half of this century is that curious semi-exhibitionist, semi-expiatory, quasi-Dostoievskeian craving on the nobility's part to share the companionship, the caprices, and even the costume of the proletariat. Marie-Antoinette's dairy at Trianon and the Prince Regent's hobnobbings with the riffraff of the London sporting world are less violent manifestations of this, no doubt. Godoy has been credited with reducing the *baroquismo* of the aristocracy—who detested him—to seemly standards. "African ardour," observes his French apologist Colonel d'Esmenard grimly, "was confined by him within the limits of civilised gallantry." Retired military men of field-rank are notoriously puritanical. The Colonel's opinion (1835) is deemed romantic by the best authorities.

Over the Church in Spain reigns a slumbrous peace, with an undersong, as it were, of plump canons droning the seven daily Offices in the cool dusk of vast, gold-encrusted choirs, and the antiphonal rise and fall of the voices of doctors of philosophy in echoing transepts, engaged in those formal disputations, *oposiciónes*, which Spaniards love. The religious Orders, overcrowded by every middle-class family's desire, as Godoy says, "to see at least one of its children a theologian or a lawyer," are responsible for a large amount of the cultural achievements cited in the

Godoy

Memoirs as a proof of Godoy's munificent patronage of letters, arts, and sciences. The Inquisition lingers on as the State department it had always been, carrying on its traditional defensive functions; picturesque, bureaucratic, obsolete in all philosophical eyes, active against public enemies of religion and morals, hampered or curbed equally by antagonists in power like Roda, Godoy (to some extent), and Urquijo, and by enemies of the Faith in its own bosom; to the Left intelligentsia a standing exasperation, to the vast majority of Spaniards of every degree still the *muro de la Iglesia, columna de la Verdad* of Fray Luis de Granada's panegyric. Less popular with the average Spaniard at this period is the monstrous plague of lawyers which infests the land. Spain is overrun, in Godoy's words, by "a swarm of attorneys, notaries, registrars, special pleaders, and officers of justice, with a multitude of inferior agents and solicitors aspiring in their turn to preferment; unproductive consumers living at the public's expense." Great landed and inherited wealth co-exists with great poverty, and the absence of any authoritative encouragement for agriculture and commerce makes life grindingly hard for the peasantry and the lower classes; without, however, extinguishing the national spirit. Though Catalonia makes no separatist trouble and Valencia will rise in 1802 in defence of its traditional exemption from militia-service, the leap of all Spain to arms against the French invader with historic fervour and ferocity, confounding all the prophets, will show Europe a few years hence that it is never safe to presume with the Spaniard.

Such, lightly sketched, is the background of Godoy, which the reader may fill in further, at pleasure, with towering snow-capped sierras and purple vineyards, cork-forests and orange-groves and vast brooding mauve-tawny plains; with tall and splendid Gothic and Romanesque cathedrals, ablaze with gilding, and blue-tiled Moorish palaces musical in the noonday heat with fountains; with bullfights and processions, monks and contrabandistas, alcaldes and alguazils, gipsies and bandits, *majos* and *majas*, and in fact all the vibrant company painted and etched by

Goya, whose portraits of Godoy, Maria Luisa, and Don Carlos are hardly less vital and arresting than those of her Grace of Alba, or the Conde de Fernan Nuñez, or the Lady in the Yellow Scarf, or the Water-Girl, or the redoubtable guerrilla El Empecinado—"The Turbulent One"—or the holidaying Madrilene crowd in the Pradera de San Isidro.

To gain some idea of the mental processes of this vivid humanity is less easy for the average modern Englishman, cut off from mental and spiritual contact with Europe at large for the past four hundred years. We may remind ourselves that then, as now and always, Godoy's countrymen are strongly marked with what Jorge Guillén has called "the fatality of being a Spaniard"; that is to say, possessing a deep, mystical attachment to religion and national roots, a dour and democratic chivalry, a bulldog individualism, an ironic, humorous realism, a disdain for most of the chimeras bombinating in foreign vacua, a proud consciousness of belonging to a race apart, and a capacity for heroic piety and blackest nihilism, sometimes disconcertingly mingled—a striking example occurring to me being Goya's production, in his infidel old age, of that work of inspired devotion *La Comunión de San José de Calasanz*, now in the church of San Anton Abad at Madrid.

"The 'idea' of Spain," remarks a French observer, Jean Cassou, "is close-packed, like the densest of metals; compact, resistant, and profound";[1] and it is notable that even to-day colloquial Spanish has practically no slang, but is almost as rich in ancestral proverbs as the talk of Sancho Panza. This fact alone replaces pages of analysis, and is one of the marks of Spain eternal.

It was in 1784, in the last years of Carlos III, that the elegant, penniless young provincial from Estremadura came up to Madrid with a letter of introduction to one of the Court ladies-in-waiting, and by her favour entered the Royal Bodyguard, the *Guardias de la Real Persona*, a corps reserved for men of birth, as a private-

[1] *Panorama de la Littérature Espagnole Contemporaine*, Paris, 1931.

cadet; the equivalent in rank, though not in pay, of an ordinary colonel. It may be reasonably assumed that hardly had the first tightness of his decorative crimson-and-silver uniform and the last rusticities of his accent worn off before the kindling black eye of Maria Luisa, Princess of the Asturias, his elder by sixteen years, had noted this agreeable recruit. Godoy had certainly become her lover before she became Queen on the death of Carlos III, in December 1788. It is apparently true that he succeeded his brother Luis in this office, and it is possible, as has been suggested, that the Queen's passion was largely maternal. The brief, demure passage in the *Memoirs* describing and dismissing this début is worth quoting:

Admitted in 1784 by Sr. Don Carlos III into the Royal Body-guard, my taste for literature and the fine arts was not weakened by Court distractions.

Remembering which model conduct, Godoy pauses to pay a tribute to his late tutors, all clerics, and pays it sincerely. "I was seldom seen at the theatre," he adds. "More rarely still did I partake of Court diversions, or the amusements of the metropolis. Gambling I always held in utter aversion." A pattern, in fact, for youthful Guardsmen of all time.

On the accession of Carlos IV Godoy was immediately promoted adjutant-cadet. His affair with Maria Luisa was long since public property, and the lampoons flew round. Whether the new King, who had taken a fancy to him which was to develop into nearly fifty years of sincerest admiring affection, knew the facts at this time or not, he knew his wife, and ignored the affair. Goya's famous group of the Royal Family in the Prado lacks only the presence of Godoy to complete its flavour of satire, and although Goya's satiric intention seems to me to have been somewhat exaggerated by commentators of a later day, reading into it their own wishful thoughts, one may agree at least that the honest dullness of Carlos and the watchful concupiscence of Maria Luisa are luminously apparent in this canvas. Carlos IV was a heavy, conscientious, kindly man, like his cousin Louis XVI, and addicted, like Louis, to tinkering at manual crafts; an excruciating amateur violinist, a passionate lover of field-sports, eminently accessible, in the Spanish Royal tradition, and possessing a certain genial breadth of mind.[1] He may have missed the satire of his Court painter at his family's expense owing to slowness of uptake, but when the audacious Goya presented the *Caprichos* to him some time later, and it was pointed out by courtiers that some of these etchings were outrageous caricatures of the mighty, the King, having thought the matter over for three months, accepted the *Caprichos* and had a special edition pulled for himself. "Our Goya is amusing himself, that's all." A mediocrity, perhaps; too much ruled by his wife, certainly; but by no means the fumbling nonentity some historians have made him.

The Bastille fell on July 14, 1789, and the chill wind of apprehension which swept the Courts of Europe pierced even Spain's lethargy. In 1791 the reigning Prime Minister, the aged Floridablanca, issued a stringent decree controlling all Frenchmen in Spain, clamped down a Press-censorship, declined to recognise the new French Constitution, and informed the French Ambassador that he no longer regarded Louis XVI as his own master. To avoid a clash with France, Floridablanca in the next year had to go. The Queen, who detested him, was responsible, and Godoy regretted it, he says, profoundly. He was by now swiftly advancing in the Royal favour; a *brigadier*, or sergeant, in the Guard, of the King's own making; an acknowledged power at Court, already, according to the sour Zinoviev, Russian Ambassador, making a snug fortune by selling places, already suggesting candidates for the "inner Council" to the Queen; the recipient of showers of presents (including a handsome coach-and-six from Maria Luisa, the target of many epigrams), and the

---

[1] " A stout, healthy Prince with a good heart and a clear head; but by a neglected education, and a continued suite of childish amusements, neither the one nor the other does him credit " (Harris, British Ambassador to Madrid, 1770).

centre of a group of flatterers. And although Godoy still regarded himself, he says, as purely a soldier, he was becoming almost daily more immersed in State affairs. His first personal experiment in that field succeeded. The Queen's chaplain suspected him, not inaccurately, of Voltaireanism and sympathy with the French Jacobins, and complained to her. Godoy had him replaced by a less angular type.

Meanwhile Floridablanca had been succeeded by the seventy-four-year-old Conde de Aranda, a seasoned statesman, a correspondent of Voltaire's and a violent Freemason—like half the statesmen of Europe—who had brought about the expulsion of the Jesuits from Spain under Carlos III and destroyed their Ideal State in Paraguay.[1] Aranda was the King's choice because there was no one else. Carlos also vaguely hoped, apparently, that Aranda's influence with the Lodges might conceivably be of service to Louis XVI, now a prisoner in the Temple awaiting trial. One of Aranda's first steps on taking office was to object violently to a proposed grant of Royal lands to the upstart Godoy. He failed, and Godoy was one of the first to observe that the old man's policy, after some vacillation, of doing nothing whatsoever was weak and humiliating. In the early part of 1792 the Russian Ambassador reported to Catherine the Great that while the King was hunting and Aranda experimenting with a new type of diving-suit, the rest of the ministers were "closeted with the Queen, to ascertain her views and those of Godoy."

The Favourite was now due for another step. Giving the Corps Diplomatique no excuse henceforth for omitting Godoy from despatches, the King created him a sergeant-major in the Guard—equal in rank to a general—and a Grandee with the title of Duke of La Alcudia, soothing his fellow-Grandees' feelings by recalling the Godoy family's services to the Crown in the early Middle Ages and their descent, though now impoverished, from the Visigothic kings. And indeed the theme-song of some of Godoy's enemies on the topic of his low birth seems oddly

[1] Cf. R. B. Cunninghame-Graham, *A Vanished Arcadia*.

absurd, if only because his brothers Luis and Diego, before being admitted to the Military Orders of Spain, had been required in the routine manner to furnish documentary proof of nobility for at least eight generations.[1] If the King seems infatuated, it must be remembered on Godoy's behalf that apart from youth and audacious charm he has energy, reasonable culture, brains, and a supple gift for diplomacy, whereas Spain's other available statesmen are an aged and, with one or two exceptions, a sorry crew.

In November of this same year, 1792, Aranda was gently relieved of his office, and into it, by Royal proclamation, stepped twenty-four-year-old Don Manuel Godoy, Duke of La Alcudia.

2

One is naturally curious, when a man's fortune takes such a swift and surprising leap, to hear his own explanation. It is possible that when dictating his *Memoirs* in extreme old age fifty years later, Godoy may have forgotten much. What he does recall is reasonable enough so far as it goes, and despite its obvious dressing for the defence. He owed his luck to the French Revolution.

The close vicinity of the two kingdoms led to perpetual fear lest the conflagration should spread from one to the other. Carlos IV looked round him, dreaded to rely on his own resources, and knew not on whom to repose his confidence. . . .

It does not become me either to excuse or to blame this irresolution. I merely observe that such was their Majesties' state of mind. They could have wished to alight upon a man who should be wholly indebted to them for this elevation, a true friend, attached and devoted to their persons and their House . . . a subject, in short, whose private interest should identify itself with that of his masters.

[1] "If I enter into these details, it is certainly not because I attach any intrinsic value to them . . . but to reply once for all to those who have accused me of borrowing mythical genealogies and affiliations" (Godoy).

Pointed out to their attention by the name I bore, by the very nature of my daily functions, I was admitted to the palace of my Sovereigns with a degree of familiarity far more usual in Spain than will be credited by those who are ignorant of her manners.

One may pause to meditate a moment on this last essential point. The Spanish Throne has been unique in this respect from the Reconquista in the fifteenth century down to the abdication, so crudely engineered, of Alfonso XIII in 1931. Side by side with an ancient, monstrously rigid, and involved etiquette went an accessibility to the subject which makes the White House or the Elysée Palace look by comparison like the shrine of the Dalai Lama. This explains the swiftness of Godoy's intimacy with the King, an affable and easy man who would welcome a blunt peasant like Goya with open arms, embrace him, discuss Aragonese agriculture with him, and treat him and any other visitor without a trace of affectation or morgue. But let Godoy conclude.

I was, no doubt, as anxious as others to raise myself to distinction. But all my dreams of fortune were limited to hopes of my gradual advancement in the military career; and before I became acquainted with the King's intentions in my regard, I can safely affirm that I received with alarm the distinctions and favours which in the short space of a few years were lavishly heaped upon me.

A sense of humour rarely deserted Don Manuel Godoy. Does it seem impossible that after dictating that final phrase— *recibí con temor los favores y las gracias*—those still-handsome eyes did not emit a sparkle of sincere amusement? The figure of the modestly ambitious young soldier caught up to power and glory despite himself is surely laid on a trifle too opulently? Let it pass. A piece of admirable baroque in the manner of Valdés Leal is coming; purple thunder-clouds and red lightning, the agony of the fallen House of France and the imminence of European catastrophe:

It was thus, as it were, in the midst of a convulsion of Nature, on the brink of a volcano whose dark smoke portended an immediate explosion, when terror was at our gates and agitated every mind, that I was unexpectedly summoned—O God!—to the helm of the State.

And so, there being nobody else available, the Favourite takes office, with deprecating modesty. There is a portrait of Godoy painted in this year, artist unknown. It shows calm, oval, regular, clean-shaven features; large, intent, intelligent dark eyes, smooth dark brows; an imperious nose. The hair is still powdered in the conservative fashion. On the Ministerial coat sparkle the jewelled insignia of two Orders. It might represent a born diplomat in repose instead of a young soldier ignorant of the first elements and surrounded by hostility. But as Godoy had not been to any extent a reader of ambassadors' memoirs, it did not occur to him, presumably, that international diplomacy is anything very difficult.

His policy on taking office was clear and difficult enough. The most urgent obligation was to rescue Carlos' cousin, Louis XVI, and his family from their increasingly obvious doom. As the combined forces of Spain amounted at the moment to barely 36,000 men, direct action was unthinkable. To move the Jacobins to an act of chivalry, the handing over of the French Royal family to Spanish custody, seemed a practical alternative. The Convention, to whom Ocariz, the Spanish envoy in Paris, presented this mediæval suggestion in December 1792, rejected it with roars of contempt. Even discreet bribery with Spanish money on a lavish scale failed to humanise the tiger. Louis' head was removed on January 31, 1793, and on March 7 the Republic, whose emissaries had been particularly busy for some time in Northern Spain, declared war on the Spanish Bourbon with a list of seventeen grievances.

Godoy accepted the challenge with the King and country behind him. Spanish response was enthusiastic, from Grandees to smugglers. Monastic and cathedral plate was freely melted down. The nobles, including Godoy himself, raised and equipped regiments of their own. Volunteers rushed to the colours. Even the blind ballad-singers of Madrid contributed their quota to the war-chest. On April 17 General Ricardos crossed the frontier and attacked in the Roussillon, and by November had driven the French back to Perpignan. The Spanish fleet, sent to co-operate with the British at Toulon, had less success, and the allies, as allies will, parted in reciprocal dislike.

Before long the ancestral croakings of old Aranda prophesying doom culminated (March 1794) in an offensive outburst in the Council, and he was dismissed to his native Aragon. By this time Aranda was not alone in his jaundice. After the French had rallied in 1794-5 and in bitter fighting driven the Spanish forces back into Catalonia, Spanish zeal for the French Bourbons began notably to cool. Revolutionary propaganda had, as we have noted, made some headway among the intelligentsia, though the Terror was turning many Jacobinesque enthusiasms back on Spain. A movement among extremists in Madrid to provoke and welcome a French invasion was detected by Godoy's police and the ringleaders banished to the Indies. Spain's anti-Republican allies were losing their fervour, and Spain might well, it seemed, have to meet a mass-onslaught of the fanatic French with no help at all. It was time to withdraw with honour, and Tallien of the Committee of Public Safety—husband of *Notre-Dame de Thermidor*, whose father, the Conde de Cabarrús, was one of Godoy's principal advisers—was able before long to convey to Godoy that the Republic, also, was not averse to peace. By a peace treaty signed at Bâle on July 22, 1795, the presumed death of the little Dauphin in the Temple having removed Spain's last excuse for continuing the war, the French restored all Spanish territory and fortresses lost in the recent campaign, and (in secret articles) agreed to hand over Madame Royale to Spanish safe-custody and to accept Carlos IV as mediator with the Holy See.

Apart from the cession of Santo Domingo, a bad blunder, and a clause allowing the French to skim the cream of the famous Andalusian stud-farms, young Godoy had done remarkably well, as even his few friends admitted. The King rewarded him with fresh honours, including the curiously liturgical title of *Principe de la Paz*, the Order of the Golden Fleece, and half a dozen rich new estates, and proclaimed him Captain-General. The snarls of the hostile were temporarily drowned in public rejoicings.

With some complacency Don Manuel could reflect that he was now the second man in Spain. His levees at the palace which is now the Ministry of Marine at Madrid, adjoining the Senate, were thronged. The routine at these receptions was royal, in that the entry from his private apartments of the Prince of the Peace, wearing Captain-General's uniform and carrying baton and cocked hat, was the signal for silence and the formation of a double line of those to be received. Suave, easy, and graceful, the Prince frequently enjoyed a joke with his suitors, and when the levees were over he was well aware that his late flatterers were ardently competing in abuse of him with the populace of Madrid, who would have disliked the *novus homo* had he been a model of probity. With hardly less vigour the leading nobility declined to address Godoy with the second-person-singular *tú* used among equals. Feeling against the parvenu was not yet crystallised and directed, so to speak, by dark young Prince Ferdinand, heir to the throne and Hamlet of the piece, but Godoy was already realising that to receive, as Wilde said of Whistler, every insult save popularity is not without charms to a man of taste.

A serene and smiling mask enabled him, like Brummell, to disappoint his enemies unforgivably. His successes with women, notorious already, were no great aid to popularity either. They were soon to annoy his Royal mistress, herself no fanatic for fidelity. Nevertheless the indignant Gallic pen of Bourrienne, recording that censorious judgment I have quoted at the head of this chapter, seems to be dipping into fantasy. So far from Godoy's introducing any Juvenalesque orgies into the Court of Madrid, he was poise personified, apart from which the tradition of the Spanish Court would never countenance any breach of decorum. No doubt Bourrienne is thinking of Godoy's extra-regial amusements. It is the Favourite's lot to have inflamed the enmity of Napoleon-worshippers, a waspish tribe, to such a degree that confusions of this kind readily occur. Lord Holland, who met him at this period and continued to admire him, describes his deportment as a mixture of dignity, propriety, elegance, courtesy, and ease. "Despite his humble origin," adds the eminent Whig kindly, "he seems born for high office."

It is significant, and should be remarked early, that Lord Holland, a shrewd observer, awards Godoy high marks for "humanity and magnanimity," two traits not invariably found in careerists. Of Godoy's fundamental generosity there is no doubt. A notable *gracia y simpatía* is one of his principal assets, shared with St. Teresa, with whom he has little else in common. He hated cruelty and injustice. How far he is to be lauded for preventing the Inquisition from prosecuting Aranda and one or two other militant Francophile atheists will depend on the observer's attitude towards the theory, enunciated by the King of Brobdingnag to Gulliver and approved by Dr. Johnson, that "a Man may be allowed to keep Poisons in his Closet, but not to vend 'em about for Cordials"; a question obviously not for discussion here. Godoy's critics are justified in pointing out that his policy of curbing the Inquisition in the spirit of enlightened liberalism was not entirely disinterested, since he himself was a public scandal, notoriously of the type for whom the Inquisition still existed. In 1778 a militant atheist named Don Pablo Olivade had been prosecuted by the Holy Office, despite his powerful connections, and sentenced to banishment from Court and eight years in a monastery (it is hardly necessary to remark that by that time burnings under the juridical code had gone out of fashion all over Europe, except in England).[1] Hence the motive of Godoy, himself to attract the Inquisition's notice in due course, may be deemed somewhat mixed.

Kindness certainly inspired him directly to at least two achievements in that impressive list which occupies a hundred pages or so of modest self-congratulation in his *Memoirs*. However valuable may be the making of good roads, the building of factories, the foundation of medical and veterinary colleges, however desirable a relaxed Press-censorship, technical and industrial education, and the encouragement of arts, letters, and sciences, they can hardly be compared as services to humanity with the reorganisation of an establishment like the Foundling Hospital at Madrid, La Inclusa, and the alleviation of the misery of the deaf-and-dumb.[2]

Apropos whom, Don Manuel could have been tempted to wish, perhaps, on beginning to tackle national finances, that large numbers of his countrymen had been temporarily thus afflicted. The Treasury was low, the country impoverished, and the Minister a neophyte dependent on the financial advice of Saavedra and Cabarrús. Yet Godoy's guiding principle seems sound enough by all modern standards, being, in a consecrated phrase of current politics, to soak the rich. "The working-class was held, as it were, sacred," he says, anticipating the ideals of a later day. With Pius VI's approval he had no difficulty in trimming the higher clergy of some of their surplus wealth. The nobles and landowners disgorged rather furiously. "It is from this epoch (1795) that must be dated the hatred, the *system of calumny*, of my enemies." The proletariat, and especially the agricultural portion of it, which Godoy subsidised with ardour, displayed

[1] Cf. the Newgate Calendar. Up to the thirtieth year of George III (1790), the punishment for women convicted of husband-murder or coining was burning at the stake. They were first strangled by the hangman though not in one case reported in the Calendar.

[2] A minor example of Godoy's good-nature is his taking the trouble to acquire a kind of sign-language to converse with Goya when severe deafness conquered the artist, whom Godoy greatly admired.

"gratitude almost amounting to enthusiasm," or so it seemed to Godoy fifty years later. Six national loans and a brisk economy-drive in all public departments, among other innovations, completed a financial policy resulting in such marked improvement that Spain was able to enter the coming war properly equipped.

For war was, of course, inevitable, though Spain's sudden operational treaty in 1796 with France threw the British Cabinet into vehement indignation and aroused the aged Burke, champion of Marie-Antoinette, to trumpeting-pitch. "Spain has become a fief of the Regicides!" cried Burke. Godoy's long list of "intrigues, threats, provocations, and insults" inflicted on Spain by Pitt's Government since the signing of the Treaty of Bâle seemed a sufficient answer to most Spaniards, though one or two modern historians agree bitterly with Burke. A modern theory (British) that Carlos IV hoped by a French alliance to succeed to the throne of France on the collapse of the Republic, still deemed possible, is oddly fantastic. The perpetually low flashpoint of Spanish pride is constantly overlooked by other Europeans; and on the other hand it is always difficult for any Englishman—though less difficult for any Celt—to realise that British foreign policy does not invariably enjoy abroad that reputation for rugged, selfless virtue it enjoys at home. Nor were many thoughtful Spaniards unaware that Britain, mistress of Gibraltar and the seas, had an eye on the Indies, and that the imminent conflict would be, like the war with England in Philip II's time, a commercial one.

In August 1796 Godoy, with the approval of the King and the Council ("much more the Council's work than mine"), signed the treaty of San Ildefonso with the French Directory, and on October 6 Spain duly declared war on Great Britain. Thiers has put the situation with Gallic neatness. "The sentiment of the Court of Spain would not and could not be favourable to the Republicans, but it regarded their friendship as the most certain mode of being protected against their principles." And in fact the Directory proved amenable and even conciliatory, ceasing all revolutionary propaganda south of the Pyrenees and receiving with relative politeness Spanish representations on behalf of the Holy See.

The war lasted six years and cost Spain Trinidad, a smashing defeat by Admiral Jervis off Cape St. Vincent, and severe losses in beating off British attacks on Cadiz, Teneriffe, Cuba, and Porto Rico. On the credit side Godoy could set the damage done to British shipping by Spanish and French privateers, the clearing of the Mediterranean, and the thousands of tons of British merchant-shipping taken as prizes in Atlantic and Mediterranean alike. But when Godoy announced as early as July 1797 that the price of peace with England, concerning which feelers were being put out from London, was the return of Gibraltar and Trinidad, with Jamaica thrown in, the French let him down. Spain was excluded from a tentative Franco-British peace conference with a bland promise from the Directory to "look after Spanish interests."

After September 4 (18th Fructidor), with the revival of the Terror and the triumph of the Republican war-party, "intoxicating Bonaparte with joy,"[1] a breach between Spain and her new ally began to form and widen. The first of the Napoleonic whirlwinds to strike Europe had already struck Italy and forced Pius VI, who had ill-advisedly resisted in arms, to yield up his chief temporal possessions, the choicest Vatican art-treasures, and a million and a half sterling, after the Papal envoy had been received by Bonaparte with expressions of "the profoundest personal reverence for the Holy Father." Godoy had ordered Azara, Spanish Ambassador at Rome, to intercede with General Bonaparte, who otherwise might have been, no doubt, harsh. For not obtaining better terms Godoy was violently abused in Spain. But greater trouble for the Minister was already brewing.

We have not been noting, so far, the progress of Godoy's affair with the Queen, to which he owed everything. It was developing rather stormily. On the one hand the multiplicity of

[1] Bourrienne.

Godoy's amours, on the other the possessive jealousy of Maria Luisa, notwithstanding her own adventures, made for an atmosphere of sulks and quarrelling. Despite which, and the additional possibility that the Queen was annoyed at Godoy's influence over her husband, hitherto her own property, her infatuation continued. During one of their estrangements, and by the efforts of a naval officer named Malaspina and some of Maria Luisa's friends, a memorial was drawn up for presentation to Carlos IV containing charges against Godoy more than sufficient to ruin him. At the last moment the Favourite's charms once more prevailed, and Malaspina was arrested for conspiracy and banished. Hardly had the sky cleared when a darker thundercloud loomed. Godoy was anonymously denounced to the Holy Office as a notorious evil-liver who had not fulfilled his Easter duty for the past eight years.

It is necessary to recall that in Spain, a Christian country, the private life of a public man matters, and may be challenged; as indeed was done even in Great Britain, in a modest way, in the memorable year 1936.[1] By the immutable law of the Church, any of the faithful failing to perform his minimum or Easter duty, which consists, as already noted in the case of Louis XV, in confessing and receiving Holy Communion at least once a year, generally between Ash Wednesday and Low Sunday, automatically forfeits all spiritual rights and privileges and is self-excommunicate. For a man in Godoy's position such a charge, if proved, spelt the end of his career, and it is difficult to see how this easy-going hedonist of Voltairean tinge could have cleared himself.

The ultimate source of the attack is not known. It quite likely came from the bitter Infante Ferdinand. Equally possibly Maria Luisa, who had recently discovered a new affair—according to Madrilene gossip, even a secret marriage—on her lover's part, may have inspired it in a fit of rage. The lady concerned was

[1] A pushing of this principle to extremes was one of the principal errors of Wyclif.

Doña Josefa Tudó—"Pepita" to the populace—the beautiful daughter of a penniless Andalusian artillery officer for whom Godoy had procured a Court appointment. Whoever set the machinery of the Holy Office in motion, it had to go on. The case was laid before the Inquisitor-General, Cardinal Lorenzana, who nervously hesitated to prosecute the head of the Ministry and was at once delated to Rome by the Cardinal-Archbishop of Seville for neglect of duty. Pius VI ordered Lorenzana to proceed. The Brief conveying the order fell into the hands of the French, then occupying Papal territory, who passed it on to Godoy, who quietly suppressed it.[1] The matter dropped, and the Queen made Doña Josefa one of her ladies-in-waiting. So that cloud passed over, undoubtedly with the connivance of the King, who could not afford such a rousing scandal. It was Godoy's suave revenge to despatch the Inquisitor-General with the Archbishop of Seville and another hostile ecclesiastic before long on a mission of sympathy and moral support to the Holy See, when the French marched into Rome.

The Directory meanwhile was becoming suspicious. Godoy was clearly not playing the French game, and had already checkmated *ces Messieurs* by refusing to annex Portugal with the aid of French troops when Portugal, having broken with England and declared neutrality, incurred French anger by trying to close her harbours. A subsequent suggestion from the Directory that Godoy might temporarily care to become Grand-Master of Malta Godoy rejected. He was unable to reject his friend the King's own plan for his immediate future, which was to marry him forthwith to Maria Teresa de Vallabriga, Condesa de Chinchon, Carlos' niece. The marriage—"I obeyed in this, as in all the acts of my life," says the bridegroom fatalistically, "with loyalty and submission"—duly took place in September 1797. If he had really contracted a secret marriage beforehand with Josefa Tudó, Godoy's meditations must have been disturbing. In Spain at this

[1] Quite possibly, suggests Ruíz, he had one or two protégés in the Holy Office as well.

period a troth—*palabra de matrimonio*—plighted in the presence of witnesses, after the Scottish manner, but in a church, was considered binding, though naturally not sacramental.[1] Plainly there can have been no true ceremony; but Godoy's enemies added the charge of bigamy to his dossier, and a growing Anglophile party at Court, headed by the Duke of Osuna, continued cheerfully to work for the Favourite's downfall.

He had recently strengthened his hand by inviting Jovellanos and Saavedra to join the Ministry. Both were statesmen of experience and hidalgos *à la* Velasquez of the old school; grave, dignified, upright, formal, frigidly condemning their Prime Minister's very public private life; on which topic, indeed, Jovellanos, a distinguished lawyer and intellectual, Minister of Justice and one of the great Spaniards of his age, was only just prevented by Saavedra, Minister of Finance, from addressing a personal remonstrance to the Queen on taking office. In that long and bitter verse-satire by Don Gaspar Melchior de Jovellanos called *Mensaje a Arnesto* (a Message to Ernest), there is a glimpse of Godoy ("Fabio") and his Royal mistress ("*una maja*," equivalent here to "a trollop") pacing together towards the alcove where

Ronca el Cornudo y sueña que es dichoso. . . .[2]

Jovellanos has a prose-impression of the Favourite equally unfavourable:

. . . On his right, the Princess [his wife]; on his left, the Pepita Tudó. This spectacle completed my desolation. My soul could not suffer him; I could not eat, or speak, or calm my spirit.

To which the cry in the *Mensaje* at the plight of Spain is a natural footnote:

O infamia! O siglo! O corrupción![3]

---

[1] Human witnesses were not essential, as appears from the well-known poem by Zorrilla in which the *palabra* is spoken before the historic crucifix at Toledo called the Cristo de la Vega, in the church of that name.

[2] "The Cuckold snores, dreaming that he is fortunate. ..

[3] "O infamy! What an age! O corruption!"

Godoy might smilingly ignore the grim brows of the Elders, but a more redoubtable critic now enters the Ministry "by the back door," one José Antonio Cavallero, viciously described by the normally indulgent Godoy as a drunkard, an adulterer, an enemy to every virtue, and a smooth, crooked rogue. It was Cavallero's self-appointed mission on attaining office, backed by the Directory's energetic new ambassador, Truguet, to gain the King's ear and to have Godoy ejected as a double-dealer and a standing obstacle to Franco-Spanish understanding. At their urging Carlos shortly afterwards ordered Godoy to publish a decree banishing all French refugees to Mallorca, though without a time-limit. The attempt to placate the Directory only partially succeeded, for Godoy asserted himself by simultaneously revoking the banishment of the Jesuits of Spain, decreed by Aranda and Carlos III during that epidemic of Jesuitophobia which, as noted already, was sweeping the Lodges and the Cabinets of Europe in the 1760–70's.

Godoy should seemingly have won himself a little relative popularity by, as he says, allowing "so many venerable men, who had lost all hope of seeing their country again, to be restored to their families." The principal result was to infuriate Freemasonry in general and the Directory in particular, and to redouble Truguet's activities. And over Spain hung the imminent threat of a British landing in Portugal and a French demand for passage through the Peninsula.

Quite suddenly the Favourite's enemies struck. On March 28, 1798, an acrid clash took place in Council between Saavedra, who proposed disbanding part of the army to relieve the strain on the Treasury, and Godoy, who demanded more extensive military preparations. To Godoy's surprise and dismay the King, who seemed oddly fearful of the Directory, backed Saavedra. When the Council adjourned Godoy had no alternative but to ask to be relieved of his portfolio. Carlos had the dismissal-letter ready in his pocket, dated that day and containing warm acknowledgments. He handed it to his Prime Minister. There was no more to be done, except to shake hands (the King had tears in his eyes) and pass the keys to Saavedra, who now took office. On perusing the letter of dismissal later, Godoy perceived it to be in the handwriting of Cavallero. The Directory had removed the obstacle.

3

To unemployed British statesmen of a more cultured age than ours, enforced leisure has generally meant a long-desired opportunity for making, in Max Beerbohm's phrase, "without wish for emolument, a flat but faithful version of the Georgics, in English hexameters." To Godoy, and possibly to his amusement, dismissal brought an increased zest for the game of politics, which had got into his blood.

Almost daily the carriage of the Prince of the Peace drew up at the Palacio Real, that massive domed and towered granite pile, rebuilt after the fire of 1734 by the Italian architect Sacchetti, which is one of the sights of Europe by moonlight, whether viewed from the Plaza de Oriente or from the valley of the Manzanares below. Almost daily Godoy's urbane and elegant figure, now growing noticeably portly, was ushered into tall-windowed damask-hung apartments commanding the vast tawny plain, the distant Escorial, and the high snow-capped peaks of the Sierra de Guadarrama, and fortified against the icy draughts of Spring by superb bronze or silver braziers in which would be smouldering with a flickering blue smokeless flame, diffusing an agreeably aromatic warmth, olive-stones heaped on glowing coals. Here, over the pre-luncheon glass of manzanilla, with his ample furred cloak temporarily flung off—"Till the fortieth of May don't put your cloak away"[1]—Godoy might discuss the new Government's latest follies very comfortably.

It is said that the King, whose conscience cannot have been too easy at this moment, grew irritable before long and spoke of forbidding his pervasive nephew-by-marriage the Palace pre-

[1] *"Hasta el cuarenta de Mayo no te quites el sayo"*—Old Madrilene saw.

cincts. The mood soon passed. When the Court left Madrid in due course for Aranjuez, the Escorial, La Granja, or some other country retreat, Godoy's letters followed his Royal friends indefatigably. Composed in the consecrated idiom of the Spanish Court, they have been dismissed as lackeyish by those unacquainted with the tradition. "Your Majesty be thanked! You remember and respect your poor vassal. . . ." It may be of interest to recall that even to-day a Spanish business-letter may end by kissing hands in the approved formula, *Q.B.S.M.* Godoy's advice continues to be offered his master without ceasing, especially on military affairs, and he views the new Government's subservience to France with the liveliest misgivings.

Eleven months after Godoy's fall the Saavedra-Jovellanos ministry fell likewise (February 1799) owing to the illness of both aged Ministers, promptly attributed in the usual quarters to a poison-plot engineered by the Queen and Godoy. Actually forty-seven-year-old Maria Luisa, now at the haggish stage, was pushing the fortunes of a new love, handsome Mariano Luis Urquijo, one of Saavedra's secretaries, a thirty-year-old Biscayan, a furious *sectaire* of Jansenist tinge and Francophile. When Saavedra, after a temporary recovery, resigned definitely a few weeks later, Urquijo found himself head of the Government; the King having given in, as once before, with the comforting thought that this would be agreeable to the French. And then, with the *coup* of the 10th Brumaire and the emergence of Napoleon as First Consul, the whole atmosphere suddenly changed. Here at last was a hope for Europe's peace, a French Executive free from atheism, regicide, and revolutionary skulduggery, with whom Spain could collaborate without qualms. "He is a Catholic, like me!" said Carlos IV in naïve delight when, on his returning Napoleon's compliments and gifts with a troop of Andalusian blood-horses, the First Consul ordered that their Spanish cavalry-escort were to be given all facilities for hearing Mass daily on French territory. It was not long before Carlos learned that a Bonaparte did not lavish silver breakfast-services, Paris gowns, and other expensive gifts on his foreign friends for nothing. Under the second Franco-Spanish treaty of San Ildefonso, signed by Urquijo on October 1, 1800, Spain exchanged rich Louisiana[1] and six battleships for a larger Parma, increased by Tuscan territory for the benefit of Carlos' young cousin, its ruler. The Corsican had amply covered his tradesmen's bills.

Meanwhile all the Madrid coffee-houses noted that Bonaparte's first gift had been sent not to any of the Royal family but to Godoy, in the shape of a suit of nobly damascened Renaissance armour. Could it be that Godoy's star was on the rise again? Godoy himself was perhaps aware that he would not remain in total obscurity much longer. Urquijo was plainly over-reaching himself in his desire to injure Rome. The Papal Nuncio, having protested against the official launching of a translation from the Portuguese of a book attacking the Vatican Chancery, was handed his passports. He appealed to Godoy, who spoke to the King. The Nuncio stayed, but Urquijo continued his offensive, so zestfully as to cause the newly elected Pius VII to address a personal remonstrance to his Most Catholic Majesty on ascending the throne in March 1800.

However, the bell was soon to ring for Urquijo. Apart from affronting the Spanish conscience with his drive against the Holy See, he was proving a disappointment to the Queen. No doubt it is difficult, as Essex discovered with Elizabeth Tudor, to simulate ardour for a crone; and Maria Luisa was now, as has been delicately hinted, approaching the category of those ghastly superannuated charmers in Goya's *Las Viejas* who smirk into a mirror inscribed on the back "*Qué tal?*" ("How goes it?"), hovered over by a sardonic Father Time.

Urquijo, apparently, was not even trying, and soon after Her Majesty had selected another playmate from the Guards, a handsome young coxcomb named Malló, he managed to embroil himself with the First Consul by ordering the Spanish naval contingent blockaded in Brest by the British to break out and

[1] Sold by Napoleon to the United States in 1803.

concentrate at Cadiz, which was not Napoleon's plan. Lucien Bonaparte was despatched to Spain post-haste to protest. Godoy, construing this as an act of pressure, urged Urquijo to protest formally to France beforehand; but Lucien arrived in Madrid before this could be done, and Carlos dismissed Urquijo forthwith and asked Godoy to suggest his successor.

With becoming deference Godoy, having run through the list of possibles with the King, suggested Ceballos, a cousin of his by marriage, pointing out nevertheless that this fact was likely to make Ceballos unpopular. The King waved the objection aside, and Ceballos succeeded Urquijo. Godoy's next unofficial duty, at his master's request, was to charm Lucien Bonaparte, which he did without difficulty. Charming the First Consul was likewise, at this stage, fairly simple, and achieved, at Godoy's suggestion, by despatching the young Prince of Parma, Carlos's son-in-law-elect, to ask Napoleon's blessing on his marriage with the Infanta Maria Luisa. As further evidence of Spanish friendship Napoleon almost immediately demanded action against Portugal, England's ally, who needed to be dealt with before his great European game could begin. The perturbed Carlos, whose other son-in-law was on the Portuguese throne, at once consulted Godoy, who pointed out that unless Portugal were subdued by the Spaniards she would certainly be annexed by the French, an evil a thousand times worse. As the Portuguese obstinately rejected this reasoning, Spain had no option but to declare war on them in February 1801. The operation was planned and the Spanish invasion force of 60,000 commanded by Godoy in person as newly-appointed Generalissimo.

It is difficult to discern, amid the contemptuous laughter of the experts, exactly how much of a commander in the field the ex-sergeant-major of what the Madrilene populace derisively called the Chocolateros proved himself. The "War of the Oranges" (*la Guerra de las Naranjas*), so styled from Godoy's present to the Queen, after invading Portugal, of two orange-branches from the fortress of Yelves, then under siege, ended nevertheless after four weeks' fighting with the capitulation of the Portuguese, so Godoy's command can hardly have been so amateurish as it is held to be in some quarters.[1] Moreover, if his object was to side-step the French he succeeded. The 8,000 French troops concentrated under Gouvion-St. Cyr at Cuidad Rodrigo under the recent treaty had nothing whatever to do, to Napoleon's fury. For Napoleon vehemently wanted Lisbon and Oporto, whereas French pickings from Godoy's peace-treaty with Portugal turned out to be only an indemnity of twenty million francs and the closing of the Portuguese ports against British shipping. In vain the First Consul tried to stop the ratification at Badajoz, swearing that French troops should be kept in Spain till the treaty was altered to his liking. Ultimately, after a typical Napoleonic carpeting—of the type later developed by Hitler—of Azara, Spanish Ambassador in Paris, and a sequence of typically Napoleonic despatches to Lucien Bonaparte, the Portuguese indemnity was increased by five millions, plus most of the Braganza crown jewels, and Gouvion-St. Cyr marched his troops back into France. It was not until a much later date that documents published by the Marqués de Lema revealed a highly discreditable ending to Godoy's conduct of the campaign; namely, a private transaction (not mentioned in the *Memoirs*) between himself and Lucien Bonaparte in the matter of the Portuguese indemnity; what is now in financial circles called a rake-off, profitable to both and detrimental to their employers.

Godoy seems to have emerged from his initial round with the First Consul with the complacent assurance that he was henceforth a match for Napoleon and the fox Talleyrand combined; a conviction heightened perhaps by his new reputation—at least with the Queen—as a warrior. "He gives himself the airs of a Souvarov," remarked Napoleon, who had already placed a black mark in his tablets against the name of the Favourite who had

[1] One military critic, General Gómez de Arteche, awards him high marks for skill and speed.

outsmarted him. His opinion of Godoy a little later was summed up to Lucien: "I can use him, but I despise him." Godoy apparently judged Napoleon similarly. From this time dates his dangerous game of playing off the coming master of Europe against an enemy at home twice as malevolent, and sworn to destroy him. It is perhaps time to take fuller note of the presence, looming larger in Godoy's vision every year, of the Infante Don Ferdinand, Prince of the Asturias, Carlos' eldest son and heir.

4

Cold, secretive, vengeful, embittered from boyhood, but not all bad, Ferdinand, later King of Spain, possessed a capacity for hate for which he cannot be completely blamed, and which Goya fully conveys. The long Bourbon nose, the jutting Hapsburg lower jaw, the thin straight lips, the heavy black brows, the glowering dark eyes combine to lend Ferdinand a Vesuvian aspect which a comfortable tendency to stoutness and a fresh complexion fail to mitigate.

He was about seventeen at this point of Godoy's career, and loathing the Favourite with a passion for which he was intensely popular with the masses. It takes no psycho-analyst to disentangle his motives. Contempt for his parents and detestation for the principal object of their affection had poisoned Ferdinand's life, and he was permanently obsessed with the belief, says Godoy, "that he was abhorred by the authors of his existence, that they preferred a stranger to him . . . and sought to blight his prospects and deprive him of his crown."

The blame for this persecution-mania Godoy does not hesitate to attach to a tutor selected by himself at the King's request when Ferdinand outgrew the tutors of his infancy. This was Don Juan Escoíquiz, a canon of Saragossa, a grave and prepossessing Navarrese of noble birth who had caught Godoy's eye at a levee and pushed himself subsequently into the Minister's notice. Canon Escoíquiz' testimonials represented him as a man of virtue, learning, experience, modesty, talents, taste, and what is called a progressive viewpoint. The epithets applied in due course to "this wretch" by Godoy range from "ambitious," "treacherous," and "infamous" to "demon incarnate." For Godoy's theme is that Escoíquiz deliberately turned the youth Ferdinand against his parents and nourished in him that smouldering rage against Godoy himself which was due to burst into smoke and flame before long.

Such malevolence, if Godoy speaks the truth, is rarely encountered save in Renaissance Italy and on Rural District Councils in Wales. But Godoy, as we must constantly remind ourselves, is making out a case, with a conscience none too easy. The view of Salcedo Ruíz and other modern historians is that Escoíquiz' intentions were to make his young pupil the great king of a great State, but unfortunately the Canon's zest for intrigue exceeded his capacity for translating his good intentions into fact. So far as a contemporary print is any guide, Escoíquiz looks anything but a villain. And should we ever forget that Godoy himself was a flaming public scandal, almost intolerable to millions of Spaniards?

He was fully aware of the greatest menace to his future. All the enmity Godoy had aroused so far was nothing to that of Ferdinand, a natural focal-point moreover for the enmity of every disappointed place-seeker, every jealous rival, every reluctant taxpayer, every sinecure-holder fearing eviction—in a word, of every anti-Godoy element in Spain, not excluding vast numbers of Spaniards, lay and clerical, in whose nostrils Godoy's morals continued to stink to Heaven, and the almost entire proletariat.

Braving this gathering storm with elegant assurance, Don Manuel Godoy, Generalissimo, was once again the most powerful man in Spain; technically commanding the military forces, actually the King's counsellor in all things, though he is careful in his *Memoirs* to deny that "all power was concentrated in my person."

Nothing was undertaken, even in the matter of Army reform, except through the usual Ministerial channels. Carlos IV consulted and listened to all the Ministers. . . . He never shut his eyes or acted blindly, or by routine, upon my advice. On the contrary, in certain very important matters he acted on counsels entirely opposed to mine.

A new enemy was now added to the list by Ferdinand's marriage at eighteen to his cousin, Maria Antonia of Naples, whose mother, the termagant Maria Carolina, was a bosom friend of Nelson's Lady Hamilton and—unhappily for his honour—of Nelson himself, who hanged the patriot Caraccioli at the yard-arm to please her. The new Princess of the Asturias inherited the maternal temperament and showed hostility to Godoy from the beginning. Before long the Asturias household became such a centre of intrigue that when, according to Napoleon's plan, the Spanish fleet sailed in March 1805 to join Villeneuve's squadron in the West Indies, Godoy apparently saved Villeneuve from interception by Nelson only by deliberately deceiving Ferdinand over the sailing orders. When, after Nelson had caught the French and the Spaniards off Trafalgar a little later and won England's most splendid naval victory, Ferdinand discovered how Godoy had duped him, he made a furious scene.

"Have you ever lied to my father?"

"I do not lie to my King."

At Ferdinand's answering sneer Godoy added bitterly: "And if your Royal Highness would persuade the King to dismiss me, I should take it as a favour."

"Do you want me to compromise myself?" snarled Ferdinand, and turned his back.

Very soon Ferdinand's wife was likewise raging. In February 1806 Napoleon seized Naples and placed his brother Joseph on the throne in place of her father, that detestable character Ferdinand IV. Neither Godoy nor Carlos IV had considered interference for one moment, though Ceballos had been trying hard to detach Naples from British influence. A stream of hysterical letters from Maria Antonia to her mother raving at Carlos, Maria Luisa, Godoy, and Napoleon impartially was intercepted, and when Maria Antonia died suddenly at Aranjuez in May of the same year the story flew round Madrid, and thence round Europe, that Godoy had had her poisoned. As the immediately published results of the post-mortem proved this a plain lie, few believed them.

Since self-preservation and increasing fear of Ferdinand were adequately mingled with desire to do his utmost for Spain, it does not seem to me that what Godoy's enemies call his "intriguings with Napoleon" between 1803 and 1808 can be entirely damned. The relations between them during this period were variable, but the Napoleonic eye never lost a hard glitter. In 1803 Godoy stood up to Napoleon with admirable firmness, refusing to drag Spain once more into the war with England after the breaking of the Peace of Amiens. This infuriated Napoleon, after vainly trying intimidation by troop-concentrations on the Pyrenean frontier (aided by the British Navy, simultaneously attacking neutral Spanish shipping) and by the blusterings of his ambassador Beurnonville, to such a pitch that he wrote to Carlos IV demanding the dismissal in the interests of Europe of "a man full of vices, the tool of England, the real King of Spain." This insolence Carlos ignored. By 1804, Spain having been reluctantly drawn into the Napoleonic wake again, Napoleon and Godoy were corresponding in secret over their ambassadors' heads quite amicably. Towards 1805 the recently-crowned Emperor was considering buying him off with some small independent kingdom "between Spain and Portugal," from which (as he never tired of reminding the Favourite with malicious relish) Godoy could defy his future King. Godoy was strongly allured by this proposal, prompted by himself; but when offered one-third of Portugal he dropped it, divining quite soundly that he and Spain equally would be the dupes.

A little time after Trafalgar Godoy essayed, quite suddenly, a surprising and desperate gamble. Smarting from recent Napoleonic high-handedness, he decided that now or never was the time for Spain to throw off Cæsar's humiliating yoke and to join Great Britain, Prussia, and Russia against him.

The moment was ideal for a change of sides, with the Grande Armée far away marching into North Germany against the Prussians. After immense difficulty (Godoy says) with the nervous and wavering Carlos, he gained his end and ordered full and immediate mobilisation, following some tortuous secret diplomacy with a suspicious London and a more receptive St. Petersburg.[1]

The new and inexperienced French Ambassador to Madrid, Vandeul, was extremely puzzled. What did these sudden feverish military activities mean? he asked Godoy. Archly the Generalissimo whispered *"Portugal!"* and a week or two later, *"Gibraltar!"* A long, obscure, rhetorical proclamation to the Spanish nation, issued by Godoy and unsigned by Carlos, called all Spaniards to "take oath beneath the banners of the most beneficent of sovereigns." Thus passed the summer of 1806, in increasing mystification.

On October 14 Napoleon smashed the Prussians simultaneously at Jena and Auerstadt. Biting his lip, Godoy hastened smilingly to congratulate Vandeul. "The forces of his loyal ally are at his Imperial Majesty's disposal. Where shall they be sent?" If Napoleon, scanning Vandeul's despatches, had smelt any treachery from "that fellow in Madrid," he decided to ignore it. He was, he assured Godoy's envoy at Berlin emphatically, knitting those famous brows, satisfied with his good ally's preparations for subduing *Portugal,* for an English fleet was already in the Tagus. Good luck to Spain, and she would of course bring Portugal into the Imperial boycott-ring forthwith.

[1]He had informed his future allies that he had at his disposal 200,000 troops, including 30,000 Portuguese; all the Spaniards well trained and equipped, thanks to Godoy's energy. But some think these figures existed only in his imagination.

And Godoy's plans, whatever they were, fell instantly apart. Whether shaken by a sudden fit of panic on his own part or foiled by another display of woolliness on Carlos', he bowed to Napoleon's dæmonic will and begged the King to dismiss him forthwith and appease the Imperial bully. Carlos refused, rejecting likewise Godoy's urgings to occupy Portugal at speed before the French did, for the sake of Spain's very existence. "The Emperor is a man of honour, Manuel," mumbled Carlos, and sent 16,000 troops to Napoleon's Baltic front. Then Napoleon dictated his terms. To a not-unfavourable alliance-treaty signed at Fontainebleau in due course were attached secret articles whereby Godoy was forced to grant a French army of 28,000 passage across Spain to attack Portugal, and to accept the concentration of another 20,000 French troops at Bayonne, near the frontier. Three Spanish armies would invade Portugal with the French. The allied commander-in-chief, unless the King of Spain or his Generalissimo, Don Manuel Godoy, took the field in person, would be a Frenchman.

Thus did Napoleon call the tune as usual, and Spain at last lay open to a French invasion.

5

Despite which, and the uncertainty of all mortal glory, never had the fortunes of Godoy stood higher than now. His patronage of the higher-educational theories of the free-thinking Swiss pedagogue Pestalozzi was evoking the acclamations of a small but vociferous group of the Switzer's disciples, one of whom taught his little ones to lisp a hymn to Godoy in place of the *Salve Regina*:

> *Viva, viva, viva!*
> *Nuestro protector,*
> *De la infancia padre,*
> *De la Patria honor!* . . .[1]

[1] An institute on Pestalozzian lines, staffed by Swiss and Germans, was opened in Madrid by Carlos IV in 1806. Actually Jovellanos had established the higher education in 1794.

Greater honours even than this, or Napoleon's hypothetical gift, under the Fontainebleau treaty, of a Portuguese principality under the Spanish Crown, were the Favourite's reward at this moment. He had managed to secure for his King the title of Emperor of the Two Americas and a half-share in advance of the Portuguese colonies, together with a French guarantee for the safety of all Spain's European dominions. In return Carlos IV created him Grand Admiral of Spain and the Indies, the title held previously by Don John of Austria, glorious victor of Lepanto; thus enabling Godoy to establish that Admiralty Council (1807) which benefited the navy not a little.

The occasion was celebrated by the illumination of Madrid and countless addresses from public bodies. But Godoy was—at any rate fifty years later—not dazzled, he says.

The demonstration was addressed to their Majesties rather than to me, their creature. Nevertheless it offended the Prince of the Asturias, who deemed himself slighted.

Godoy was expressing himself more fluently on this topic, doubtless, over the coffee-cups in the drawing-room of Josefa Tudó, his nightly refuge and the *bodega* or rest-house of his perturbed and weary spirit. What is called in modern jargon his sex-life had now become "set," so to speak. His relations with Queen Maria Luisa, that harridan, had long since declined into an easy, humdrum association, part friendship, part habit, part necessity. The Countess of Chinchon, the wife imposed on him by Carlos IV, was, though (or even because) she had recently produced him a daughter, one of his most intimate enemies. Contemplating her portrait by Goya, one is impressed by a fragile, childlike, pathetic unhappiness of expression which suggests that Doña Maria Teresa Godoy may have had a case as well. Josefa Tudó, the only woman Godoy ever loved and his only solace, now had a house in Madrid and had given him, so far, two sons.

We may catch a fleeting glimpse of him now, on the eve of his fall, reclining among Doña Josefa's brocaded cushions on a gilt sofa, in the attitude in which Goya painted him at Field Head-quarters during the War of the Oranges. In his forty-first year Godoy is a handsome, heavy personage, a mature Regency buck, wearing his black hair unpowdered[1]; somewhat Brummellesque, a trifle Wildeish, in well-filled snowy buckskins or black-silk tights, brilliant Wellington boots or pumps, a black-silk stock, and a gold-buttoned blue swallowtail coat of the British "Whig" pattern, made fashionable by Brummell and the Regent all over Europe, fitting snugly round an ample waist. Lassitude and resignation pervade him, though the tired dark eyes can still flash with humour and the mobile mouth is still good-natured and capable of smiles and jokes and compliments.

Don Manuel had need of all Doña Josefa's consolations. Prince Ferdinand's hate and hopes were growing. He had recently been assured by the French Ambassador of Napoleon's firm backing in any trouble arising from recent debates in Council over the succession to the Throne, from which the King reluctantly, and un-doubtedly at Godoy's continued urging, apparently contemplated excluding Ferdinand in favour of his less-difficult brother, Prince Carlos. Already, during a severe illness in 1801, Carlos was said to have signed a will appointing Godoy and Maria Luisa joint Regents after his decease. If these were facts, the rancorous Prince of the Asturias had yet more reason to brood over the machinations of the Favourite, now desperately striving to master his enemy while he could.

Early in 1806 the alleged discovery by the Queen of a mys-terious plot between the Princess of the Asturias and her mother, said to menace the lives of the King, the Queen, and Godoy, was swiftly reported by Godoy to Napoleon, at this moment himself playing a double game and promising Godoy

[1] Hair-powder went out finally in Spain, except for the usual conservatives like the Corregidor in *The Three-Cornered Hat,* about 1805-6, when Godoy made the army conform to the French military coiffure "à la Titus." But he and the King, and all the advanced young bucks, had adopted unpowdered hair, without queue, some time before. It was the badge of the liberal-minded.

full protection against Ferdinand. Meanwhile the Minister's police kept a tireless eye on the Infante Ferdinand's movements and those of Canon Escoíquez, now at Toledo and in regular correspondence with his ex-pupil. In the same summer they arrested and examined some of Ferdinand's lower domestics on the pretext (plausible enough) that the slanders concerning the late Princess's death originated in the Asturias household. Nothing more valuable emerged from the examination of the *valetaille*, who included Ferdinand's barber, than the fact that the Prince was keenly interested in chemical experiment.

Something explosive was certainly preparing. On October 7, 1807, Ferdinand in his desperation addressed a secret letter from the Escorial, where the Court now was, to Napoleon in reply to a recent confidential suggestion, via the French Ambassador, Beauharnais, that Ferdinand might marry a nineteen-year-old cousin of the Empress Josephine, Marie-Rose Tascher de la Pagerie. Respectfully welcoming this proposal, Ferdinand thanked the Emperor and invited him to interfere in the domestic affairs of the Spanish Crown, now betrayed by "perfidious egotists."

... With the utmost confidence, therefore, I implore your Imperial Majesty's paternal protection, hoping that you will not only deign to accord me the honour of an alliance, but that you will remove all difficulties in the way of the fulfilment of my wish ...

The letter was handed to Beauharnais (who loathed Godoy and had undoubtedly inspired it), and a trusty messenger was despatched with it to Paris. Napoleon can hardly have received it before a mysterious unsigned scrawl was found by Carlos IV on his dressing-table:

Haste, haste, haste! Prince Ferdinand is hatching a design in the Palace which puts the Crown in danger. Queen Maria Luisa runs a risk of poison. To defeat these plans not an instant must be lost. The faithful vassal who writes this is unable to fulfil his duty in any other way.

Blankly, Carlos showed the note to the Queen and went with her immediately to Ferdinand's apartments, taking a volume of new poetry with him as a pretext. The King did not believe a word of this melodramatic rigmarole; but on being shown the note Ferdinand's perturbation (says Godoy) betrayed him; still more his uneasy glances, revealing the presence of compromising documents. The King sent for Cavallero, Minister of Justice. The Prince's apartments were searched forthwith and a mass of papers taken away.

They were, according to Godoy, sufficiently compromising. One at least was described in the Queen's presence by Cavallero, a stickler for sanctions at all times, as a "death-warrant"; at which the Queen (still according to Godoy) shrieked and tore it from him. It was a document in which Ferdinand compared himself to St. Ermengild, Prince of the Goths, driven by conscience to oppose his father, Leovigild, and assassinated by his stepmother and her paramour.

After perusing all Ferdinand's papers, many in cipher, Carlos sat down in a whirl of emotion and addressed a personal letter to Napoleon:

SIRE, MY BROTHER,

At the moment when I was occupied with co-operation for the destruction of our common enemy, my beloved eldest son, heir to my throne, has formed a horrible plot to dethrone me, and has even gone to the length of attempting the life of his mother. A plot so terrible must be punished with exemplary rigour. The succession must be revoked. One of his brothers will be more worthy than he to fill his place in my heart and on my throne. I am now seeking his accomplices, and lose no moment in informing your Imperial Majesty, whom I pray to assist me with your wisdom and advice. . . .

Such was the Conspiracy of the Escorial, which modern Spanish historians regard with as confirmed a scepticism as that with which enlightened British historians regard the murky imbroglio of the Gunpowder Plot. Ruíz, for example, holds the whole conspiracy to be a comedy planned and carried out by Godoy, with the Queen's active connivance, to destroy the popular Ferdinand's succession to the throne once and for all; allowing simultaneously that Ferdinand's invitation to Napoleon was certainly *una incorrección*, yet a trifle (*un pecado venial*) compared with the crimes the Favourite and his Royal mistress, who hated her eldest son almost as much as Godoy did, had been committing against Spain for years past. As for the King, an honest man, he was duped.

That same October night the Infante Ferdinand was escorted under guard from his apartments, followed by his father, stout, red-faced, bewildered, furious, grief-stricken, appalled, possibly a dupe but not a figure of comedy, along those long, sombre, tapestry-hung Escorial corridors by candlelight, and lodged in solitary confinement on a charge, on which he had already undergone a preliminary examination, of high treason. Godoy was at this moment in Madrid, confined to bed with a fever. On learning the news he cried aloud and scrawled a shaky missive to the King, adjuring him half-hysterically not to make the scandal public; but a proclamation announcing that the Prince of the Asturias had been seduced into a conspiracy against the Crown was already posted on the walls of the capital. Three days later, still shaking and yellow with nerves and fever, Godoy appeared at Carlos' urgent summons in the Escorial. The Prince of the Asturias had, it seemed, confessed, bringing half a dozen notables into the matter. The name of Napoleon loomed large in the background, having been brandished by Ferdinand like a talisman against all his enemies, real and imaginary.

Godoy recovered and moved with customary skill and speed to secure the Prince's chief accomplices among the nobility and throw the onus upon them. Among them were the Duque del Infantado, alleged to have been appointed in advance by Ferdinand Captain-General of New Castile, the Marqués de Ayerbe, the Conde de Orgaz, and Canon Escoíquez of Toledo, whose most tangible share in the conspiracy was a prose-memorial depicting Godoy as a monster of infamy and disloyalty, a lecher, pimp, and bigamist; a fine piece of baroque invective. A week later, after a scene in his prison-room described by Godoy, who apparently himself shed tears on this occasion as freely as any of the serious characters of Dickens, as highly affecting, Ferdinand grovelled to his father and sued for forgiveness. Since Napoleon was likely to intercede for his protégé within a few posts, Carlos saved him the trouble. "The voice of Nature disarms vengeance," began a Royal proclamation of November 5, informing the Madrid populace that all was forgiven; and Carlos was shrewd enough to allay popular feeling by publishing Ferdinand's confession, for what it was worth, simultaneously.[1] Maria Luisa, to whom her son had made (says Godoy) abject appeals, pardoned him likewise. The idol of the Spanish populace was a humbled spectacle, it seemed; apart from the tremendous public ovations greeting him on every appearance.

It remained to take up with Napoleon that portion of the conspiracy (or as some call it, Godoy's Last Card) involving him. Carlos did so, requesting with frigid courtesy to know to what extent Prince Ferdinand had been in negotiations with his Imperial Majesty, and strongly censuring Beauharnais. Napoleon flew into a thunderous rage, denied to the Spanish Ambassador all knowledge of the Escorial letter, vowed protection for Ferdinand henceforth, and menaced Godoy, the real enemy, with reprisals. But such displays were a habit with the Emperor, as his frail, indomitable old prisoner Pius VII was later to remind him with a smile ("Commediante! . . . Tragediante!"). Napoleon was well aware that Marshal Junot's army of 23,000, marching through Spain towards Portugal and now at Salamanca, was liable to be harshly handled if he went too far, and the Fontainebleau treaty was not yet ratified. He replied in writing to Carlos IV, also with frigid courtesy, that he had never received any communication from the Prince of the Asturias, and had, indeed, no knowledge of him, direct or indirect. This statement Carlos with a shrug

[1] "Probably written by Godoy" (Ruíz).

accepted, and the Treaty of Fontainebleau was ratified on November 8. Godoy's net had meanwhile closed on the half-dozen principal Escorial conspirators, who were duly tried and—since the King forbade Prince Ferdinand to be called as a witness, and equally forbade any mention whatsoever of Napoleon or Beauharnais during the trial—duly acquitted; a highly popular verdict.

Napoleon had now made up his mind finally about Spain, to annex which, one of his confidential agents on the spot had recently reported, an army of 30,000 would be more than enough. It seemed to Napoleon that Spain, solidly clamouring for Ferdinand, was ripe for plucking and the insupportable Godoy for long-merited sanctions.

By November 29, 1807, Junot had pushed through the Peninsula, after having his forces reduced to some 5,000 by the terrible winter storms of the Sierra de las Batuccas, and entered Lisbon with 1,500 grenadiers, to find the Portuguese Royal family away on the high seas, bound for Brazil with a British naval escort. Godoy had dutifully carried out his co-operative commitments under the Fontainebleau treaty, but something ominous was happening just over the Pyrenean frontier. The swelling French reserves under Dupont at Bayonne were establishing contact with another two divisions under Duhesme concentrating on Perpignan, and demonstrating sinister intentions of a southward move. From Bayonne over the Pass of Ronces-valles into Navarre, from Perpignan along the coast into Catalonia. . . . the objective of Napoleon, who had just annexed Etruria, the kingdom of Carlos' widowed daughter, was becoming plain. Carlos, Godoy, and the entire Cabinet now had no illusions, though Godoy's calmness, we gather from the *Memoirs*, was tonic.

Chaos prevailed in the seat of Government. Carlos IV stood alone. In such an extremity I knew my own ruin was practically certain, but . . . I deemed it infamous to abandon the King.

Even were it certain (I said to myself), that Bonaparte's design was to place the Prince of the Asturias on the throne, he would not do so without reward; Spain's integrity, so happily preserved hitherto amid the transformations of Europe, would not long escape his claws.

Of the plans for staving off invasion which occurred to Godoy, thinking feverishly, the first and most obvious was his own instant disappearance from State affairs, thereby freeing the King and his newly-reconciled son from further association with the principal object of Napoleon's vengeance. Carlos once more refused to dismiss him, foreseeing that Europe would construe Godoy's exit as yet another Napoleonic *coup*. The King likewise refused to allow Godoy to surrender command of the army, though agreeing that he could, if Ferdinand agreed, hand over command of the fleet. Ferdinand, with what must be construed as a sudden impulse of generosity, refused to listen to this, and begged Godoy not to desert them.[1] While these urgent discussions were still going on, Dupont's army (27,000) at Bayonne, pompously called the Second Corps of Observation of the Gironde, crossed the Bidassoa without notice and began to advance slowly towards Valladolid, welcomed everywhere by the populace—and especially, it was noted, by the clergy—with an enthusiasm significant of the depth of Spanish loathing for Godoy, the Queen, and all their works. The cheering, the flower-scattering, the fireworks, the bellringing continued as Moncey followed Dupont with the Corps of Observation of the Ocean Coast (30,000), Grouchy commanding the cavalry. At the same time Duhesme's two divisions, French and Italian, began moving unostentatiously from Perpigan into Catalonia, in the direction of Barcelona. "Spain was appalled by this sudden massing of silent, mysterious armies," says Mr. A. G. Macdonell in his admirable study of the Napoleonic dynamo.[2] But Murat's despatches to Napoleon make it clear that the Spaniards as a whole saw in the traditionally-detested *Gavachos* only the champions of

[1] Godoy's account.   [2] *Napoleon and his Marshals* (London, 1934).

their martyred Ferdinand and the deliverers of Spain. It was not the people who were appalled.

The Spanish Government certainly was. Under the strain, Carlos IV, implored passionately by Godoy in Council to appeal to one of the articles of the Treaty of Fontainebleau by which he might at least suspend this invasion till Napoleon's return from Italy, turned suddenly old, haggard, stubborn, stupid, and irresolute, hesitating to sound a national call, refusing to dismiss Godoy, complaining pettishly of Ferdinand ("embarrassed when I converse with him . . . speaks of Bonaparte with enthusiasm"), and of certain Ministers' "coldness and evasiveness." In February 1808, almost simultaneously with Marshal Junot's declaration, at Napoleon's order, that the House of Braganza had ceased to exist, Duhesme threw off pretence and, half by force and half by finesse, occupied four Spanish fortresses; Pamplona, San Sebastian, Figueras, and Barcelona. This did not provoke any immediate revulsion of feeling outside Catalonia, where the French had been greeted with marked coolness and growls, the Catalans being a difficult race at all times. News, moreover, travelled slowly in those days, apart from the interest which the governors of the seized fortresses had in hushing the affair up as much as possible. Nor did the spectacle, immediately after-wards, of the gay and gallant Murat gasconading into Madrid itself, at the head of a gaudy Staff and a large force of infantry and cavalry, cause much adverse comment among the citizenry, since Murat's mission, carefully advertised, was essentially pacific and concerned with explaining the amicable nature of Duhesme's move.

The real ultimatum arrived swiftly. An indictment of Spanish policy under eighteen heads, reaching years into the past, was handed by Talleyrand to Don Eugenio Izquierdo in Paris. The gist of Napoleon's discontent was as follows:

1. Peace having been established by his Imperial Majesty in Northern Europe, the South was now his preoccupation; and

although it was plain that England (*l'ennemi du genre humain*) was about to create trouble in Southern Europe, the attitude of the Spanish Court continued to be unsatisfactory [a list of complaints followed].

2. To protect his troops from an unfriendly populace his Imperial Majesty had been reluctantly forced to occupy certain Spanish fortresses, in a peaceable and friendly manner.

3. The intrigues of the Anglophile party in the Spanish Court, and their imputing to his Imperial Majesty of iniquitous designs, were of grave consequence, and obliged him to protect himself against any possible change in Spanish policy.

The master of Europe proceeded to a proposal. He would hand over Portugal entire to the Spanish Crown in exchange for the Spanish provinces between the Pyrenees and the Ebro, namely Navarre, Aragon, and Catalonia. Alternatively, he would agree to these provinces being turned into a buffer-State.

Except that Napoleon was dealing with Spaniards, with his troops on the march all the time, his scheme for Spain—at present—was not without material advantages. Kinglets in Germany had accepted even complete submission and were thriving on it. Carlos IV rejected the proposal totally, protesting with dignity against French aggression, referring his Imperial Majesty to the Treaty of Fontainebleau, and assuring the Emperor that Spain was not to be coerced. Godoy added a last-minute inspiration to the effect that the Ebro provinces might be made into a viceroyalty, or even a separate kingdom, under a Spanish prince.

Napoleon's reply was curt rejection and a final insistence on his terms. From this moment Godoy's star begins its downward swoop, and his Royal master's accompanies it. The trumpets of the French armies now steadily converging on Madrid curiously resemble those announcing the final *suerte* of the bullring. Had Napoleon only guessed, they proclaimed the beginning of the end for him as well.

6

Bedevilled, bemused, and prematurely aged, Carlos IV still had a plan, agreed after frantic urgings by his wife and Godoy. By staying in Madrid he would become the prisoner of the French in a matter of days. By removing over the Sierras to Andalusia immediately he could possibly collect his troops and rouse all Spain. There was never, Godoy affirms, any intention whatsoever of Carlos' seeking refuge, like the Braganzas, in the New World. At the worst he hoped to make a final stand in the Balearics.

Couriers having been sent galloping along the roads to Portugal with orders to all Spanish generals to converge at once on the Royal headquarters, the King and Queen quitted Madrid in the ordinary manner for Aranjuez in *la Tierra de Maria Santisima*, their country seat just outside Seville, the lovely city. They had left Godoy in Madrid, and Madrid itself humming with conjecture and hostility, skilfully fomented by the swarming agents of Beauharnais. On arrival at Aranjuez, in no mood for enjoying the celebrated moonlight, the roses, and the nightin-gales of those delectable gardens, so exquisitely translated into music in our own day by De Falla, Carlos found an anonymous note warning him finally to beware of Godoy and to trust the Emperor. Divining its source, he sent for Ferdinand, summoned Godoy post-haste to Aranjuez as well, produced the note, and made Ferdinand an offer, with surprising firmness and clarity.

"I will withdraw permanently from the capital, on the ground of ill-health, and appoint you Regent with full powers. If you can save the country I will associate you henceforth with me in ruling it till the day I die. If you fail, I will resume the burden without reproaching you. Disunion between us now means the ruin of Spain."

Looking trustfully at Godoy, pale and impassive in the back-ground, the King resumed.

"Manuel here agrees with me. He is ready here and now to divest himself of the power which has subjected him to so many unjust attacks. Reflect, my son."

Ferdinand's reply (according to Godoy, the only recording witness) was to burst into tears and swear that his only desire was to obey and follow his beloved father in all things. Then, embracing Godoy impulsively and calling him *amigo*, Ferdinand begged him to save Spain "as you have done before", after which affecting scene he left the Palace. It seemed to Godoy in old age that he had meant it, at the time.

Confusion followed immediately. As the last of the Madrid garrison and Household troops took the road to Aranjuez, increasing alarm and conflicting rumours swept the capital. A hurried proclamation by Godoy, explaining that these and any other troop-movements were merely to make things more convenient for the friendly troops of Spain's ally, was rejected scornfully by the Cortes of Castile. All this time Godoy was imploring the harassed King to rally his army. As he wrung his hands, news came that Duhesme's forces were nearing the gates of Madrid. Carlos growled that this settled it. "We shall be caught between two fires! What is the use of exasperating everybody and being taken by the French in addition? I will not move." And he sent for Ceballos forthwith and dictated a proclamation to that effect to his subjects at large, received in due course with huge plaudits by the Sevillan populace as the King bowed and waved from the Palace balcony.

This irrevocable decision Carlos repeated firmly to Ferdinand and to Beauharnais, who took it that any projected flight or resistance was now abandoned. But was it? None of the troop movements was cancelled, and the road to Madrid was blocked with them. Suspicions reawakened. What was in the Royal mind? Godoy himself did not know, he says.

On the night of March 17 Godoy left the Palace at about ten o'clock, the King being resigned and apparently almost cheerful, and after supping moodily in his own mansion, near the suspension-bridge at the north-east end of the Royal Park, with his brother Diego and a colonel of Hussars, retired at midnight. As he began undressing a distant pistol-shot—or, according to some authorities, a trumpet-signal—cracked the silence of a starless night, followed by a muffled hum, rapidly increasing. Below him, a few moments later, Godoy heard the guard being turned out. Flinging a cloak over his shoulders, rushing upstairs to a garret overlooking the Park, peering out towards the Palace, he turned to find that his valet had locked him in and fled. Hardly had he discovered this before the beat of feet, the roar of many voices, and the crash of bursting wood and glass announced that the crowd was breaking in, overpowering the guard, pouring through the corridors and howling for blood. How Godoy's garret escaped their notice seems extraordinary. It did, nevertheless; perhaps some faithful servant was able to avert public attention at the last moment. A story that the mob actually broke into this garret and that Godoy was just able to hide in a roll of carpets seems unlikely. Balked of its prey, the populace, having handed out Godoy's terrified wife with marked respect—was she not royal, and a victim of El Choricero?—sacked and wrecked the main apartments thoroughly and, towards dawn, streamed up the avenues to the Royal Palace, howling, "Long live the King! Death to Godoy!"

The King and Queen, with Ferdinand, had passed these hours awake, fully dressed, helpless and in suspense. It might have been, it nearly was, another Tuileries. Had the King, while Ferdinand, the people's idol, was assuring the mob from the balcony, by the light of a candelabra, that Godoy was not there and had been dismissed, an assurance received with yells and cheers—had the King not confirmed this with a hasty decree, posted up on the main doors, relieving the Prince of the Peace of all his functions and ordering that he was free to go where he pleased, the Palace might easily have been stormed. The decree allayed popular frenzy for the moment. As the cry arose, "*Viva el Rey!*", the travelling-carriage of Beauharnais came at a gallop up the avenue and he was recognised. "*Viva Napoleón!*" yelled the mob. . . . The patriotic savageries of the War of Independence were only a couple of months away.

Smooth Beauharnais, making anxious inquiries concerning their Majesties' health and safety, found Carlos bowed and broken, wiping red eyes. "Manuel is gone. I do not know where he is. He has served me twenty years. If only no harm has come to him!" At that moment Godoy in his garret across the Park was draining the last drops of dirty water from a broken pitcher and waiting for nightfall. Some time after dusk a woman servant and a man unknown burst his door open, snatched up a few belongings without a light, and left without seeing him, flattened against a recess-wall. Shortly afterwards Godoy collapsed in exhaustion. It is hardly for those who have never been sought by a mob to curl a lip at his condition. Waking in broad daylight, mad with thirst after his thirty hours' ordeal, he crept downstairs, found a sentry at every door, and gave himself up. Escorted by a half-squadron of the Guard under an officer, he was taken to the adjacent barracks at a brisk trot to escape the fury of a pursuing crowd which tore and struck at the prisoner with every missile it could lay hands on, so that he arrived staggering, streaming blood from two knife-thrusts, dazed, breathless, covered with mud, and half in rags.

He had been able to note that some of his most energetic assailants wore the livery of the Infante Antonio de Bourbon, Ferdinand's uncle and most enthusiastic backer. It was made clear a little later by whom this popular uprising had been inspired and directed. The Conde del Montijo, a leading enemy of Godoy, had been seen mixing, disguised as a proletarian, in the crowd watching the troops arriving earlier in the day and claimed all the credit. The Infante Antonio was said to have spent a large sum on organising the whole affair.

Meanwhile at the Palace Carlos IV, informed of the arrest of the Favourite, cried in a passion to Ferdinand to see to Manuel's

safety, and was only just prevented from tottering out himself.
As Ferdinand entered the Guards' barracks Godoy, stumbling
up the staircase with his escort's help, turned and fell half-fainting
at the Prince's feet.

"I grant you your life, Manuel," said Ferdinand contemptu-
ously.

"Are you . . . are you already King?" gasped Godoy.

"Not yet; but I soon shall be."[1]

The Prince went out on the balcony and informed a cheering,
enormous mob that "this man" would shortly be tried and
punished according to the gravity of his offences. "*Señores, yo
respondo de este hombre!*" A surgeon was sent to Godoy: not
Carlos' personal surgeon, as he had ordered, but the regimental
one. The old King, in fact, was now set aside and in some danger
himself. Furious hands cut the traces of a travelling-coach drawn
up ostentatiously before the barracks, apparently—the rumour
flew—to convey Godoy to safety in Granada. A myriad voices
hooted the King, many cried to him to abdicate. The Ministers
were in conclave at the Palace, debating nervously which master
they should obey. As the populace was wild for Ferdinand, and
as Cavallero reported that the Household troops could not be
relied on, Carlos within an hour or two made up his mind. At
half-past four that afternoon (March 17) proclamations of "free
and spontaneous" abdication, already announced to the politicians, were posted on the Palace gates and public buildings, and
the populace was roaring "Long live King Ferdinand!" That
night the mob of Madrid sacked the house of Godoy's brother
Diego in the Calle de Alcalá amid public rejoicings, street
demonstrations, and cries of "Death to Godoy!" Elsewhere in
Spain the same.

On March 24, 1808, King Ferdinand VII entered Madrid to
uproarious acclamations, such as had the day before welcomed
the entry of Spain's deliverers, 40,000 French troops headed by
Marshal Murat, who was under the fixed impression, vociferated

[1] Godoy, again.

with characteristic recklessness, that he was conquering Spain for himself.[1] Within six weeks the gutters of Madrid were to be awash with French blood.

7

Y riase la gente. . . .

"And everyone laughs. . . ." Gongora's sardonic refrain, adaptable to so many historic exits, might well be heard echoing, with a ghostly plucking of guitars, over the rest of Godoy's story, which, since he has quitted the public stage, may be briefly set down.

It was his first misfortune, one may well believe, to miss the pain and glory of that national struggle which broke out just after his fall, and in which he would perforce have taken a leading part as Generalissimo of the Armies of Spain, unless the troops and the guerrillas objected; and the fierce whiskered glare of Goya's El Empecinado somehow suggests that the command of the Warrior of the Drawing-rooms (*militar de salón*), as a professional called him, could not have lasted long. Nevertheless Godoy lacked neither patriotism nor courage, nor had his conduct of the War of the Oranges lacked efficiency.

Quite likely vanity alone might have nerved Godoy to a display of heroism sufficient to disappoint his enemies, one feels. To hear, biting his nails across the frontier, of those epic two sieges[2] of Saragossa, *la siempre heroica*, and to picture their splendid fury—the Joan of Arc of Aragon, Maria Agustina, serving her cannon with Uncle Jorge Ibort and Mariano Cerezo, black with powder and drunk with glory; the clashing tocsins of Our Lady of the Pillar, of the Seo, of Santa Engracia, of San Gil, of San Pablo; the soldiers and the citizens and the monks, even the old women and children fighting back the French from balconies and street-corners to the cry *"Viva Maria del Pilar!"*; the curate Don Santiago Sas charging a platoon of French grenadiers with tucked-up cassock and whirling sabre; stout

[1] Bourrienne.   [2] June–August and December–February, 1808–9.

Palafox roaring "War to the knife!" in reply to the French call
to surrender; the eighteen thousand seasoned troops of Lannes,
Mortier, Moncey, and Junot slowly clearing house after desper-
ately-defended house; the suburbs piled high with dead; the
smoke, the din, the starvation, the stench . . . to contemplate all
this in his mind, and not to have been there, may well have been
more bitter to the ex-Generalissimo than either of his countrymen's attempts to lynch him. But Spain had no further use for
Don Manuel Godoy. He was, indeed, fortunate to have got over
the frontier with his life.

Rescued by Murat's soldierly decency from King Ferdinand,
who had designed parading his vanquished enemy through
Madrid, Godoy had been removed from Aranjuez on March 23
to the castle of Villaviciosa on the Portuguese frontier, still in
rags and bloodstained bandages, with a six-inch beard. In April
a ray of light pierced his darkness. A message to him from Carlos
IV, now in retirement at the Escorial with the Queen, deserves
immortality as a monument of true and simple affection; or, as
some would say, senile infatuation:

Incomparable Manuel, how we have suffered at your sacrifice!
To-morrow we start to meet the Emperor. We will intercede for
you, that we may live happily together. Always your friend,
CARLOS.

By this time Godoy had been taken across the French frontier
and handed over to Napoleon, who lodged him near the Imperial
chateau of Marrac, outside Bayonne on the Biarritz road, and
received him with elaborate courtesy and concern, deploring
their past misunderstandings, denouncing Spanish ingratitude,
proclaiming his determination to restore Carlos IV forthwith,
and offering Godoy complete vengeance on all his enemies;
which offer Godoy stoically declined, he says.

Ferdinand VII was already waiting at Marrac for the family
conference; somewhat apprehensively, having accepted Napoleon's invitation (says Bourrienne, who, having been the

Emperor's private secretary, should know) with hesitation, and only after being beguiled by "most deceitful promises" and assurances of Napoleon's backing, though how Ferdinand could possibly have refused such an invitation Bourrienne does not explain. Five days after Godoy's arrival came Carlos IV and Maria Luisa, received by Napoleon, their best friend and ally, with sincere effusions and all the honours of their rank. For Carlos was now reconsidering the abdication which had been lately thrust upon him.

"Where is Manuel?" was one of the ex-King's first questions on getting out of his coach at Marrac on May 1. The Royal triangle had hardly been joyfully reassembled, the reception-ceremonies were barely over, Napoleon had not yet found time to settle the Spanish succession (being determined in advance, he assured Godoy, to throw Ferdinand off the throne for good, for Ferdinand's unfilial conduct at Aranjuez and his evident lust for power had disappointed and disgusted Napoleon) when, in the afternoon of May 5, one of Murat's staff officers came galloping hell-for-leather along the road from Hendaye, bringing the news to the Emperor that three days previously Madrid had risen *en masse*, with bloody street-fighting, against the too-insolent French, and that Spain was aflame.

O corona de Iberia! Alza la frente! . . .[1]

Quintana's battle-cry and Goya's brush still convey some of the authentic exaltations of the *Dos de Mayo*, 1808, a date as illustrious in the Spanish national calendar as Lepanto.

While Napoleon stamped and raved and accused Ferdinand of trafficking with the British behind his back, a painful family scene took place. Threatened simultaneously by his distracted old father's walking-cane, stormed at by his hateful mother, Ferdinand stubbornly denied any responsibility for the shedding of French blood. The bark of Napoleon finally dominated the tumult. "If you have not recognised your father by midnight as

[1] "O Crown of Iberia! Lift up thy head!"—Manuel José Quintana, *Al Armamento de las Provincias Españolas, etc.*

King of Spain, and notified the fact to Madrid, you will be treated as a rebel!" When Napoleon had stormed out, and Ferdinand had followed him, Carlos sent for Godoy. "Manuel, I have resigned the crown. Such is the reward of twenty years' devotion to my people."

Godoy went white at the shock. "Surely, Sir," he stammered, " this proposal is not yours?"

"No," said the poor old King, victim of his own weaknesses, and wiped his weary brow. "No. The Emperor offered to restore me by force. I refused to trample on my people's bodies. 'Very well,' he said. 'If you will not reign, your son certainly shall not.' It's all over, Manuel. Let him take everything."

"Sir! Sir!" cried Godoy. "Think again!"

Carlos brushed him irritably aside. Maria Luisa added her shrill bitterness to Godoy's. While they were still disputing a draft treaty was brought in by Duroc for signature, and the Spanish Crown passed to Napoleon Bonaparte. A pension of seven and a half million francs, the provision of the Chateau of Chambord, small pensions for the Infantes, and promises to safeguard all Spanish religious and other rights were among the Emperor's undertakings. Ferdinand and his brother Carlos were to live at Valençay.

So Joseph Bonaparte, lately King of Naples, known to his derisive new subjects as "Joe Bottles" (*Pepe Botellas*), ascended the Spanish throne, and Godoy went into exile with his Royal friends, sped by a tempest of curses from Spain, since Carlos' surrender of the Crown was at once laid exclusively to his charge. His entire estates and fortune had already been stripped away. His wife remained in Spain with their daughter Carlota, hating him. Doña Josefa Tudó, wafted immediately northwards by the gallant Murat to rejoin her lover—to be soon, after his wife's death, her husband—was received by Maria Luisa with her two children into the Royal household when it moved, with Godoy, to Compiègne in the following June and, four months later, to the kinder climate of Marseilles.

The exiles moved on to Rome in 1812, but at the particular request to the Holy See of Ferdinand VII, re-established on the Spanish throne by British bayonets after the ignominious defeat and exit of "Joe Bottles," Godoy had to leave, and went to Pescaro. When Murat, on Napoleon's return from Elba, invaded the Papal States, Carlos and Maria Luisa moved to Verona, where Godoy and his family rejoined them. Carlos in his afflicted seventies was growing morose and childishly senile, and his affections variable. In 1817, learning that Godoy meditated settling at Vienna, where Metternich had gladly consented to receive a man he admired, Ferdinand viciously intervened once more. A rather squalid interval of ingratitude and bickering followed, thanks to Ferdinand's ascendancy over his father's enfeebled mind and his secret agents' tireless activities, which enabled Ferdinand to harass Godoy and Doña Josefa very pleasurably with accusations of having stolen some of the Spanish Crown jewels, missing since the French invasion. Ferdinand VII was not what we call in Great Britain "a public-school type," though not without his points.

A formal declaration by Maria Luisa cleared Godoy of theft. Her death shortly afterwards, in January 1818, and the death of poor old doddering petulant Carlos three weeks later, was possibly a relief to their friend. Remorsefully the Queen had bequeathed him everything she possessed in the world "for the many great losses he has suffered in obedience to our orders, and our refusal to allow him to retire into private life." A copy of her will was duly submitted by Godoy to Ferdinand VII for sanction. His Majesty, discovering that this act of justice lacked his father's *imprimatur*, was delighted to toss it into the nearest brazier.

So Godoy, now in his fifty-first year, facing poverty and already forgotten—successive Spanish Ministers took no notice whatsoever of communications from him—moved on resignedly to Paris, that final refuge, with his wife, Doña Josefa, and their surviving child. By 1833, the year of the implacable Ferdinand's death, Doña Josefa had grown weary of shabbiness and exile.

In that year she returned to Spain and comfort with her son, leaving Godoy penniless and quite alone. Neither she nor his daughter, Doña Carlota, who had been granted some of his Valencian estates and had married a Roman prince, took any interest in him henceforth. But for a timely 6,000-franc pension from that frugal bourgeois Louis-Philippe, in recognition of Godoy's generosity to French refugees in the past, the ageing Prince, once master of Spain and the Indies, might have starved.

His last admirer, Lord Holland, who had called on him in Verona and had written to him cordially in Spanish after Carlos' death to inform him that the British Government was, unofficially, quite agreeable to his settling in England if he chose, called on him in his drab fourth-floor Paris lodgings in 1838 and found him much altered, but good-humoured, jovial, and hearty. "Bad French and a chuckling voice, and an arch expression in his eyes." Godoy shrugged off his material misfortunes with a laugh, but he obviously still suffered painfully from Doña Josefa's desertion, and brooded over it continually. "He had no great complaint of Napoleon," noted Lord Holland in some surprise. "He spoke with less bitterness of Ferdinand, and with more of Don Carlos, than I had expected." In Spain a group of sympathisers was actively at work in his behalf, headed by Ramón de Mesonero Romanos, the archivist of Madrid. The late poet Juan Meléndez Valdés, whose long, indignant, laudatory ode to Godoy is so freely quoted in the rambling and discursive memoirs of the Prince's old age, had begun this reaction some years before.

At last, in May 1847, Isabella II signed a decree restoring all Godoy's titles and estates. But before a swarm of lawyers could complete this complex task Godoy—"Monsieur Manuel" to children in the Tuileries—was dead, at the age of eighty-five. He is buried among the other Spanish exiles in that corner of Père Lachaise Cemetery known as *l'île des Espagnols*, with a simple tablet over his grave.

8

"The hatred of the people," muses Bourrienne in his *Memoirs of Napoleon Bonaparte*, "is almost always the just reward of favourites, the very character appearing to announce abjectness of sentiment and base servility. If this be true as regards favourites in general, what must have been the feeling excited by a man who, to the knowledge of all Spain, owed the favour of the King to the favours of the Queen?" From which it will appear that M. de Bourrienne probes to the root of this matter.

That the populace—any populace—will never stomach an upstart who owes a brilliant fortune to a start like Godoy's is a recurring phenomenon. Lord Henry Wotton's conjecture in *The Picture of Dorian Gray*, that "the masses feel that drunkenness, stupidity, and immorality should be their own special property, and that if any one of us makes an ass of himself he is poaching on their preserves," no doubt bears the stamp of a vanished pre-democratic age, but it has still, perhaps, a tiny, horrid grain of truth in it. A tinge of envy mingling with moral execration is not invariably exclusive to the bourgeoisie either, perhaps. Notwithstanding which, who can deny the Spanish populace was justified? Even in our own broad times we have seen a President of the United States climb to power by scrofulous means and become nationally execrated. Even Mexican Reds have been known to blush for their Calles.

So Godoy's services to Spain were and are outweighed by his odious reputation. The extent of those services is still a matter of debate. Briefly reviewing Godoy's foreign policy recently, Don M. Fernández Almagro, of the Royal Academy of History, dismisses him as a rhapsodist (*fantaseador*) and, in his relations with France, an unskilful and unblushing opportunist; acknowledging his valuable service to the Navy in the establishment of the Council of the Admiralty in the year before his fall, but noting that even this was partly due to Napoleon's naggings.[1]

[1] *Política Naval de la España Moderna* (*Revista de Estudios Políticos,* IX, 18, Madrid, 1944).

I have not paused to examine all the diplomatic double-shuffles of which he is accused, rightly or wrongly; still less to note all the private scandals attributed to him (the young Infante Francisco de Paula, for example, was believed by half Spain to be his son). For his beginnings alone the mass of Spaniards never forgave him, and they were right. However debased the age, the populace prefers decency in high places. With that weary patience which aroused G. K. Chesterton's admiration it may accept without murmuring (for example) the bequest of a deceased hero's concubine as a national charge, but there is no evidence that it does so with relish.

Centuries ago a poet cried out against a scandalous intrigue likewise involving a throne:

> . . . *Well you wot that of such life*
> *There comes but sore bataille, and strife,*
> *And blood of men, and hard travaille!*

The worst of the ancient platitudes, as Godoy discovered, being that they are true.

IV

POTEMKIN

"I should like to be surrounded only by heroes."
                              (CATHERINE THE GREAT, to Grimm.)

"The most extraordinary man I ever met."
                              (THE PRINCE DE LIGNE, on Potemkin.)

> *"Or who in Moscow, toward the Czar,*
> *With the demurest of footfalls,*
> *Over the Kremlin's pavement bright*
> *With serpentine and syenite*
> *Steps, with five other Generals*
> *That simultaneously take snuff,*
> *For each to have pretext enough,*
> *And kerchiefwise unfold his sash,*
> *Which, softness' self, is yet the stuff*
> *To hold fast where a steel chain snaps,*
> *And leave the grand white neck no gash? . . ."*

NOTHING half so choreographic as Browning's fantasy marked the removal of Tsar Peter III of Russia, husband of Catherine the Great, by the good offices of her lover Orlov in July 1762. The drunken young half-German cretin[1] to whom this capable girl had been married at sixteen by a lucky mother gave himself up to his executioners, as Frederick-William II of Prussia remarked, like a child being sent to bed; moreover Peter III was murdered not at once and spectacularly, in his palace of Peterhof, but quietly and in the country a week later. Thus did his immensely intelligent widow assume the Russian imperial crown and become Voltaire's "Semiramis of the North" and a commanding figure in Europe.

Orlov (Grigori Grigorievitch) comes third in order of succession in the roll of Catherine's twelve principal and pen-

[1] Previously Duke of Holstein; grandson of Peter the Great; nephew of the Empress Elizabeth of Russia; brought up in Germany.

sioned lovers.[1] Potemkin (Grigori Alexandrovitch), who comes fifth, towers over them all like a fir-tree in a shrubbery. The parallel of Maria Luisa and Godoy would be more striking, perhaps, had Catherine been a Slav. But Catherine, born Sophia-Frederika, was a German, a Stettiner, daughter of an obscure Prussian princeling of the house of Anhalt-Zerbst; a Nordic of orderly mind to whom Slavonic extravagance and exaltation were as distasteful as Austrian *Schlamperei*. Her highly un-Teutonic sense of fun chimes oddly with her doggedly Teutonic lyricism in affairs of the heart. For each of her paramours in turn she had, like a female Werther, such a love as she could scarcely utter. When she duly failed to find in each of them that transcendental ideal, coupled with obedience to her will, she sought, she crossed him neatly off her list, like a housewife shopping at the stores, and tried another. Only Potemkin continued to master her and to dominate the Russian scene long after passion died, and for that reason takes his place with the other subjects of these pages.

So grossly has Catherine the Great been flattered by Voltaire and the *philosophes*, so absurdly has her sensualism been be-glamoured by a cloud of romantics into that of a kind of northern Messalina—"Etna in eruption," said Grimm—that it may be as well to strive for a reasonable view of her here and now. She was completely amoral, yet not so much lascivious as eupeptic. Her very warm and generous heart and senses functioned like her brains and her digestive organs, regularly, unostentatiously, efficiently, like a clock. Catherine's amorous affairs were not the unbridled Oriental orgies of one or two notorious Tsarinas before her, inevitably recalling Diaghilev's productions of *Tamar* and *Schéhérazade*, but, so to speak, matters of State routine, ordered with dignity and a strict regard for decorum. Queen Victoria herself could have conducted an amour (*si j'ose m'exprimer*

---

[1] No. 8 deserves a passing mention, being Count Ivan Nikolaevitch Rimsky-Korsakov, a forbear of the composer, and himself a talented musician.

ainsi) with no more propriety than Catherine conducted a whole long sequence, nor was any ritual at Buckingham Palace in the Victorian Age more rigorous than what might be called the Protocol of the Russian Imperial Bedchamber. Having singled out a likely candidate, Catherine had him first of all invited by an intimate woman-friend, known to the Court as the Tester (*l'Éprouveuse*), to a dinner-party at which the Empress would arrive at the last moment, and without warning. Having, as we should say nowadays, thoroughly vetted the young man for deportment and conversation, Her Imperial Majesty signified approval or otherwise to the Tester with a look and withdrew. Two more strict tests awaited the successful candidate. On passing them he was at once promoted to apartments in the Palace prepared for him, and on the day following his installation the world was officially notified of the appointment by his appearance, with the Empress on his arm, in the State apartments, wearing a plumed hat and splendid clothes, and followed by all the Court bareheaded.

This methodical German streak in Catherine, a woman of virile intellect, gives her an obvious link with Victoria. They have other traits in common, such as good sense, prudence, autocracy, an instinct for stability, and a sincere passion for music and correspondence.[1] Had Catherine been given an Albert she would possibly have been as blameless a wife and mother as Victoria. It was her earliest misfortune to be married to an impotent driveller, and a hated Holsteiner to boot, and after Peter's removal she was apparently unable, for all her seeking, to find an affinity strong enough to risk matrimony with a second time. Among her undoubted qualities the taming Western influence she exercised on the Russian temperament deserves the highest praise. A very few years before her accession her tigress aunt-by-marriage, the Empress Elizabeth, had had an unfortunate lady-in-waiting, Madame Lapoukhine, whose principal offence

---

[1] Apart from her services to State opera, Catherine wrote five opera-libretti; music by Fomine, Spartini, and others.

was her beauty, involved in a Court plot, stripped naked before the crowd in the public square by the common hangman, knouted into a bloody wreck under the Empress's eyes, deprived of her nose, and banished for life to Siberia. Such Asiatic vivacity, common enough before Catherine's accession, ceased thenceforth save for one massacre of revolting serfs on the grand scale.

Catherine's portraits in her bloom display other similarities to Victoria, such as an opulent majesty of figure and bearing, a firm chin, a benevolent but imperious blue eye. Catherine had the advantage in looks, as in brains. In her twenties, according to Official Lover No. 2, the handsome Poniatowski—Stanislas Augustus, unfortunate last King of Poland—she was actually a beauty, with a dazzling white skin, large blue eyes, dark hair, vivid colouring, long black eyelashes, a slim figure, perfect hands and arms, a charming voice, a gay laugh, and "a mouth that seemed to crave for kisses;" which seems not to be entirely Polish gallantry, for Poniatowski was deeply enamoured and never forgot her. He alone of all her lovers was her social equal and an eligible *parti*, and he seems to have urged her passionately in 1762 and later to marry him. But she had ascended her throne quite unexpectedly—owing, it was officially announced, to the regretted sudden death, from natural causes, of Tsar Peter III—and her position had to be consolidated; and the dashing, amusing, careless Pole did not entirely fit in as a consort with her plans for Russia.

These, as might be expected, were prudent, conservative, and absolute, despite that liberalism of outlook which won Catherine so much adulation from the French intelligentsia. For Utopians babbling as only Russians can babble, till the last candles gutter out, and dawn breaks over the snowy streets, and the last empty bottle of sweet Crimean champagne is hurled away, and the yawning gipsy orchestra begins packing up, she had a serene contempt; nor did her ardour for the Encyclopædists, which waned markedly with the advent of the Revolution, affect her judgment that

what eighteenth-century Russia needed was a firm maternal hand
and no novelties.[1] At the back of her mind was some benevolent
notion of liberating one day those swarming millions of serfs at
the mention of whom pained white hands were raised in every
advanced European drawing-room, and especially in France and
in England, where the Negro slave-traffic reached its most
prosperous peak in the 1780's; but this could wait, and meanwhile the serfs must behave themselves. Whether or not she
shared the low opinion of the Russian peasant common to observers like Dr. Astrov, of *Uncle Vanya*, and other nineteenth-
century pessimists (and how different the Russian serf's characteristics from the manly independence of the hinds of her
native Prussia!), she was careful never to display it. For a
foreigner of Lutheran upbringing Catherine combined, in fact,
private enthusiasm for the French philosophers and a strict
public observance of Orthodoxy with a remarkable grasp of certain patriarchal aspects of the Russian serf-owning system, and she
was aware that, as with Western serf-owners in the early Middle
Ages, the average Russian squire knew and fulfilled some of his
obligations at least. He might in a fit of ungovernable rage, like
testy Admiral Lyesovsky in the memoirs of Rimsky-Korsakov,[2]
bite off the nose of an offending serf, but a moment later might
equally see him kneeling in tears, begging forgiveness of his
victim in the name of Christ and making all reparation possible.
Amid the cruelties inflicted on its myriad serfs by our modern
industrial civilisation such eccentricities as remorse and reparation have no place, but the most ardent worshipper of Progress
will admit their picturesqueness.

Undoubtedly Catherine was well-advised, in her time and
place, to ignore the philosophers, much as she grieved her
friends, Voltaire, Diderot, Grimm, Helvetius, and the others

[1] Though she made two attempts to westernise the Russian judicial code.
One, based on Montesquieu, was foiled by the nobility. The other, based on
Blackstone, partially succeeded.

[2] Not Catherine II's favourite No. 8, but his descendant Nikolay Andreye-
vitch, the composer (1844–1908).

thereby, though their grief was partly assuaged by her generous presents. The impact of the smart new French philosophies on an hysterical intelligentsia reacting on millions of ignorant and barbarian peasantry could hardly suit her book. Nor did she swallow all French prescriptions herself, on examination. Having invited her idol Diderot to St. Petersburg, lodged him luxuriously in the Hermitage Palace, and loaded him with flattery and favours, she shrewdly probed the philosopher's mind and rejected his sophistries. In her own words some years later: "I talked long and often with Diderot, but with more curiosity than profit. . . . If I had believed him, everything in the Empire would have been turned topsy-turvy. Legislation, administration, politics, finances—all to be upset in exchange for a set of implacable theories! . . ." The philosopher's playful habit of pinching women's knees in intimate conversation may or may not have contributed to this coolness. Having parried his attentions more than once with a laugh and moved farther away, Catherine was eventually forced (she often recalled) to place a table between them. Nevertheless, she sent Diderot back to Paris with three thousand gold roubles and a set of priceless sables, among other expensive presents. Impulsive generosity was Matushka's[1] ruling passion, as all her paramours agreed; as did also Sir Joshua Reynolds, on receiving a magnificent diamond-studded gold snuff-box and an autograph compliment in recognition of *Discourses on Painting*.

2

The début of Potemkin as Favourite lacks the romance of Orlov's, which the late Alfred Savoir amusingly exploited in his satiric comedy *La Petite Catherine*. Looking from a window in the Winter Palace one day early in 1760, the frustrated thirty-one-year-old consort of Peter III perceived a handsome, gigantic young Guards officer gazing absently in her direction. On being

[1] *Matushka*—"Little Mother," a term of endearment used by Catherine's lovers and the Russians generally.

duly presented, he turned out to be precisely what her soul craved, as she proclaimed to her philosopher friend Grimm. Thrice wounded at Zorndorf against the Prussians, a byword throughout the Army for reckless valour . . . like the Grand Duchess of Gérolstein in the operetta, and like Maria Luisa of Spain, Catherine II *aimait les militaires*, and heroic ones for preference. Her liaison with Orlov, which began thenceforth and was kept a secret for some time, lasted ten years. Having in due course deceived her luxuriantly, beaten her excessively, and nearly broken her heart with the zest of the spoiled child he was, Count Grigori Orlov was duly retired with a marble palace, a fortune of 17 million roubles, and estates carrying some 45,000 serfs, to be succeeded in the Imperial embraces by Official Paramour No. 4, Alexander Simoneivitch Vassilchikov, a comely but mediocre Guardee who bored Catherine consummately and was discarded within a year or so, with an annual pension of 20,000 roubles and a *douceur* of some 150,000, exclusive of plate and linen. Potemkin, who now succeeded, was already an admired acquaintance, even a friend, of the Empress's, and had been so since 1762. His promotion to the Bedchamber is relatively banal.

Little else about Potemkin could be described as banal. An attractively and essentially Russian type, he might in some aspects have burst straight from the pages of Dostoievsky or Tchekov. That cosmopolitan Prince Charming, connoisseur of life and men and citizen of Europe, Marshal the Prince de Ligne, who accompanied Catherine and Potemkin in their celebrated musical-comedy progress through the Crimea in 1787 and also saw Potemkin in action (or at that period, inaction) against the Turks, has summed up "the most extraordinary man I ever met" in a justly admired series of brilliant and daintily balanced antitheses:

A Commander-in-Chief who looks idle and works incessantly, who has no desk but his knees, no comb but his fingers; constantly reclining on his couch yet sleepless night and day, driven by zeal for a Sovereign he adores. Timorous for others, for himself fearless; alarmed when danger approaches, gay in the midst of it; sombre amid his pleasures, made unhappy by his great fortune, surfeited with everything, easily disgusted; morose, inconstant, a profound philosopher, an able Minister, a sublime politician, and a ten-year-old child; free from vindictiveness, asking pardon for any wrong he inflicts; believing himself to love God, afraid of the devil, beckoning with one hand to women who attract him and crossing himself with the other. . . . Prodigiously rich and not worth a sou; talking divinity to his generals and strategy to archbishops; reading nothing, but pumping everyone he talks to; extremely affable and extremely savage, having alternately the bearing of the most arrogant Oriental satrap and the politest of Louis XIV's courtiers. . . . Fantastic in ideas of time, in his meals, his leisure, and his tastes; wanting everything like a child and knowing how to do without it like a great man; gnawing his nails, apples, and raw turnips. . . . Sometimes going barefoot in a shabby dressing-gown, sometimes in a superb coat with diamonds the size of your thumb. . . . Stooping, almost bent double, when at home; tall, erect, proud, noble, majestic, fascinating when with his army, like Agamemnon among the kings of Greece.

What is his magic? Genius, genius, and again genius; natural abilities, an excellent memory, an elevated soul, practising malice without injury and artifice without craftiness; a happy mixture of caprices, in his good moments, which attracts every heart; great generosity, gracious and just in award; an abundance of tact, the gift of guessing what he does not know, a consummate knowledge of men.[1]

Another intimate, equally fascinated, the Comte de Ségur, French Ambassador, adds in his memoirs one or two more strokes to de Ligne's portrait. To Ségur Potemkin is East and West bewilderingly alloyed:

A big heart, a caustic wit. Avaricious and ostentatious, despotic and popular, inflexible and beneficent . . . nothing could equal the vigour of his mind or the indolence of his body. He

[1] *Lettre sur la dernière Guerre des Turcs, III* (1788).

was weary with the burden of his own existence, envious of everything not done by himself, disgusted with everything he did. In conversation he astonished alike the scholar, the artist, the mechanic, and the divine. . . . Sometimes, shut up in his room for weeks on end with his nieces and intimates, he would lounge on a sofa without speaking, or play at chess or cards with bare legs and unfastened shirt, wrapped in a dressing-gown, knitting his brows, like a squalid Cossack. At other times he affected the courtier in magnificent clothes, covered with ribbons and orders, displaying diamonds of extraordinary size and brilliance and giving splendid entertainments without any motive.

A third intimate, Mr. James Harris, later first Earl of Malmesbury, had less opportunity, perhaps, during five arduous years (1778–83) as British Ambassador at the Russian Court, to indulge in analytical character-portrayal. Harris's diaries and correspondence nevertheless confirm here and there the impressions of Ligne and Ségur. Like them he was charmed, fascinated, and baffled by "this very extraordinary man, who every day affords me new matter of amazement and surprise . . . a mixture of wit, levity, learning, and humour such as I never met in one man." The Favourite's avarice does not escape Mr. Harris's comment, nor yet that passion for the arcana of Orthodoxy which clashes so violently, in Western eyes, with the feats of a paladin of the alcove more worthy of a tomb at "Saint-Satyr by Sancerre" than Villon's Michault le Bon Fouterre himself.[1]

From Harris's successor at the Embassy, Mr. Alleyne Fitz-Herbert, first Baron St. Helens, one of Catherine's principal guests on the famous tour of 1787, one might reasonably expect some diverting Potemkiniana, since Mr. FitzHerbert, son of one of Dr. Johnson's friends, was gay and amusing and a notable raconteur. Unfortunately FitzHerbert's private papers perished in a fire in 1797, and his despatches surviving in the Foreign Office archives are stiff with discretion, even in cipher. Only once, so far as I can discover, does he break out, relatively, with a

[1] *Grant Testament,* lxxxi.

reference (in a letter to Charles James Fox) to Potemkin's "haughty reserve and superciliousness, joined to a variety of capricious and tyrannical exercises of authority," at that moment evoking growls at G.H.Q. No doubt FitzHerbert's lost diaries were more revealing.

3

Grigori Alexandrovitch Potemkin was born near Smolensk on September 14, 1736, the only son of Alexander Potemkin, a retired colonel and landowner of the small nobility and of modest means. The Colonel, in middle age a reputed bigamist, was of morose disposition and violent and uncertain temper, perpetually shouting and weeping, insanely jealous of his young second wife, accusing her constantly of infidelity; an open-air type faintly recalling General Khvalynsky in *A Sportsman's Tales* or, more justly, a synthesis of half a dozen pop-eyed military and land-owning eccentrics in as many Russian novels. A difficult character, making life difficult for all around him; and from the Colonel his son possibly derived some of his own wayward temper. His talents and his rich confusing personality were his own, and his rage for Byzantine theology remained a dominant all his life.

One should realise that the singularity of such a hobby is, or was, no more noticeable in Russian eyes than (for example) the eminent professor of chemistry Borodin's spare-time addiction to composing superb opera and the similar diversions of nine-teenth-century naval and military officers and Civil Servants like Rimsky-Korsakov, César Cui, Moussorgsky, and others. As with the Spaniard, past and present, religion with the Russian of the old régime could be a *raison d'être*, and the spectacle of a young Guardsman, as Potemkin soon became, rushing away after parade to vest as an acolyte and swing a thurible at Mass or Vespers at a neighbouring church, or to engage in long, absorb-ing debate on the Filioque Clause or the Council of Nicæa in a monastery parlour, was nothing unusual right down to the collapse of the Russian Empire in 1917. Had young Grigori actually become a seminarist, as did a modern personage of note named Djugashvili, *alias* Nizheradze, *alias* Chizhikof, *alias* Ivanovitch, *alias* Stalin, he would quite likely have made a very good bishop, and, so far as the traditional subservience of the Orthodox Church to the State would permit, a memorable one.

Destined by his father at first for Orders, Potemkin's temperament very early convinced his tutors at the University of Moscow that the energies of their brilliant, lazy pupil would be better directed towards a military career. The Colonel accordingly entered him as a trooper in a cavalry regiment of the exclusive Guards. Promotion to a cornetcy followed very quickly, and zeal for theology did not prevent his joining in all the gambols of the fashionable young rakes of his regiment. He attained a lieutenantcy without difficulty, and towards 1762 attracted the eye of the new Tsar's uncle, Peter, Duke of Holstein, who attached Potemkin to his staff as an aide-de-camp. It was in this way that the efficient young soldier came in contact with the handsome giant Count Orlov and his equally enormous and inseparable four brothers, at this moment about to carry out the operation which removed the young fool from Holstein and gave Catherine the Russian throne.

It does not seem that Potemkin took any notable part in the *coup d'état* of June 1762, in which a large number of influential people were involved, including the Archbishop of Novgorod. The business had been carefully organised some time before Potemkin's arrival on the scene. Grigori Orlov, Catherine's lover, was the principal operator, Count Nikita Panine wrung the abdication from the terrified Tsar at Peterhof, and Alexis Orlov attended to him with a glass of poisoned vodka at Ropcha on July 5 and finally strangled him with a scarf, more or less in the Browning manner.[1] Peter III was more easy to kill than the

[1] Voltaire's comment in a letter to Mme du Deffand is worth quoting: "I am well aware that a few trifling reproaches concerning her husband are being levelled at Katy [Catherine]; but these are family affairs, in which it is my rule never to interfere."

satanic Rasputin, whose return to fighting life, after apparently dying of poison, makes such a macabre story. Before the murder Catherine, who had nearly been arrested at the last moment by Peter's orders, had been proclaimed Empress in the Cathedral of Our Lady of Kazan. As Potemkin's name is among those rewarded by her subsequently with a shower of roubles and serfs, it is evident that he had not been entirely quiescent during the complicated events of June and July.

When and where his personal contact with Catherine began is also uncertain. There is a story of his lending her a sword-knot and exchanging a few words with her on the first day of the *coup*, as she was reviewing troops. There is another early story of Potemkin's delighting her, shortly after being presented, with a clever parody of her own voice and manner; which, when one remembers a freezing story of Queen Victoria in similar circumstances, places Catherine in a rather agreeable light. In November 1762, at all events, we find Potemkin, a colonel and a Gentleman of the Chamber with the title of "Excellency" and a stipend of two thousand roubles, being despatched on a brief errand to Stockholm to inform the Russian Ambassador there of current events. On his return Potemkin resumed his duties as a *Kammerjunker* and, despite his careless lack of polish, began impressing Catherine more and more with his extreme intelligence and his strange amusing charm. Another step in military rank followed before long.

Catherine's interest in him was growing, though as yet without any sentimental tinge. Potemkin's great muscular frame naturally pleased her. His shrewd, round, big-nosed, thick-lipped Slavonic features, hardly improved about this time by the loss of his left eye, for which accident there exist three separate explanations,[1] could apparently be rendered highly attractive by the magic of his smile. His range of picturesque moods, his colossal

[1] He is said to have (1) run a pin into his eye while reducing a swelling brought on by quack treatment, (2) lost his eye at tennis, and (3) lost it in a fight with the brothers Grigori and Alexis Orlov. No. 3 has been adjudged correct.

GENERAL FIELD MARSHAL PRINCE POTEMKIN TAURIDA &c. &c. &c.

Engraved from the Original Picture in her Imperial Majesty's Collection by James Walker Engraver to her Imperial Majesty, and member of the Academy of Arts B.r Giacobino

Potemkin

vanity, his habits of biting his nails, ignoring Court etiquette, and forgetting to speak French when addressed soon became a standing joke with the Empress. His gift for mimicry and his enormous appetites made her laugh heartily. His brains, as I have said, impressed her increasingly.

On Potemkin's side the boredom of the Court was for some time offset by its showy luxury, which appealed to him. He had a curiously feminine passion all his life for fingering jewels, gloating over glittering stars and Orders, and polishing the mountings of his rings. He loved choosing sumptuous clothes and liturgical vestments, designing mitres of cloth-of-gold and silver for episcopal friends. His opinions on interior decoration were decided, and are conveyed at great length in a letter to one of his mistresses for whom he was planning a house. "A peristyle of pierced and sculptured columns, treated as delicately as lace. . . . . A large, dimly-lit hall, from the depths of which will be heard the murmur of a fountain. . . . Everywhere paintings in the most vivid colours. . . . Draperies of the softest pale green. . . . Windows of the clearest aquamarine crystal. . . . Sofas, richly furnished with cushions, covered in white muslin relieved by raspberry-colour. . . . " For the most part his taste was ardently rococo, and the Winter Palace was full of rococo; perhaps overfull.

Like every other northern Court of the period, Catherine II's founded itself more or less self-consciously on Versailles. As the Winter Palace dated only from 1732 (the previous palace of Peter the Great, at whose order St. Petersburg arose from the marshes, stood on the site of the present Hermitage), it of course displayed none of that authentic Byzantine blaze, that rich, hot Muscovite magnificence so brilliantly evoked in our own day by Bakst, and even more by Bilbilin in his Kremlin settings for a memorable Parisian production of *Boris Godounov*, towards the end of Chaliapin's reign. Nevertheless gold and silver ikons encrusted with jewels, heavily-gemmed clocks and samovars, a recurrence of rubies, emeralds, and diamonds the size of plovers' eggs, and a rather lamentable over-indulgence in malachite and porphyry, serpentine and syenite, could strike a valiantly Russian note against a relatively European background, itself banal and emphatic enough and suitable to a parvenu city like St. Petersburg, yet often failing to attain that note of gorgeous vulgarity which stuns the eye in Frederick the Great's palace of Sans-Souci at Potsdam, where hardly an inch of space is left untortured by caprice or unloaded with bright paint and thick gold.

It was not easy, even in the last days of the unfortunate Tsar Nicholas II, I have gathered from a Russian connoisseur, to imagine what the enormous Imperial barrack on the left bank of the Neva looked like in Potemkin's day. The palace of 1732, reconstructed by the Italian architect Rastrelli a few years later, was burned down in 1837 and restored conjecturally by Stasov and Brulov, two native architects of elaborate fancy. *Un décor d'opéra*, remarks a French critic of the 1900's, wincing even in the Art-Nouveau period at an undoubted masterpiece of nineteenth-century baroque. The Hermitage Palace adjoining, built by a Frenchman, Vallin de la Mothe, for the entertainment of Catherine's foreign philosopher-friends without Court etiquette, continues to shame it by a classic sobriety. The conjectural interior restoration of the Winter Palace in the 1840's was fairly faithful, apparently. It is permissible to doubt whether the impact of vast salons of this kind—whether draped in heavy crimson velvet brocaded with gold Byzantine two-headed eagles, or studded with plaques of gold and enamel, or dazzling as a colossal wedding-cake with pillars of white marble—on a moody and impressionable nature like Potemkin's can have been invariably happy. Even His Britannic Majesty's ambassador, Mr. James Harris, was jolted out of his diplomatic calm by the Winter Palace. "The entertainments, the apartments, and the number of domestics are *quite Asiatic*," he wrote home in 1777.

Yawning amid the splendour, bored with the etiquette, amusing and fascinating enough when the mood took him, Potemkin seems to have made up his mind very early to replace

Grigori Orlov in the Empress's favour, and his first too-obvious manœuvres to that end led apparently to that brawl with two of the Orlov brothers in which he lost his eye. Catherine's reception of the newcomer continued markedly encouraging. How his rivalry with Orlov would have developed had Potemkin remained at Court one cannot judge (huge and heavy as he was, Grigori Orlov could support his eighteen-stone on one hand amid the Court's evening romps, a mortifying thought). Nor, possibly, could Potemkin have made much sentimental headway at present, for Catherine was fully and anxiously preoccupied with establishing herself, amid intrigues, treacheries, and menaces within and without. The ghost of Peter III was looming over her oppressively. Little Father was not dead, the peasantry murmured, scratching themselves vigorously on their stoves at evening; he had escaped the knives, he would return soon. False Tsars began cropping up, like false Dauphins after the French Restoration, but more formidably. Russia has always been a rich soil for pretenders.

The principal impostor, a dashing Don Cossack named Pougatchov, more redoubtable than any Naundorff or Perkin Warbeck and hardly less so than the False Demetrius of Boris Godounov's reign, familiar to every opera-lover, commanded a considerable army of brigands, deserters, escapees from Siberia, disaffected troops, and miscellaneous riffraff. After Pougatchov had raised a vast revolt of serfs in the Urals, overrun nearly all south-eastern Russia, assumed Imperial style and honours, taken Samara, sacked the holy city of Kazan, and conquered a string of fortresses, Catherine's nervousness, though she put a stoic face on the matter to Voltaire and affected to jest, became extreme. Fortunately for her, the Cossack Tsar drank day and night like a Cossack, as his proclamations perhaps indicate. Example:

If God leads me to St. Petersburg I will send my wife [Catherine] to a nunnery, where she can implore pardon for her sins. I will deprive the boyards of all their villages and property and give them money in exchange. As for those who have deprived me of my throne, I will hang them all.

It took Catherine two years to put down Pougatchov's rising, with excessive bloodiness, and in January 1775 the Cossack Tsar was duly hanged, to be romanticised half a century later by the poet Pushkin, among others. The Cossack's exit left only one outstanding thorn in Catherine's pillow, for the rightful heir to the Russian throne, Ivan VI, whom his aunt Elizabeth had imprisoned for life, had been murdered in 1764 in the fortress of Schlusselberg. The remaining menace was an adventuress of some personality with half a dozen aliases and a European following who claimed to be Princess Elizabeth, the late Empress's daughter, and may have been a Turkish agent, as Catherine conjectured. The Princess was captured in May 1775 and succumbed to rigorous prison-conditions six months later.

By way of relief from these domestic troubles Catherine had been giving the Turk, between 1769 and 1774, a hearty drubbing, evoked by a heaven-sent Turkish ultimatum, at the appeal of desperate Polish patriots, on the subject of withdrawing from Poland the Russian troops and swarming secret agents who had helped to place her vassal Poniatowski on the Polish throne. The peace-treaty of Kainardji (1774) was merely a pause. To expel the Turk from Europe and to extend Russian frontiers to the Black Sea, and farther, will be Catherine's almost lifelong preoccupation; and not entirely a vulgar or imperialist one, since it ultimately envisaged the old Orthodox hope of wresting back Byzantium.

"Allah! Catherina!" wrote Voltaire to his friend on learning of the naval victory of Tchesmé. "Your Imperial Majesty, by slaying the Turks, gives me a new lease of life!" It was not only the eminent French crusader's heart which was thus uplifted. Catherine knew what she was about. Down to half-way through the first World War (1914–18), when the merest fickle caprice of Fate, as dons would say, saved the Dardanelles and closed the Allies' road to Constantinople, the possibility of crowning Hagia Sophia once more with the Cross was no vague mirage in the Russian heart but a vision bright and glowing, at intervals, as the frescoes of San Marco. In Catherine's day it was only three hundred years since the Turk stormed Byzantium and Constantine XI, last of the Imperial Palæologues, died like a soldier in his purple shoes before the Cannon Gate. Twenty years after this disaster Tsar Ivan III, marrying a refugee Palæologue princess, made the Kremlin heir and legatee to the Byzantine Empire, its religion, autocracy, ceremonial, bureaucracy, and to some extent its virtues, vices, and arts. It was Ivan's firm conviction that with the twicrowned bicephalous eagle, the symbol of Byzantine imperial pride, he "transported to Moscow the soul of Byzantium and the seat of Orthodoxy,"[1] and the Russian Church has ever since cherished, with the Byzantine Liturgy, the traditional Byzantine jealousy and sectarian hatred of Rome. Catherine the Great was exploiting the deepest and most sacred emotions of her subjects when she seized her first opportunity to harry and drive the Turk. Her second grandson, with admirable foresight, was christened Constantine in due course.

Sick of biting his nails at Court, sighing at the blue flash of Catherine's eyes, and fuming over the obvious impossibility as yet of ousting Orlov, Major-General Potemkin welcomed the outbreak of the Turkish war with relief, and as soon as possible left violently for the front with Catherine's permission and a letter to Marshal Count Roumiantsev, G.O.C., in her own firm hand. Roumiantsev, an elderly professional soldier of some eminence, grimly appointed the newcomer his personal aide-de-camp, as ordered, and took little trouble to conceal his opinion of Court favourites, thereby sowing the seeds of lifelong enmity. Though his post gave him few opportunities of acquiring

[1] Auguste Bailly, *Byzance*, Paris, 1939.

glory in the field Potemkin was gazetted in due course, and it seems deservedly, for ability and courage, and the delighted Empress at once gave him another step. And General Potemkin had not worn his new insignia long before persistent rumours began arriving at G.H.Q. that the days of Count Grigori Orlov's reign at Court were at last numbered. Applying for leave, granted without difficulty, Potemkin rushed back to St. Petersburg, to find that Catherine had already appointed Orlov's successor to her embraces, the handsome but vapid Vassilchikov.

It is difficult to judge whether Potemkin's fit of typically Slavonic temperament on discovering this disappointment was genuine, counterfeit, or both. Undoubtedly he was now in love, in his strange way, with Catherine. ("When she enters a dark room," he said adoringly of her about this time, "she lights it up.") How far thwarted egotism added to his furious chagrin, how far he was acting a part, who can say? He ostentatiously removed himself from Court to a small house in the suburbs, growing long hair and a beard, living like a hermit behind locked doors, absorbed day and night in theology and, it was said (undoubtedly the rumour was inspired), determined to become a monk. The heart of Catherine, who had welcomed him back with ardent pleasure, was pierced on learning that the absentee, tortured with passion for an inaccessible love, had renounced the world. Potemkin was given tactfully to understand by an emissary that there was no need to despair. His immediate and very skilful move was to retire to the great monastery-fortress of St. Alexander Nevski, and the story flew swiftly round St. Petersburg that he had already entered the novitiate under the Rule of St. Basil. Catherine, in high alarm, sent him the blunt assurance that his unsatisfactory rival was already, so to speak, out on the doorstep. Within a few days General Grigori Potemkin, back at Court, cropped, shaven, brilliantly dressed, and beaming, was officially proclaimed the reigning lover of Catherine the Great.

4

When, with unerring psychological skill, the German General
Staff in the spring of 1917 packed Lenin into a sealed railway
carriage and sent him speeding east over the frontier like a V-
bomb, it is recorded that the future master of Russia was terrified,
and his right-hand man, the Jew Zinoviev, yellow with fright.
Neither of them was prepared for that state of mystic, nightmare-
like paralysis which delivered Russia into their hands like a dazed
sheep. It is significant that Rodzianko, last President of the
Imperial Douma, speaks seriously in his survey of the last years
of the Russian monarchy of "occult forces" directed by a power-
house of militant evil, emanating from Rasputin and his associ-
ates, which influenced the entire governmental machinery of
Russia, nominated and gave orders to Ministers, and operated
everywhere.[1]

No such devilry darkens the memory of Potemkin, and his
influence over the Empress Catherine has none of the satanic
terror of Rasputin's over the Empress Alexandra Feodorovna.
Witchcraft was (and is) not unknown in Russia, as in Lapland,
and in our own time we have become aware of that great cloud
of evil, sweeping over Europe from the Mongolian deserts, so
oddly foreseen by one of D. H. Lawrence's characters.[2] But
Potemkin's acts are as free from sorcery and sortileges as his
mistress's. He dominated her, during their brief amour, by a
skilful mixture of roughness and tenderness which presents no
problems to Harley Street. Matushka's itch for letter-writing
evoked a sequence to Potemkin of which many specimens are
preserved. They are the kind of letter any lovesick girl would
write. "My Cyclops, my bow-wow, my pigeon, my golden phea-
sant. . . ." And less embarrassingly: "You have infatuated me. . . .
I love and will love you till eternity, against your will. . . .
Love me just a little, for I am yours. . . . I pray God I may

[1] Mikhail Vladimirovitch Rodzianko, *Le Règne de Raspoutine*, Paris, 1927.
[2] *St. Mawr.*

die at that very hour when you cease loving me. . . ." She wrote usually thus to big attractive men. In Potemkin's case, however, she soon divined that his ambition was greater than his love, and it shocked her. "Dear one, how shameful! . . ." His strong, cunning common sense was meanwhile making plans against the day of satiety. Within a little over two years he was no longer the Empress's official paramour. By that time his influence over her was so firmly established that he could, and did, nominate successors to the Imperial Bedchamber; at a reasonable fee, and not without some admirably acted chagrin to begin with, which stirred Catherine to remorse, pity, and rich consolations.

Potemkin, then, conquered by no occult means, but with a bizarre, erratic, and fundamentally boyish genius which, outside Russia, as his friend Ségur, the French Ambassador, remarked, would probably have got him nowhere in particular. The diplomat and statesman glittering like a cathedral *ikonostasis* with every jewelled Order procurable, native and foreign—he loved these massive trinkets dearly, as already observed, and was sincerely piqued at being unable to add to his collection the Garter and the Golden Fleece—remains, like the administrator and soldier, his favourite rôle, a brilliant amateur.

Nevertheless he had one fiercely definite objective, which began to emerge soon after his accession to the Imperial embraces, and particularly after he had consolidated his position at Court by ensuring the ejection of all—or at least all he knew—who could in any way embarrass him; including such leading conspirators of 1762 as Count Panine, Minister of Foreign Affairs, and above all the Orlovs. His victory over the Orlovs —though he did not succeed in destroying their prestige entirely —was particularly gratifying after the long effort of smooth dissembling which their predominance at Court had forced upon him. As already noted, this subtle warfare had at least once broken into a bout of fisticuffs in which Potemkin lost an eye, though vanity always made him attribute this accident to other causes (he had perhaps been lucky to escape so lightly when two of the gigantic brothers fell upon him like a landslide). However, the Orlovs were now swept out of his path and his way was clear. It has been suggested that his twin goal from the beginning of his preferment was to make Catherine II totally dependent on him, and ultimately to make himself Tsar. The first objective he nearly achieved; never quite. The second remains doubtful, though a few years hence, as we shall perceive, he got close enough to inspire strong rumours of a secret marriage with the Empress.

About one of his earliest and most flaming ambitions, as I have said, there is no doubt at all. "It was about this time," says the anonymous author of his Memoirs, "that Potemkin inspired Catherine with the gigantic project of driving the Turks from Europe" (more likely it was the other way round). And in fact, but for his addiction to recurring and typically Slavonic spells of paralytic indolence, seizing him unexpectedly amid his most energetic labours, and an equal tendency to drop everything without warning and go off on a large-scale orgy, Potemkin—or at least the professionals under him, like Roumiantsev and Souvarov—would probably have made short work of the forces of the Sublime Porte, now owing allegiance to the semi-imbecile Sultan Abdul Hamid IV, who had been kept forty years in a cage.

Potemkin flung himself into action with cyclonic zeal, stirring up new trouble for the Turk in the Crimea, Moldavia, Wallachia, and even Egypt by a spirited secret-service propaganda drive. His next concern was the reform and re-training of the Russian army, for which purpose Catherine appointed him President of the War Council. Apart from Cossacks, some 300,000 formidable but ill-equipped regulars made up the war-establishment. Potemkin cropped the Army's luxuriant hair, issued it with modern arms, uniform, and equipment, doubled its strength, and reorganised its training on the French model with the advice of two foreign experts, a British officer named Major Semple[1] and

---

[1] A shady character, also notable for trying to blackmail the bigamous Duchess of Kingston.

an Irish officer named Newton. A more important British coad-jutor, granted general's rank by Potemkin, was Samuel (later Sir Samuel) Bentham, naval architect and brother of the Utili-tarian Messiah, who had been sent to Russia by Lord Lansdowne to study naval problems. According to the diaries of that sober gossip Joseph Farington, R.A., what brought Bentham to the Favourite's notice was the invention of "a machine which he travelled in by Land, and could convert into a Boat when he wished to cross a River"; the direct ancestor, one observes, of the British Army "duck" which figured so prominently in the final stages of World War II.

Potemkin's next moves against the Turk were the fortifying of a chain of towns along the Russo-Crimean frontier, the extension of his propaganda-drive to embrace the Orthodox Greeks and Armenians in the Turkish Empire itself, and finally a demand for free access to the Black Sea, backed by the concentration of an army corps on the Crimean frontier. Towards the end of 1782, the invasion and annexation of the Crimea was finally decided.

During these five or six years of preparation some enjoyable and ultimately profitable diplomatic manœuvring in his spare time had increased Potemkin's already high opinion of himself and gratified his mistress equally. Frederick the Great, the Philosopher-King, who greatly esteemed Catherine's brains and had made a treaty with Russia in the 1760's to frighten Austria, had recently condescended to deal with the Russian Favourite as man to man, approaching Potemkin with the suggestion that Russia should annex Swedish Finland while he, Frederick, dealt simultaneously with Swedish Pomerania. Potemkin advised Catherine to reject this as a trifle unworthy of consideration. A better offer was coming.

Thanks to the military genius and cold astuteness of "Old Fritz," Prussia was now one of the current five Great Powers, the others being Great Britain, France, Austria, and Russia. Frederick's working ally and pupil at the moment was Joseph II, son of Maria Theresa of Austria, a personage hardly less arid, coldly ambitious, egotistic, and atheist. In 1772, the two philosophers decided to carve up helpless Poland by an Act of Partition, with the assistance of Catherine the Great, despite the tears of the noble and honourable Maria Theresa and the European appeals of Poniatowski.[1] By the deal of January 5, 1772, based admittedly (like the two subsequent partitions which finished Poland twenty years later) on "liberal" grounds, since all Polish patriots were and are fervently Catholic, Russia took 42,000 square miles of Ruthenia and Inflanty with 2 million inhabitants, largely Orthodox. Austria took 27,000 square miles of Galicia and Sandomir with 3 million Catholic Poles. Lutheran Prussia took 13,000 square miles round Posen, Pomorze, and Masuria, with 600,000 Poles, also Catholic. Joseph II, unsatisfied, next cast his eyes on Bavaria, whose Elector had just died, and here the bandits quarrelled. A war which neither particularly wanted broke out between Prussia and Austria, and towards 1779 it seemed desirable to each party to angle for Russian support.

There was money in this, and Potemkin received the overtures of both sides with haughty composure, waiting for the highest bid. Frederick eventually offered him the Duchy of Courland. Joseph, less frugal and knowing his man, offered a handsome bribe in gold, which Potemkin accepted. Catherine duly received Joseph II at Mohilev, concluded an alliance, and enlisted Austrian help against the Porte, and Potemkin almost immediately realised that his love of cash-down had perhaps spoiled his chance of a bigger prize. "Once I had got Courland," he growled to one of his entourage, "it would not have been too difficult to get Poland!" However, if it was now too late, he was able to console himself almost immediately with another highly profitable deal, this time with the British Cabinet, via our Ambassador, Mr. James Harris. The affair has its entertaining aspects, like other Potemkiniana.

[1] To whom George III replied that he had better expect no help but that of God Almighty.

Bribery was, of course, as normal a branch of eighteenth-century diplomacy and politics as dining out, and Thackeray's quip about the noblemen of England slipping Lord North's presents so elegantly under their ruffles applies, *mutatis mutandis*, to Europe at large. At the Court of Catherine II, which Mr. Harris very early perceived to be "one continued scene of intrigue, debauchery, iniquity, and corruption," the system had attained almost cynical perfection. Hardly a member of Catherine's entourage, from Ministers to scullions, was not receiving money from some Embassy or other; apart from a cosy informal arrangement among the Corps Diplomatique for the benefit of members desiring advance-information from their colleagues' confidential servants. More than once Harris complains to a relatively tight-fisted Whitehall of the financial competition against him, notably from Count Goertz, the Prussian Minister, to whom expense was no object, and from the Chevalier de Corberon, French chargé-d'affaires, who was indelicate enough in 1779 to boast of "having the wherewithal to buy Prince Potemkin," which seemed to Mr. Harris a typically Gallic lapse from good form.

Harris's task, which was, first and last, to wean Catherine the Great from armed neutrality under mainly Prussian influence to active military and naval alliance with Great Britain, was unspeakably complicated, laborious, and unenviable. A sequence of Russian promises given and broken, abortive conferences, tergiversations, procrastinations, subterfuges, face-savings, and other disappointments finally—abetted by the Russian climate—broke down the health of this capable and by no means humourless British diplomat. *Ce rusé et audacieux Harris*, as Mirabeau had already described him at Berlin, with unwilling admiration, had to return home on sick-leave in 1782 with his mission unfulfilled, and was subsequently transferred to The Hague. His predecessor Sir Charles Hanbury Williams had had no better luck. Nor had his immediate successor, Alleyne FitzHerbert.

"Every day produces me fresh difficulties and new enemies,"

reported Harris to Lord Weymouth as early as November 1779, and indeed the obstacles facing him were insuperable. His three major problems were Count Panine, Catherine's as-yet-unousted Foreign Minister, a man hiding vitriolic hate of everything British under the blandest of masks and, as everyone in Court and diplomatic circles knew, deep in the pocket of the King of Prussia; Panine's enemy, the powerful Favourite, open to financial suggestions from any quarter, perpetually expressing cordiality towards England and—quite sincerely—warm personal friendship for *mon cher Harris*, and perpetually, when brought by Harris to the point, slipping away like an eel; and finally Catherine herself, swayed, despite her intelligence, by her vanity and her passions, jealous of British power and glad to see Great Britain involved in Continental troubles which gave Russia a free hand in the Near East; willing at times (and especially when tentatively offered Minorca as a bribe) to listen to Harris and to flatter and charm him, but ever dreading the loss of the great Frederick's esteem and equally, says Harris sardonically, the epigrams of the French; a *maîtresse femme* who, "with many eminent and superior qualities," wrote his Excellency wearily to Lord Mountstuart, "frequently degenerates into an ordinary woman, and often plays with her fan when she thinks she is wielding her sceptre."

Little wonder, then, that before long Harris was forced to fall back seriously on the strongest of diplomatic arguments. He had no great difficulty with Lord North's Government in this emergency. Like Joseph II, North knew his Potemkin, thanks to the most efficient spy-service in Europe. On April 11, 1780, Harris writes to Lord Stormont at the Foreign Office a despatch divertingly dry and of the period:

My Lord,

If on further inquiry I should find, as I almost suspect, that my friend's [Potemkin's] fidelity has been shaken, or his political faith corrupted, in the late conferences, by any direct offers or indirect promises of reward, I shall think myself in such a case not only authorised but obliged to lure him with a similar bait. . . .

Warning Stormont that if Potemkin comes under Prussian control "the tide will turn powerfully against us," and adding that while awaiting instructions and subsidies from London he will proceed suitably with the Favourite and encourage his expectations, Harris comes to the point:

You will be pleased to recollect that I have to do with a person immensely rich, who well knows the importance of what is asked, and whose avidity, not necessity, is to be paid. He will require, perhaps, as much as Torcy proposed, but without success, to Marlborough.

Whether the British gold Potemkin duly received was equivalent to the 100,000 *louis-d'or* in which Torcy tried to interest Marlborough at The Hague in 1709—one of the bribes Marlborough certainly refused—Harris does not reveal. He must have paid the Favourite a substantial sum very soon after writing to Stormont. For the slightly melodramatic sequel we may quote Potemkin's anonymous biographer:

His [Harris's] exertions were baffled by a singular stratagem. He had given a long memorial to Potemkin, who promised to hand it to the Empress and back it with his recommendation. However, a young female of the name of Guibald, who was about the nieces of Prince Potemkin and lived on a very familiar footing with him, took the paper by stealth out of the Prince's pocket and carried it to her employers. They immediately enriched it with marginal notes, which victoriously opposed all the arguments of the British Minister; and the writing was then without discovery returned to the place whence it had been taken. The Empress, on reading the memorial, naturally supposed the notes had been added by Potemkin; which confirmed her determination to maintain armed neutrality.

Dismissing this story years later as fiction, Lord Malmesbury adds that the young female of the name of Guibald was one of Potemkin's "low mistresses", in the pay of Panine. At the time his Excellency could hardly withhold (in a despatch to Stormont of February 1781) a shrug of polite contempt for a report in certain foreign gazettes "taxing me with having attempted to bribe the Russian Ministers (*sic*)." On the whole it seems not impossible that the young female's right to life, liberty, and the pursuit of happiness had been increased by some such service to Panine as the story indicates. What is quite certain is that all Harris's arduous diplomacy went for nothing—through no fault of his own, as Whitehall handsomely admitted—and that the British Government wasted a great deal of money; and Potemkin, having locked its gold away, turned with renewed zest to deal with the Turk, whom he had left alone, by a convention, during the late byplay with Prussia and Great Britain.

Towards the beginning of 1783 the Ottoman authorities, at last fully aware of Russia's plan for them, were bestirring themselves, scrambling their forces together and trying to stiffen their ramshackle defences. But if the mullahs howled exultantly for a holy war Abdul Hamid's ministers hung back, fearful of taking the initiative, even when some of the Mahometan Tartar tribes of Tauris rose opportunely against the Orthodox menace. The rising was put down by Potemkin's cousin Paul, a general, with exemplary verve, the surviving Tartars flying *en masse* over the frontier, and the Crimea was duly occupied. Potemkin's immediate move was to provoke the Porte once more to combat by demanding its signature to a highly prejudicial treaty which the Turks accepted with disappointing alacrity, throwing open the Black Sea to Russian shipping as it had never been thrown open before and recognising the Crimea as a Russian province.

After these feats, and a preliminary development-plan for the Crimea, including the foundation of the port of Sebastopol, Potemkin could justifiably relax for a space under the fresh showers of roubles, serfs, and jewels, and the titles of Prince of

Tauris and Governor-General of the Crimea with which a grateful mistress rewarded him.[1] Her gift of the specially built Taurida Palace in the Embassy quarter, on the left bank of the Neva, he likewise accepted with easy grace. It is a confection in the Russo-Classic style of white-stuccoed brick, with a tall colonnaded portico, long, low wings, and a Pantheon-like central dome of copper; during the last years of the Empire it was occupied by the Douma. Though not so outwardly impressive as the Marble Palace built by Catherine for Grigori Orlov in admirably sober French taste near the Troïtsky Bridge, the Taurida, with its great columned hall, winter garden, ballroom, and orangeries, was admirably adapted for gorgeous entertaining and the display of massy treasures, and its upkeep cost Potemkin nothing, thanks to Little Mother's loving care. His personal fortune was piling up—some authorities place the final figure at fifty million roubles—and he was increasing it from home and foreign sources with that shameless avidity which, simultaneously with a frenzied extravagance which frequently left him short of ready money, is one of his principal characteristics.

In 1784 it was strongly rumoured that the current Imperial paramour, one Lanskoi, who died very suddenly, to Catherine's passionate distress, had been poisoned by Prince Potemkin, and that he had secretly married the Empress. Neither rumour was true, but it has seemed to most historians that Catherine's behaviour at this moment justified the marriage-theory to some extent. By the whole Court Potemkin was seen lounging in and out of her apartments in a dressing-gown. Catherine likewise frequently visited him on the floor below in a négligée. His manner towards her was becoming more peremptory at intervals, and he was ordering the Court about likewise with increased haughtiness, though it must be said in his favour that he was invariably kindness itself to the humbler officials. No doubt the principal obstacle to any marriage-project on Catherine's part was her fear

[1] He had been created a Prince of the Holy Roman Empire by Joseph II of Austria, at Catherine's request, some time before.

of the nobility, who would never have endured it. She may have thought of it, but she refrained.

To all appearance, however, Potemkin was now occupying the position of a husband of brevet rank. Catherine had long since begun turning to him in troubles great and small. In addition to his official salary, as Favourite, of 12,000 roubles a month, his entertainment expenses were also paid by the Treasury. He had the Taurida Palace free of all charge. His wines came in enormous quantity from the Imperial cellars, his liveries were supplied by the Court. Whenever he was in ready-money difficulties, as he was regularly, a word to Catherine removed them, for above all he was her refuge in her disappointments of the heart. To assuage her grief for Lanskoi took him nevertheless a few months. He eventually selected a young and attractive Guards lieutenant named Yermolov, and turned with relief to more profitable matters.

A typical Potemkinesque performance followed immediately. Before proceeding with the colonising and industrialising of his province of White Russia, he drew three million roubles from the Treasury for himself. On discovering this, his enemies at Court seized their opportunity and the fond Catherine was forced to listen to them. With frank and ·disarming simplicity Potemkin agreed that he had indeed borrowed that sum, being in temporary need of it. His proposal to Catherine to draw three millions more from the Treasury immediately for public works and to pay back his private debt in the near future she accepted, and no more was heard of the matter. He placed a black mark in his diary forthwith against the name of Yermolov, whom he suspected to be at the bottom of this persecution. When, a little later, one of the Russophile ex-Khans of the Crimea complained to the Empress that Potemkin had pouched his pension, and Catherine turned distinctly frigid, Potemkin had no doubt of it. But he knew his Catherine. Another admirable dramatic performance wrung the Imperial heart, indignant as it was. Bowing humbly before her displeasure like an errant moujik, the Prince of Tauris mournfully quitted all his posts and withdrew once more into retirement. Within a week or so he was back at Court, jaunty as ever. During his disgrace he had managed to set on foot an advantageous commercial treaty with the French Ambassador, thus showing Catherine and her pet, so to speak, whom was whom. And immediately he presented his ultimatum. "Yermolov goes, or I." Catherine authorised him to order Yermolov out then and there, and Potemkin's ensuing choice on her behalf of another attractive Guardee, one Mamonov, was made with greater circumspection.

4

And now the time seemed ripe to him to afford Catherine ocular proof of his recent work in the Crimea. Towards the end of 1786, accordingly, arrangements were completed by Potemkin for that famous tour of inspection which has ever since surrounded his name with the halo of a theatrical producer on the gigantic scale, something in the class of Reinhardt, and has turned Catherine's voyage into a comic legend. Even shorn of fantasy it remains an impressive performance; a combination, one might say, of Cleopatra's passage down the Cydnus, a Potsdam review by Frederick the Great, Queen Victoria's opening of the Great Exhibition, and the Sahiba's progress in *Kim*.

On the morning of January 2, 1787, in seventeen degrees of frost and amid the mingled roar of cannon and crowds, the Empress of All the Russias, muffled in her sables, left the Winter Palace in a huge gilded travelling *berline*, a luxurious combination on wheels of drawing-room and library. By her side were Mlle Protassov, principal lady-in-waiting, and the new lapdog, Mamonov, quarrelling constantly. Behind her followed a train of fourteen coaches and a hundred and sixty sleighs conveying some fifty carefully selected guests—among them the Prince de Ligne, Mr. Alleyne FitzHerbert, British Ambassador, the Comte de Ségur, French Ambassador, and Count Cobentzel, Austrian Ambassador—and a small army of lesser diplomats, courtiers, musicians, and servants. Potemkin had gone ahead as advance-manager. Young Grand Duke Paul Petrovitch, Catherine's only legitimate son, heir to the throne, whom his mother and Potemkin kept sedulously in hand and in the background, stayed in St. Petersburg.

After a halt of three days at the Imperial country palace of Tsarskoïe-Selo, the cortège proceeded south according to strict schedule, starting every morning at nine, halting for luncheon at twelve, and resuming the journey at three; soon after which hour the Russian winter sun set in splendour over vast snowy wastes, to be replaced by the torchlight of flaming trees on either side of the highroad, making the scene almost as brilliant as day. In the early evening, at the end of each stage, Catherine's guests found a magnificent banquet awaiting them either in private mansions or in houses belonging to the Crown, all richly furnished and decorated for this purpose; or, if no suitable house stood near, in elegant temporary pavilions of wood. In every town of any dimensions the procession halted for one or two days while Catherine surveyed the place, asked the provincial Governor and the municipal and police authorities a thousand searching questions, and distributed praise or blame. It is possible that the enormous cheering crowds in holiday attire who thronged Matushka's passage may have given her some illusions. She would not be the first or last ruler in that position.

At Kiev, where Potemkin hastened to greet the Imperial cortège after putting the finishing touches to the Crimean scene and placing all the troops, the festivities in their sumptuous variety recalled those famous celebrations at Versailles a century earlier for which Molière composed *Les Plaisirs de l'Isle Enchantée*. The beaming *régisseur*, who as usual had spared the Imperial Treasury nothing, received ecstatic compliments from his sovereign, who christened a superb new regiment of cuirassiers with his own name, a unique favour.

The next stage of the Empress's progress was to be by water, and a fleet of eighty vessels, escorting seven magnificent galleys, was already riding at anchor on the Dnieper. That noble river itself had received Potemkin's attentions, hundreds of its worst sandbanks and rocks in the Ukraine stretches having been removed or blown up by armies of serfs. As for the brightly painted and gilded galleys, each with its large and smartly uniformed crew, conveying Catherine and her guests, no expense had been spared in their fitting, as the Comte de Ségur conveys:

In our galleys we each had a bedroom and a *cabinet de toilette*, of which the luxury equalled the elegance; a comfortable divan, an admirable bed upholstered in speckled taffetas, and a mahogany escritoire. Every galley had its own band. A crowd of boats hovered constantly around and alongside the squadron, which looked as if it had come out of a fairy-tale.

Aboard the Imperial galley their Excellencies dined daily with Her Imperial Majesty, Potemkin, and other notables. Once a week Catherine invited all her guests together to a dinner of fifty or sixty covers. Gay and good-humoured, remarking laughingly to Ségur that "they tried to frighten me off with stories of the fatigue of this journey, the bleakness of the deserts, and the unhealthiness of the climate"—this did not impress Ségur particularly—the Empress was the life and soul of the party and Potemkin one vast smile. For Nature herself, it was remarked, was collaborating loyally with the fortunate impresario, as arranged. The exquisite Russian spring was just breaking into a foam of green. The birds were in full song, the lilacs full of perfume, the flowers new-enamelled, the sky a pale, pure blue, the sunshine lavish. The melted snows were broadening and deepening the mighty Dnieper. The pastures on either bank were vast and lush. The flocks and herds were sleek and plentiful. The villages . . .

So we come to the traditional peak of comedy. Those smiling riverside villages of the Ukraine at which Catherine gazed from her deck-pavilion with delight and approval, so bright and neat were they, so solidly prosperous, so swarming with cheerful, well-fed, well-clothed, enthusiastic peasants—were most of them mere façades of stone or even lath-and-plaster, hastily erected for the occasion? Those shops in the new riverside towns, bursting with produce of every kind—were their sacks and bales stuffed with rubbish? And the gaily-garbed inhabitants of these Arcadian places—were they imported from all over the Empire, rushed from point to point by night, with or without their cattle, reappearing like a stage-army?

It seems that nobody has found the complete answer, though the Prince de Ligne, a man highly curious of novelty and not easily fooled, supplies most of it. He made several discreet excursions ashore by himself during the voyage, and was satisfied that with a certain amount of reality Potemkin had mixed certain "legerdemain-tricks." Catherine herself was not deceived for a moment, the Prince conveys quite clearly. The show was, after all, aimed at the ambassadors, and through them at all Europe, and in any case large areas of the Ukraine benefited instantly and for years afterwards by the slow passage of this lavish and opulent procession. And the Prince de Ligne adds, very fairly, "I discovered many things with which even the Russians are not acquainted: superb establishments in their infancy, growing manufactures, villages with regular streets surrounded by trees and irrigated by rivulets. . . ." Ségur was seemingly no dupe either, as he briefly conveys:

Every trick by which his [Potemkin's] vivid imagination, un-limited power, and profound knowledge of his Sovereign's character enabled him to exalt her imagination and to flatter her pride was employed with consummate skill.

And Ségur hastens to award the Favourite a deservedly high mark for that "real miracle of activity," the creation of the port, town, and forts of Sebastopol within two years of the occupation of the Crimea; a remarkable feat, viewed from any angle.

The unofficial impressions of agreeable Mr. FitzHerbert, which may have accounted for some scintillating passages in his diary, are not available, as we have noted, owing to an unlucky fire. If it is permissible to read between the lines of a letter of May 27 to the Marquess of Carmarthen, a certain demureness becomes perceptible:

The Empress seems to be extremely well satisfied with the state of things in this province, the improved condition of which is, in fact, something wonderful, considering that but a few years (*sic*) ago it was an absolute desert. Prince Potemkin has naturally taken care to set off everything to the best advantage. . . .[1]

With which Mr. FitzHerbert, after glancing very briefly at one or two imminent entertainments, proceeds to other matters.

As business men would say to-day, the Crimean exhibition was possibly fifty-fifty. If only half those "Potemkin villages," soon to become an international proverb, were bogus, Potemkin's "production," in theatre-language, was still masterly. Moreover one factor seems to me to have been strangely under-estimated. It would ravish Potemkin's elfin sense of humour to fool their Excellencies—already captivated, as Ségur records, by Catherine's "continual flow of graciousness, wit, and gaiety," and "a thousand different amusements, curious and original stories told us by the Empress, the clever reflections of Mr. FitzHerbert of the British Embassy, the follies of the Master of the Horse," and many other diversions—in this manner; a jest of the choicest, and all for the good of Holy Russia. It may even be that Potemkin and Catherine planned the entire Dnieper comedy together in gales of laughter. It may be, also, that their Excellencies of Europe were not fooled after all.

At Kanev, Catherine's old lover Poniatowski, King Stanislas-Augustus of Poland, met her to present his saddened homage. At Kanev, also, storm-clouds veiled the sunshine and Potemkin's stage-management went wrong for the first and only time. An overlooked rock and an unruly current nearly wrecked the Imperial galley, shaking Catherine's nerve so much that, after reaching Kaïdaki, where Joseph II of Austria awaited her, she

[1] *Foreign Office Records*, Public Record Office, 65/15.

decided to continue by land. At Kherson, her new Crimean capital, more magnificent junketings celebrated her arrival. The port was thronged with Russian and foreign shipping, the shops crammed with rich merchandise, and to complete Catherine's delight, Potemkin smilingly drew her attention to one of the ancient stone gates of the town inscribed in Greek: "*This way to Byzantium.*" What omen more fortunate? From Constantinople hastened the Russian and Austrian ambassadors forthwith, by order, to confer with her and Joseph II, while the perturbed and angry Turk protested with a futile naval demonstration off the mouth of the Dnieper. Catherine had never been more happy.

When the show was over Potemkin judged it time to get seriously to grips with the Turk, and by a diplomatic offensive to begin with. Boulgakov, the insolent Russian ambassador at Constantinople, was given a free hand to bribe his way into Ottoman Cabinet secrets, always a simple matter. Notes were showered simultaneously on the Turkish Government, demanding, among other things, the reason for Turkey's warlike preparations, to which the Turk replied not unreasonably with a similar question of his own. As he still did not declare war, Potemkin forced his hand by violently rejecting all Turkish explanations and proposals as ludicrous, and the unfortunate Abdul Hamid, prodded from behind by Great Britain and Prussia (France had just signed a commercial treaty with the Porte), replied at last by throwing his Excellency Boulgakov into prison, after which the Grand Vizir raised the Green Standard of Mahomet and the mullahs renewed their frenzies, lashing the Turkish troops and populace into the desired condition. In August 1787 a large Turkish army crossed the Danube, and in October attacked the fortress of Kinbourn in the Ukraine.

Potemkin had been, perhaps, a trifle precipitate. Conflict raged in the Russian High Command. Catherine's leading generals, the brilliant Souvarov and Repnine and Roumiantsev, who had always detested the Favourite, refused to obey the orders of an amateur with no field experience, and it took some time to settle the commands. Ultimately two Russian armies took the field, one commanded by Potemkin, with Souvarov under him, the other by Roumiantsev. While Potemkin invested the strong Turkish fortress-town of Otchakov, the Turks at Kinbourn were superbly routed by Souvarov. A sudden attack of mental jaundice afflicting Potemkin at this news thickened into nihilist gloom at the news that the Black Sea fleet had lost two ships in a storm. He took it hard. The Fleet was done for.

In vain Catherine kept urging him to cheer up and take Otchakov. No Russian despairs by halves. Biting his nails moodily in front of Otchakov, it seemed to Potemkin that the only solution, after handing over to Roumiantsev, was to evacuate the Crimea. Catherine, to whom he put this in a sequence of letters, soothed and flattered and cajoled him like a sick baby, begging him to hand over more routine-work to subordinates:

It is true that I have more resource than you at the moment, but I am in good health, and you are ill. You are impatient like a five-year-old child, whereas what you are doing needs unshakeable patience.

Whatever happened (added Matushka lovingly) she could never lose her high opinion of her best friend and pupil; which had no effect whatsoever. Winter had come, and the snows, the long dark nights, and the traditional Russian winter lethargy. The Prince de Ligne, visiting Potemkin's headquarters at this period on behalf of Joseph II, who had an army corps supporting the Russians, formed that gay epigrammatic impression of him I have already quoted; in which, it may be noted, there is as much admiration as cynicism. Spring arrived, to find Potemkin still inactive and a prey to gloom, still recommending to Catherine the evacuation of the Crimea. It was not till Gustavus III of Sweden, whose hostility had for some time been growing more active, declared war on Russia in this spring of 1788 that Potemkin recovered his nerve, energy, and fighting spirit. No Russian recovers by halves.

Sweden's grievances were many and Gustavus's own troubles complicated. Difficult as it is for any modern European to imagine a badly behaved Swede, the Swedish Crown in the 1780's was in some danger owing to the brawling of two powerful factions of the nobility, under the thumb of France and Russia respectively.

Towards 1787 Gustavus had managed to deal his Russophiles, the more dangerous party, a smashing blow and to regain full control of his kingdom; on which Catherine and Potemkin at once set about organising more intensive underground intrigue in the Swedish provinces bordering on Russia and in Sweden itself, ordering the Russian Ambassador at Stockholm simultaneously to make himself as obnoxious as possible. Their policy was to keep Sweden on the boil and to restore the Russophiles, but they under-estimated Gustavus's desperation. No sooner were the main Russian forces thoroughly embroiled with the Turks than the King of Sweden declared war and led an army personally into Russian Finland. Hastily despatching a third-rate corps to hold him in check, Catherine II faced the imminent threat to St. Petersburg with admirable coolness, and trebled her secret agents' gold; not without success, to which her fifth column among the nobility contributed. Several Swedish regiments led by Russophile officers laid down their arms before Frederiksham, and Swedish battleships plainly ratted at Hogland. But it took Catherine two years to conclude the highly expensive campaign.

Away at Otchakov Potemkin, on hearing of the Swedish offensive, roared with fury and turned on Catherine with reproaches and on her Council with violent abuse. He knew she would soon be demanding some of his best troops, and the extremely long and arduous process of taking Otchakov was now absorbing him in earnest; moreover he was taking preliminary steps to oust his enemy Marshal Roumiantsev and to secure the supreme command.

It was not till December 6, 1788, that the final assault on Otchakov could be made. It was highly successful. Ten thousand Turks perished in the attack, including women and children, with some thousands of Russians, reduced by Potemkin in his despatches to one thousand, for Catherine had ordered him to be sparing of Russian lives. The booty was immense. A fresh shower of roubles, gold boxes, and other loving tributes, including a jewelled sword, descended on Prince Grigori Potemkin, every officer under his command received a gold medal and every soldier a silver one, and Sultan Abdul Hamid broke his weak heart and died.

5

Those eager to destroy the legend of Lawrence of Arabia have never failed to point out that whatever that enigmatic personage achieved, he had gold behind him in large quantities. To a much greater extent this essential factor in politics and conquest gilds the feats of Potemkin, to whom the Treasury was always a milch-cow. As with Clive, whom Dr. Johnson described as "a man who acquired his fortune by such crimes that his consciousness of them impelled him to cut his own throat," the world was Potemkin's oyster, to vary our zoology, though unlike Clive he had no belated conscience in the matter of loot. In this strange man's career a frantic avarice is as powerful a motive as devotion to his sovereign. From now to the end of his life his avarice increases.

After the victory of Otchakov the conquering hero handed over to General Kamenski, who swiftly enveloped the Turkish army and finished the Ukraine campaign, after which Potemkin ordered his troops into winter quarters and returned to St. Petersburg for his ovation, which was that of an Alexander returning with the globe. But Catherine's welcome was noticeably tinged by a certain *arrière-pensée* on the subject of her hero's most recent raids on the Treasury, which even Russian resources could not withstand much longer, as his enemies were proclaiming. Resenting this, and still more furiously resenting the raffish young fop Mamonov, who was giving himself excessive airs, Potemkin gave way to stamping jealousy and demanded Mamonov's instant dismissal. Catherine refused. Potemkin raged. The dazzling diamond collar of the Order of St. Alexander Nevski, valued at 60,000 roubles and Russia's highest honour, and an effusively glowing tribute by the Empress in the presence of the whole Court, soothed him greatly. He declined nevertheless to return immediately to fresh military glory, as Catherine and Mamonov were gently urging. After some weeks of that maniac wasting of money on amusement which delighted him only a little less than receiving and refusing to pay his tradesmen, Potemkin demanded another six million roubles for the next Turkish campaign, and, after some wrangling, got it. Having advised his sovereign, very soundly—most of his advice to her was extremely sound, especially on the choice of Ministers—not to enrage the King of Sweden further by lampooning him on the stage of the St. Petersburg Opera in a piece with words by herself and music by Martini, entitled *The Awkward Warrior*, Potemkin left at last for the front; to be highly incensed, shortly after arrival, by the news that Mamonov, who had at last overstepped the mark, had just been replaced without his advice by another young Guardsman, Lieutenant Platon Zoubov, a "sweet innocent soul" (Catherine) who loved flying kites and playing with his pet monkey.

In her sixty-first year the Semiramis of the North, eupeptically and half-maternally amorous as ever, was increasingly worried by Imperial finances and increasingly beset by Ministers and courtiers crying that the Treasury was bleeding to death and urging peace at all cost with Turk and Swede alike; especially with the Turk, whose traditional fighting-quality, despite sottish leadership, had lately been stimulated by the new Sultan, Selim III, nephew of the late half-witted Abdul and a vigorous young man of bellicose and relatively westernised ideas, furiously hostile to the Giaour. Another factor favouring Potemkin's enemies at Court was the recent death of Catherine's old ally Joseph II of Austria, whose influence with his sister Marie-Antoinette had been so helpful in Russia's behalf up to the first rumblings of the

Revolution. Joseph's successor, Leopold II, was showing signs already of disliking the Russian alliance and the Favourite himself, and was suspected by Catherine of having given Coburg and his Austrian generals on the Turkish front the order not to exert themselves; which indeed they had not done so far, to any extent.

Potemkin equally wished to finish the war, but strictly *ad majorem Potemkinii gloriam.* By way of discouraging the Swedes he sent 3,000 ferocious Bachkir tribal cavalry into Finland, which was thoroughly ravaged, Swedish and Russian Finland alike; not without heavy Russian casualties. Meanwhile trouble seemed to be boiling up in Poland, where the patriots were showing dangerous signs of rising and cutting off Russian communications. Before attending to this, and before opening the spring campaign of 1789 on his main front, Potemkin coolly asked for another fourteen million roubles; partly for the Spring offensive, partly for a great new plan he had conceived of either buying the entire Turkish Government or, alternatively, assaulting Constantinople in person from the sea. Catherine could hardly stand out long against such a gorgeous inspiration. Once more the hero got everything he demanded.

His next necessity was to get rid of Marshal Roumiantsev, who was evidently preparing to steal more of the limelight. Life was accordingly made so impossible for the aged Marshal that he resigned in bitter fury; on which Potemkin assumed the supreme command, handed the Ukraine army over to Kamenski, and launched his main offensive at last.

The Turks did badly to begin with and worse in August, when that magnificent soldier Souvarov, later to win the admiration of Napoleon, with Austrian assistance gave them a tremendous thrashing at Fokchany and again at Martinechti on the River Rymnik, earning for himself the double title of Count of the Holy Roman and Russian Empires, the honorific title of *Rymnikski,* and rich gifts from Catherine. Not long afterwards Potemkin's main forces stormed two strong Turkish fortresses, Akkerman and Bender, with huge booty, and his self-esteem reattained its normal peak. His acknowledgment to Catherine of a hundred-thousand-rouble personal reward and a crown of emerald laurels was frank and genial:

Most-honoured Little Mother, you have already loaded me with all the treasures at your disposal, and I am still alive. This life, believe me, most noble Sovereign, will be everywhere and always consecrated to your service and the downfall of all your enemies. . . .

Little Mother's latest bounty and his zeal for her service did not prevent her adored warrior from becoming in due course bored with a six-months' siege of Ismail, in Moldavia, and retiring to G.H.Q. at Jassy for a spell of luxury, amid the bevy of women and parasites who surrounded him constantly.

The women were for the most part society harlots from St. Petersburg. Princess Basil Dolgorouky, Princess Theodore Gargarine, Countess Samoïlov, Mme de Witte, and Mme de Vivarais, the young French wife of an unfrocked priest, were among them, also one or two of Potemkin's nieces and his current mistress-in-chief, Prascovia, his cousin Paul's wife, who had accompanied the Favourite on the Crimean tour. To entertain what was known to all St. Petersburg and Moscow as his travelling harem— and to Catherine the Great, ever laughingly, as his hen-house (*poulailler*)—Potemkin ordered from the capital two large string orchestras, a complete Opera ballet under the maestro Rosetti, and a corps of gardeners to lay out the grounds of G.H.Q. on the English model. Heavy eating and drinking, gambling, brooding, nail-biting, and sleep at all hours filled in the intervals between his more serious amusements. While the Generalissimo disported himself thus, in such a fashion, imitated modestly by the Russian Command at Port Arthur 114 years later, as to earn a severe rebuke from the compiler of his memoirs as an Oriental voluptuary and a disgraceful example to his troops, the fuming Souvarov continued doggedly to invest Ismail and to wait for further orders.

One day at Jassy Mme de Witte, telling fortunes by the cards, discovered that Potemkin was due to take Ismail within three weeks. Galvanised into action (he was long since sick of his women), Potemkin ordered Souvarov to take the fortress in three days, and Souvarov did so forthwith, after furious fighting, putting 35,000 Turks to the sword with the loss of 15,000 Russians, and finishing the campaign in 1790 in one splendid burst.

And now, flushed with glory, master of the Black Sea and of every fortress covering Constantinople to the north, Potemkin had no intention whatsoever of obeying Catherine's reiterated orders to conclude a peace as soon as possible. But caution intervened. Scenting opposition piling up dangerously at home, he left for St. Petersburg to cajole or subdue Matushka, as so often before. Immediately on learning of his departure from G.H.Q., Catherine sent Prince Repnine, Potemkin's second-in-command, secret express instructions with powers to begin peace-preliminaries as soon as the first opportunity arrived. In the meantime another ovation on the grand scale was prepared for the homing Generalissimo. St. Petersburg and the surrounding countryside for miles were illuminated, and hordes of serfs hastily repaired the main roads leading south. Before entering the capital the conqueror was duly advised by his ally and factotum Bezborodko, Minister of Foreign Affairs, of all Court news, saving only the instructions to Repnine, which Bezborodko dared not reveal.

To describe the festivities celebrating Potemkin's return on this supreme occasion would require, in the memorable phrase of a living master, a far less brilliant pen than mine; and is anything more tedious than describing such things, save reading about them? A single item of one of the entertainments given by Potemkin for Catherine, seated on a golden throne, stands out against the Asiatic exuberance of these saturnalia and perhaps conveys their essence. In one of the salons of the Taurida Palace stood a colossal artificial elephant blazing with jewels. At a signal from the orchestra a curtain in its flank rose to reveal a gorgeous full-dress Opera ballet beginning a performance in its belly; an inspiration even an hospitable Pittsburg steel king giving a small and intimate party in the 1890's never dreamed of. Catherine described her host to the Prince de Ligne a little later as "handsome as the day, gay as a lark, brilliant as a star, and wittier than ever; apart from which he has ceased to bite his nails, and gives fêtes each more splendid than the one before it." Far away in the south Repnine had begun a strong new offensive and had already sent back a leading Turkish corps-commander in triumph, to be granted by the kindly Catherine a pension of 12,000 roubles.

Potemkin was now simultaneously sick of the Turkish war and flamingly suspicious of the machinations of a peace-party at Court working behind his latest *bête-noire*, Zubov, the current Imperial lapdog, who was annoying him in a score of ways. For this reason, in addition to his enduring passion for the delights of St. Petersburg, he deferred his return to the front as once before. Catherine, dreading a flat refusal, was too nervous to issue an ultimatum. Several Ministers and nobles of influence and standing wisely declined her invitation to undertake this dangerous mission on her behalf. Repnine's continuing successes at last supplied the necessary spur. Stung to action as ever by jealousy, the Generalissimo decided to take up his command again. The news, received on the road south soon after beginning his return journey, that Repnine had begun peace-negotiations with the Turks drove him into a frenzy. On arrival at Jassy early in August 1791 he gave Repnine a thunderous dressing-down for acting without his knowledge and consent, and to his genuine surprise Repnine turned on him, revealing Catherine's order behind Potemkin's back and refusing to acknowledge any other. But Potemkin held the whip-hand. For all Matushka's protection, Repnine was recalled by her almost immediately at Potemkin's demand and banished to his estates, and the tiger, with a growl of satisfaction, turned to the task of destroying usurped prestige.

But Prince Potemkin of Tauris was no more the Potemkin of his prime. He had often complained of his health, he was passionately devoted to quacks of every kind, and that huge frame and iron constitution could not for ever support his wild outbursts of superhuman energy, his mad orgies, his tremendous eating and drinking, and his insatiable lust, to which incest had long since been added.

Among a myriad other affairs, he cherished a violent passion for three in succession of the nieces who so continuously hover in his background, and who were all ladies-in-waiting to the Empress. Ségur's memoirs among others throw a curious light on this aspect of the ardent amateur theologian, somehow recalling one of those Chinese war-lords of the 1920's naïvely described by the British and American Press as "Christian," doubtless owing to their well-known habit, derived from mission schooldays, of reading the Old Testament with their concubines in the intervals of rapine, loot, and torture on the grand scale. Potemkin's young nieces, Alexandra, Barbara, and Catherine, were the daughters of one of his five sisters, Madame Engelhardt. Alexandra, later Countess Branicka, his favourite, seems to have become his soulmate as early as 1776, and was living with him when he died. Barbara ("Varinka"), later Princess Galitzine, captured his fancy about 1778. Her uncle's existing letters to Varinka—"My life . . . My angel . . . Little scamp . . . My soul . . . My beauty . . . Little idiot . . . My divinity . . ."—are anything but avuncular. Catherine Engelhardt, who replaced Barbara after 1779, was a notable beauty, painted by Vigée-Lebrun; for two years after her marriage to Count Scavronsky, Russian Ambassador to Naples, her uncle kept her with him.

It would seem that only in Russia, even in the Age of Reason, could such a family arrangement be possible. It was no secret to anybody, least of all to Catherine, who was extremely fond of Alexandra and gushed over her uncle as usual. The Empress's attitude to Potemkin in his last phase is in fact slightly senile. Half-resentful of the hero's peremptory manner, which had increased vastly with his successes in the field, half-adoring, half-nervous, totally fascinated, she continues to bleat (the only word) and cajole. After his demand for the dismissal of Zubov in 1791, for example, she wrote in almost a maudlin strain:

> You scolded me all day yesterday for no reason. Thank God you have found one now! . . . You have thrust a sword into my breast. . . . I have done nothing to offend you, nor have I any intention of doing so, in spite of anything which your abrupt and stormy mind makes you imagine. . . .

Matushka was not to abase herself thus much longer. The huge temperamental Potemkin-machine was now breaking down, or wearing or burning itself out. Within a week or two of his return to Jassy the Favourite found himself smitten with what seems to have been an attack of malignant malaria, to begin with, contracted possibly in the Crimea and increased by drinking. His fevers grew swiftly more virulent, and the two leading physicians of St. Petersburg, Linman and Massot, hastily summoned, could do nothing for a patient who spurned their orders and, while shaking and sweating at a high temperature, would swallow a goose or a ham, two or three fowls, and a half-gallon or so of wines and liqueurs at one sitting. Potemkin had little use for eminent physicians. He dismissed the Faculty at length in a rage and began to prescribe for himself. A diet of salt smoked ham and his favourite raw turnips, washed down with hot wine and spirits, *quant. suff.*, failed to alleviate his condition. His mind became as inflamed as his blood, his capricious outbursts more and more ungovernable. A story that he was poisoned by Zubov has no foundation. It was his own grave that Potemkin was digging, in the homely old-wives' phrase, with his teeth.

Early in October, feeling death upon him, he determined to move from Jassy, whose climate he blamed furiously for his condition, to Ekaterinoslav, a town he had built some years ago in Catherine's honour. On the eve of setting out he dictated his last letter to her:

Matushka, gracious Sovereign, I have no more strength to endure my torments. My only chance is to leave this town. I do not know what will become of me. Your very faithful and very grateful subject,   POTEMKIN.

Catherine had no idea of his real condition, it appears. The hero perhaps seemed immortal. But his end had come. At 6 a.m. on October 15 he set out in a coach from Jassy across the misty plains with his favourite niece Alexandra, Countess Branicka, a doctor—doubtless a quack—and three attendants. Thirty miles along the highway some five hours later the coach pulled up hastily at the doctor's cry, and Potemkin was laid, gasping, "I am dying!" under a tree by the roadside. Here, a little before midday, he died in the Countess's arms.

On receiving the news by express courier Catherine the Great fell prostrate in a swoon three times in succession. To the philosopher Grimm she wrote at 2 a.m. on leaving her bed, after being bled by the Court surgeon: "I have received a terrible knockdown blow (*coup de massue*). My pupil, my friend, my almost-idol Prince Potemkin of Tauris is dead. . . ." Five years later apoplexy struck her, and she followed Potemkin to the grave.

6

Half-child, half-savage, with a strong dash of the mystic, excessively vain, combining the most brilliant and sterling qualities of brain and heart with the most crapulous vices and an insane passion for money, most ignoble of all, Potemkin remains a fascinating specimen of the genus Slav. Doubtless the tremendous eulogies poured out in Catherine's letters to Grimm and others after his death were dictated more by her heart, that expansive and hospitable organ, than by her immensely capable head. Even so, no mediocrity could have ruled such a woman so continuously, and if he only played at being a soldier Potemkin changed the map of Europe. After his death there was no such conspicuous figure on the international stage till the advent of Napoleon.

As a Favourite he towers several sizes larger than his companions in these pages, just as his background is vaster than theirs, and stranger; more barbaric, more showy, half Oriental. The Prince de Ligne accurately noted the satrap in Potemkin, who could have emerged equally naturally in the Russia of Ivan the Terrible or of Boris Godounov, possibly with the same *éclat*, possibly more briefly. To the orderly mind of Catherine the unpredictable Slav in him was a perpetual and magical surprise, I think. One could never be certain, with such a man, when he might begin to talk astounding sense, and Catherine's faith in his judgment of men and affairs was generally not unjustified. But for that fatal habit of suddenly losing interest in some passionately absorbing plan he might have achieved a great deal. An example of his energy and its limitations is his attempt to colonise the Government of Azov in the 1780's. Flaming with zeal, he began by attracting immigrants from Livonia, Germany, and even England, founding new villages and towns, establishing manufactures, supplying material, cattle, corn, implements, everything necessary to establish a flourishing colony on scientific lines, sparing neither pains nor enormous sums of money. His grandiose scheme failed before long owing to corrupt underlings, but before this he had become keenly interested in something else. His sudden languors in the middle of a campaign have already been noted. Boredom might have attacked him thus, quite likely, under the very walls of Constantinople on the eve of the final assault.

Nevertheless his fits of energy were by no means all fruitless. The great ports of Sebastopol, Odessa, and Kherson owe their existence and importance to him solely. He avoided a great deal of unnecessary bloodshed, before annexing the Crimea, by tirelessly bribing, cajoling, and menacing the principal Tartar Khans into acquiescence; it was their subordinates, who had received no Russian backsheesh, who later revolted and had to be suppressed. He nearly succeeded in extending the Russian frontier to the Caucasus. He reformed and modernised the Russian Army, and his final decree of 1786 settling military expenditure is almost Napoleonic in detail, embracing the last buckle and nosebag. The publicity value of the Crimean inspection-tour he organised for Catherine in 1787 was undoubtedly high, apart from his proportion of real achievement there. As for his military exploits, though he could not compete with real soldiers like Souvarov and Roumiantsev he was not entirely a figurehead. If he never won a pitched battle he had studied warfare, his strategy was more than respectable, and he was usually not wasteful of his men. Moreover, however lazy and vicious he could be, he never flagged in promoting his country's interests, simultaneously with his own. The Prince de Ligne, one of the most critical assessors of men in his age—and especially of unusual men, including Casanova, his friend—perceived much greatness in him.

Charm being the common denominator of all favourites, Potemkin has just enough in common with Melbourne and Godoy—and if it comes to that, Mme de Pompadour—to make all further comparison impossible. Potemkin does not belong to any world we in the West have ever known; not even to that relatively fantastic political world of Melbourne, of which the few faint remaining echoes are mixed with Dickens's laughter at the evolutions, like the change of partners in some dignified set of quadrilles, of the Coodle and Doodle Cabinets, "supposing it to be impossible for the Duke of Foodle to act with Goodle, which may be assumed to be the case in consequence of the breach arising out of that affair with Hoodle. . . ." One cannot measure him for one moment, either, against the world of Mme de Pompadour or of Don Manuel Godoy—what would a society which deemed even Englishmen to be mad have made of this exotic Caliban?

As Kipling very soundly remarked, the Russian is a delightful person till he tucks in his shirt. "It is only when he insists on being treated as the most easterly of Western peoples instead of the most westerly of Easterns that he becomes a racial anomaly extremely difficult to handle." Potemkin, who fills the bill exactly, belongs in fact to the strange universe of Posdnichev of *The Kreutzer Sonata* and Konstantin Gavrilovitch of *The Sea-Gull*, a universe of restless, wild-eyed introverts which often seems (except to the initiates of modern Bloomsbury) to be slightly deranged, whirling in a kind of dervish-dance to the feverish ache of a Tschaikowsky waltz. It is clear that Western admirers like Ségur and Ligne consider Potemkin a freak. So, a century and a half later, Western observers deemed Rasputin; not so that moujik's Imperial dupes, and masses of their subjects. Potemkin's personality, detached from its natural background, will likewise seem to a Western eye at times perverse or half-crazy. Viewed against the Russian scene of the eighteenth—or perhaps any other—century, he becomes a normal and reasonable figure.

Without doubt his fascination for Catherine, a Western product, owes a great deal to his temperament, as has been observed, and especially she responded to that flaming fidelity to the Crown he constantly flourished. Undoubtedly he flourished it sincerely, his ambition being almost inseparable from hers, his fortunes dependent on her will, his admiration of her constant, and his love of Russia fiery. It would be cynical to speculate on what might have happened had the regular Imperial gold-showers suddenly ceased to descend on a man so consumed with greed. But it has never been suggested, even by those indebted to him for favours, that Potemkin sold himself at any time, though he accepted gold as a matter of course from anyone who offered it. In a Russia traditionally given at intervals to treachery—I have not paused in this brief survey to note all the intrigues and combinations and betrayals which threatened Catherine for years after her accession—and notable, then as always, for the excessive number of raving *exaltés* and crazy messiahs among the population, Potemkin indeed displays a quite irreproachable and unswerving loyalty.

His very position as Favourite exposed him to innumerable dangers which his insupportable arrogance despised. His Imperial mistress for some time after gaining her throne (by what means we have observed) was at the mercy of one of those *coups de main* which had enlivened the Russian scene often in the past, and she had every reason to be grateful to her strong man. It was therefore only natural that when his enemy the Grand Duke Paul, whom Potemkin had always snubbed and treated like a child, assumed the crown as Tsar Paul I in 1796, one of his first official acts afforded what is called public opinion deep satisfaction; namely his having Potemkin's tomb at Kherson broken open and its contents flung to the dogs to avenge a mother's memory. Like other favourites, Potemkin had never been popular with the unsuccessful.

His death robbed Catherine the Great of an irreplaceable servant, ally, friend, and counsellor; Russia of an unrivalled and very expensive publicity-agent; and the rejoicing Turk of Mahound's greatest bugbear since Don John of Austria. Two months after Potemkin's splendid funeral Count Rostropchine remarked with surprise and pleasure that he was already forgotten. Thus his destiny repeats that of the Pompadour. All things human, indeed, as a *tropar* of the Orthodox Requiem Mass reminds us, are but ashes, phantoms, shadows, smoke, and dust in a whirlwind.

END

BIBLIOGRAPHY

THE principal authorities on which the sketches in this book are based are as follows:

For Madame de Pompadour:

Bainville, *Histoire de France,* 1924.
Gaxotte, *La Révolution Française,* 1926.
De Goncourt (J. and E.), *Madame de Pompadour,* 1878.
Leroy, *Madame de Pompadour et Son Temps,* 1936.
De Nolhac, *Louis XV et Madame de Pompadour,* 1903.
Poulet-Malassis, *Correspondance de Mme de Pompadour,* 1878.
Barbé-Marbois, *Lettres de Mme de Pompadour,* 1774; etc.

For Melbourne:

Lord Melbourne's Papers, ed. Lloyd Sanders, 1889.
Greville's *Journals,* ed. Reeve, 1875–85.
Bernard Newman, *Lord Melbourne,* 1930.
Edith Sitwell, *Victoria of England,* 1936.
The Creevey Papers, ed. Maxwell, 1904.
The Girlhood of Queen Victoria, ed. Esher, 1912.
Letters and Journals of Lord Byron, ed. Moore, 1830.
Letters of Queen Victoria, ed. Benson and Esher, 1908; etc.

For Godoy:

Mémoires du Prince de la Paix, ed. d'Esmenard, 1836.
Cuenta dada de su Vida Política, por el Principe de la Paz, ed. Peters, 1904.
Bourrienne, *Mémoires de Napoléon Bonaparte,* 1836.
Lord Holland, *Foreign Reminiscences,* 1850.
Gómez de Arteche, *Reinado de Carlos IV,* 1892.
Ángel Salcedo Ruíz, *La Época de Goya,* 1924.
Eugenio d'Ors, *Goya,* 1926.
Caballero, *En el Centenario de Jovellanos* (Revista de Estudios Políticos, IX), 1944; etc.

BIBLIOGRAPHY

For Potemkin:

Memoirs, 1813.

Prince de Ligne, *Mélanges militaires, Lettres à la Marquise de Coigny,* etc., 1795–1818 and 1914.

Robert Michel (tr. Walter), *Potemkine,* 1936.

Diaries and Correspondence of James Harris, first Earl of Malmesbury, 1844.

Despatches of Alleyne FitzHerbert, first Baron St. Helens (Public Record Office, Foreign Office Records, 65, 11–15).

Réau, *Saint-Pétersbourg,* 1913.

Ségur, *Mémoires;* etc.